BLACK CAT

GRAND THEFT MARVEL

collection editor **JENNIFER GRÜNWALD** ♦ assistant editor **CAITLIN O'CONNELL**
associate managing editor **KATERI WOODY** ♦ editor, special projects **MARK D. BEAZLEY**
vp production & special projects **JEFF YOUNGQUIST** ♦ book designer **JAY BOWEN**

svp print, sales & marketing **DAVID GABRIEL** ♦ director, licensed publishing **SVEN LARSEN**
editor in chief **C.B. CEBULSKI** ♦ chief creative officer **JOE QUESADA**
president **DAN BUCKLEY** ♦ executive producer **ALAN FINE**

BLACK CAT VOL. 1: GRAND THEFT MARVEL. Contains material originally published in magazine form as BLACK CAT (2019) #1-5. First printing 2019. ISBN 978-1-302-91920-7. Published by MARVEL WORLDWIDE, INC., a subsidiary of MARVEL ENTERTAINMENT, LLC. OFFICE OF PUBLICATION: 135 West 50th Street, New York, NY 10020. © 2019 MARVEL No similarity between any of the names, characters, persons, and/or institutions in this magazine with those of any living or dead person or institution is intended, and any such similarity which may exist is purely coincidental. **Printed in Canada.** DAN BUCKLEY, President, Marvel Entertainment; JOHN NEE, Publisher; JOE QUESADA, Chief Creative Officer; TOM BREVOORT, SVP of Publishing; DAVID BOGART, Associate Publisher & SVP of Talent Affairs; DAVID GABRIEL, VP of Print & Digital Publishing; JEFF YOUNGQUIST, VP of Production & Special Projects; DAN CARR, Executive Director of Publishing Technology; ALEX MORALES, Director of Publishing Operations; DAN EDINGTON, Managing Editor; SUSAN CRESPI, Production Manager; STAN LEE, Chairman Emeritus. For information regarding advertising in Marvel Comics or on Marvel.com, please contact Vit DeBellis, Custom Solutions & Integrated Advertising Manager, at vdebellis@marvel.com. For Marvel subscription inquiries, please call 888-511-5480. **Manufactured between 11/8/2019 and 12/10/2019 by SOLISCO PRINTERS, SCOTT, QC, CANADA.**

10 9 8 7 6 5 4 3 2 1

BLACK CAT
GRAND THEFT MARVEL

writer	**JED MacKAY**
artist	**TRAVEL FOREMAN**
flashback artist, #3	**MICHAEL DOWLING**
color artist	**BRIAN REBER**

"The Ongoing Adventures of Black Cat and Her Purrfect Purrloiners"
writer/artist	**NAO FUJI**

"Leaving Miami"
writer	**JED MacKAY**
artist	**MICHAEL DOWLING**
color artist	**BRIAN REBER**

letterer	**FERRAN DELGADO**
cover art	**J. SCOTT CAMPBELL** **& SABINE RICH**
assistant editor	**KATHLEEN WISNESKI**
editor	**NICK LOWE**

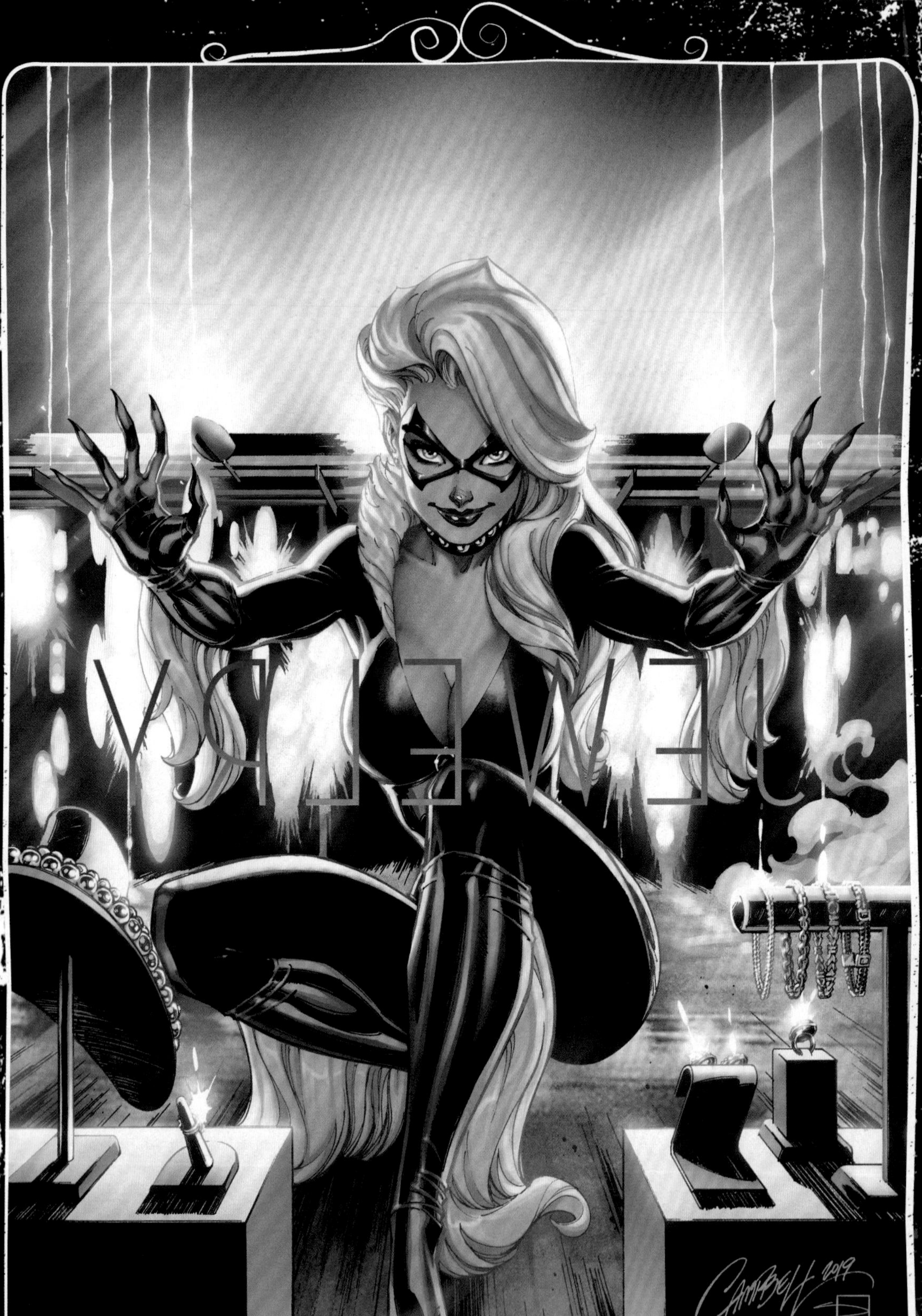
JEWELRY

1 • Thieves Like Us

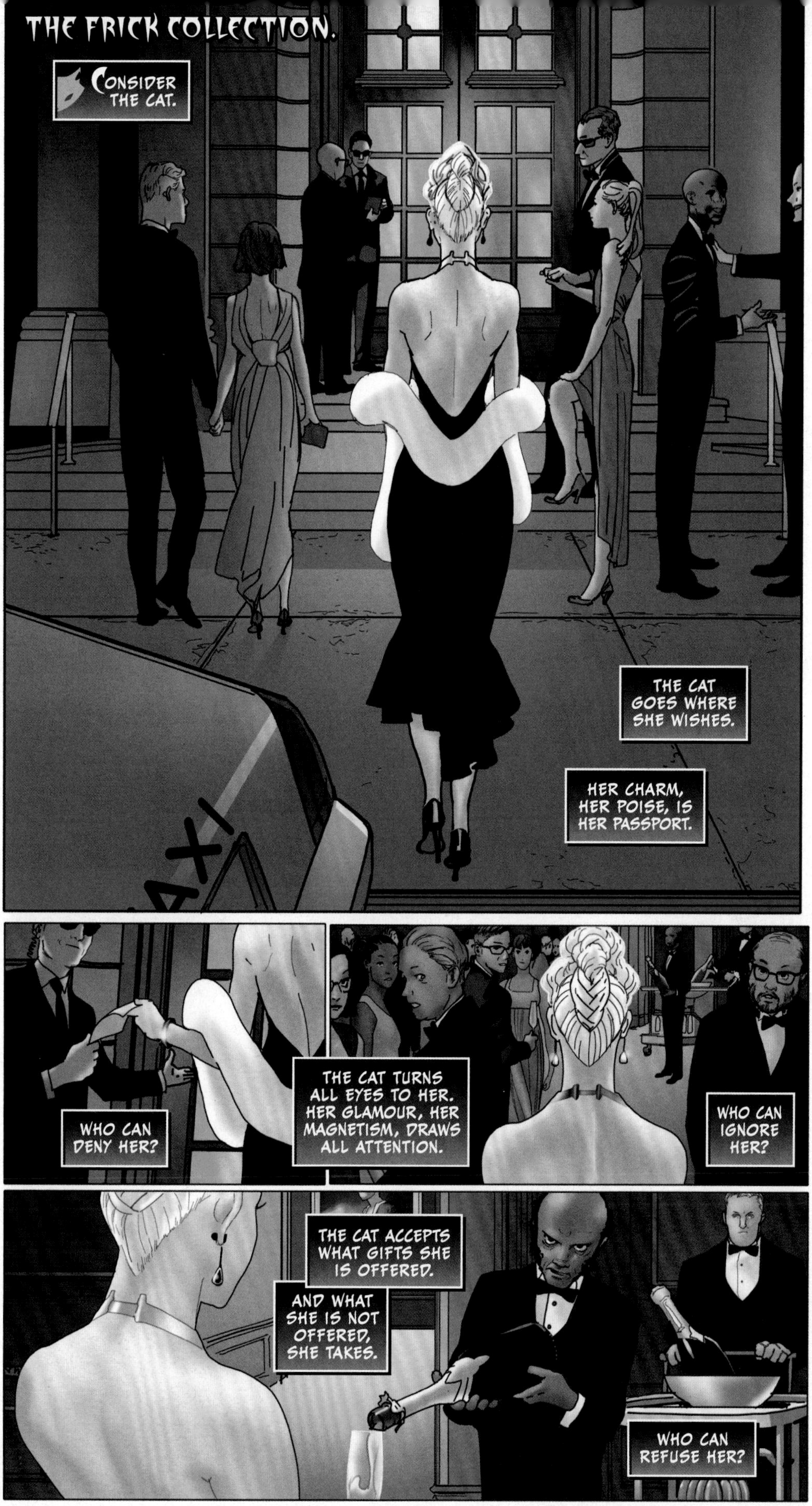
THE FRICK COLLECTION.
CONSIDER THE CAT.
THE CAT GOES WHERE SHE WISHES.
HER CHARM, HER POISE, IS HER PASSPORT.
WHO CAN DENY HER?
THE CAT TURNS ALL EYES TO HER. HER GLAMOUR, HER MAGNETISM, DRAWS ALL ATTENTION.
WHO CAN IGNORE HER?
THE CAT ACCEPTS WHAT GIFTS SHE IS OFFERED.
AND WHAT SHE IS NOT OFFERED, SHE TAKES.
WHO CAN REFUSE HER?

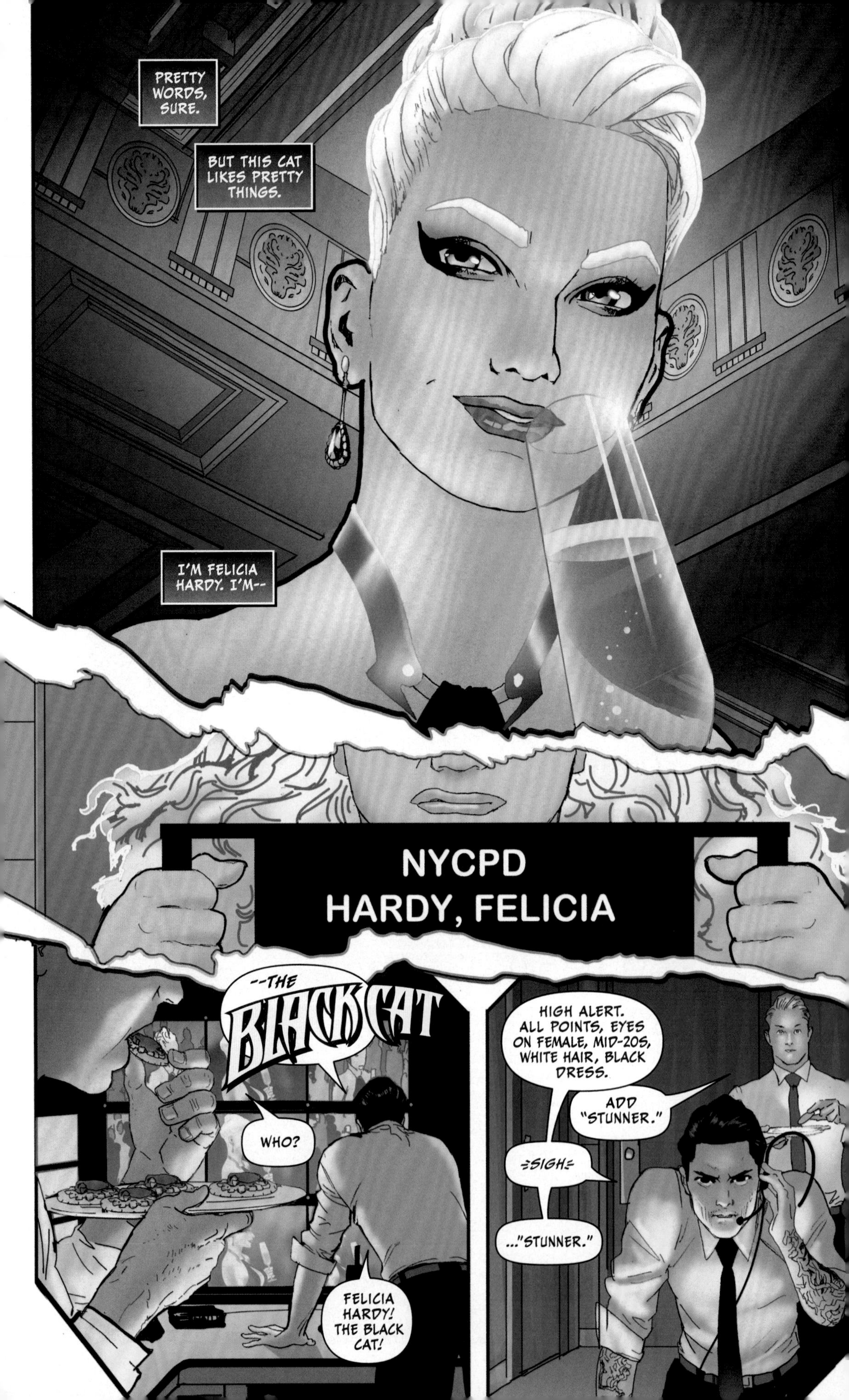
PRETTY WORDS, SURE.
BUT THIS CAT LIKES PRETTY THINGS.
I'M FELICIA HARDY. I'M--
NYCPD
HARDY, FELICIA
--THE BLACK CAT
WHO?
FELICIA HARDY! THE BLACK CAT!
HIGH ALERT. ALL POINTS, EYES ON FEMALE, MID-20S, WHITE HAIR, BLACK DRESS.
ADD "STUNNER."
=SIGH=
..."STUNNER."

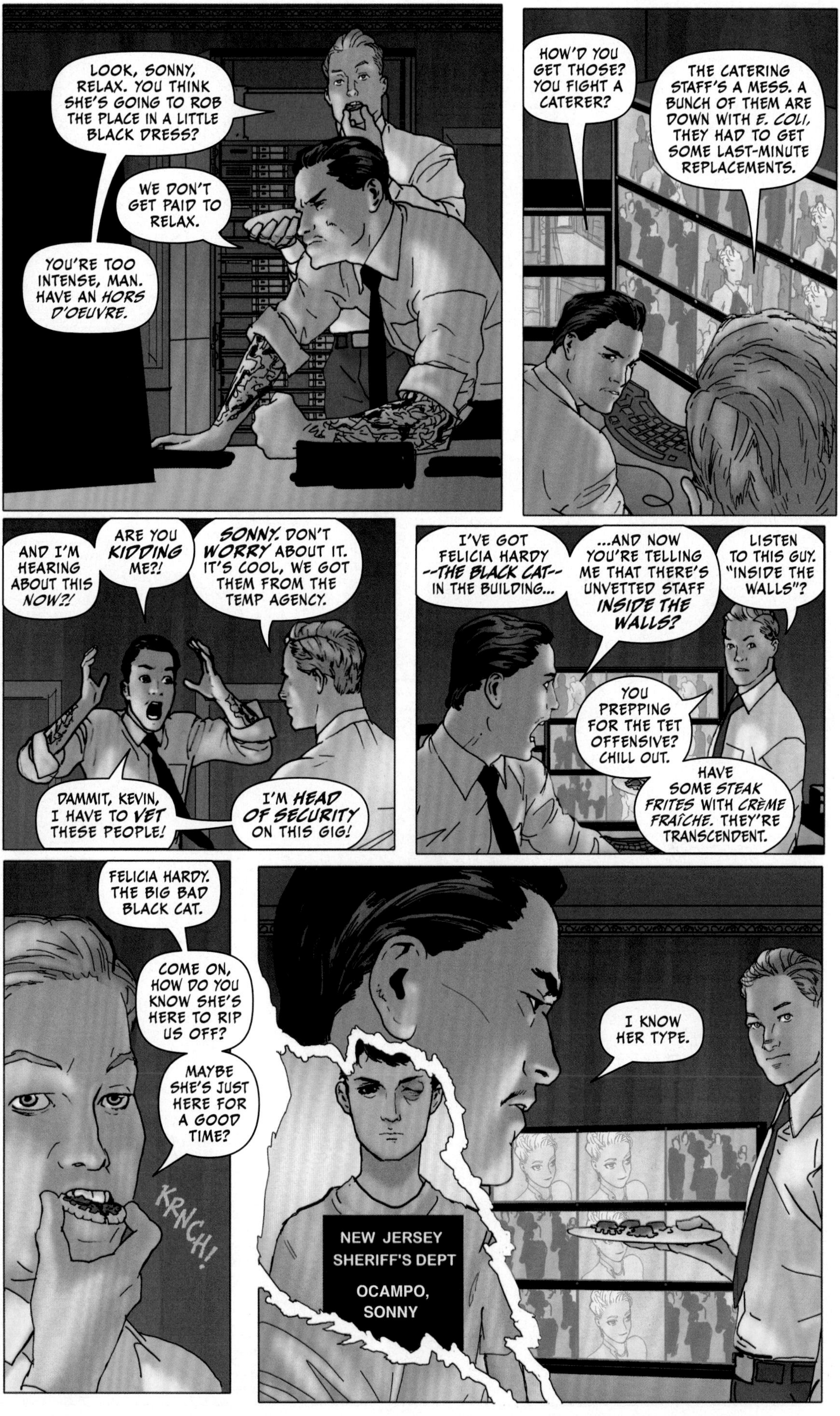
LOOK, SONNY, RELAX. YOU THINK SHE'S GOING TO ROB THE PLACE IN A LITTLE BLACK DRESS?
WE DON'T GET PAID TO RELAX.
YOU'RE TOO INTENSE, MAN. HAVE AN *HORS D'OEUVRE.*
HOW'D YOU GET THOSE? YOU FIGHT A CATERER?
THE CATERING STAFF'S A MESS. A BUNCH OF THEM ARE DOWN WITH *E. COLI,* THEY HAD TO GET SOME LAST-MINUTE REPLACEMENTS.
AND I'M HEARING ABOUT THIS *NOW?!*
ARE YOU *KIDDING* ME?!
SONNY. DON'T *WORRY* ABOUT IT. IT'S COOL, WE GOT THEM FROM THE TEMP AGENCY.
DAMMIT, KEVIN, I HAVE TO *VET* THESE PEOPLE!
I'M *HEAD OF SECURITY* ON THIS GIG!
I'VE GOT FELICIA HARDY *--THE BLACK CAT--* IN THE BUILDING...
...AND NOW YOU'RE TELLING ME THAT THERE'S UNVETTED STAFF *INSIDE THE WALLS?*
LISTEN TO THIS GUY. "INSIDE THE WALLS"?
YOU PREPPING FOR THE TET OFFENSIVE? CHILL OUT.
HAVE SOME *STEAK FRITES* WITH *CRÈME FRAÎCHE.* THEY'RE TRANSCENDENT.
FELICIA HARDY. THE BIG BAD BLACK CAT.
COME ON, HOW DO YOU KNOW SHE'S HERE TO RIP US OFF?
MAYBE SHE'S JUST HERE FOR A GOOD TIME?
KRNCH!
I KNOW HER TYPE.
NEW JERSEY SHERIFF'S DEPT
OCAMPO, SONNY

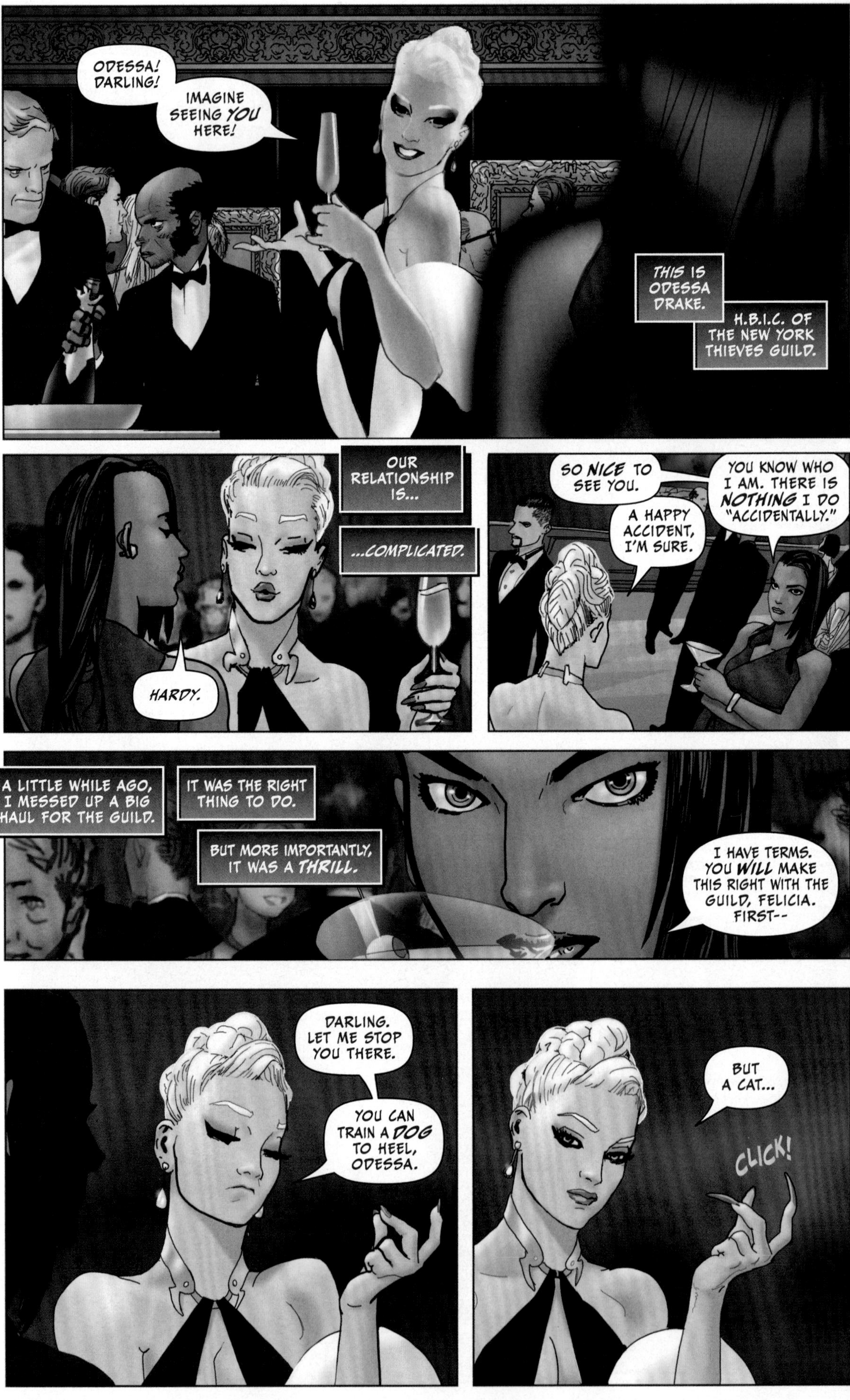
ODESSA! DARLING!
IMAGINE SEEING YOU HERE!
THIS IS ODESSA DRAKE.
H.B.I.C. OF THE NEW YORK THIEVES GUILD.
OUR RELATIONSHIP IS...
...COMPLICATED.
HARDY.
SO NICE TO SEE YOU.
A HAPPY ACCIDENT, I'M SURE.
YOU KNOW WHO I AM. THERE IS NOTHING I DO "ACCIDENTALLY."
A LITTLE WHILE AGO, I MESSED UP A BIG HAUL FOR THE GUILD.
IT WAS THE RIGHT THING TO DO.
BUT MORE IMPORTANTLY, IT WAS A THRILL.
I HAVE TERMS. YOU WILL MAKE THIS RIGHT WITH THE GUILD, FELICIA. FIRST--
DARLING. LET ME STOP YOU THERE.
YOU CAN TRAIN A DOG TO HEEL, ODESSA.
BUT A CAT...
CLICK!

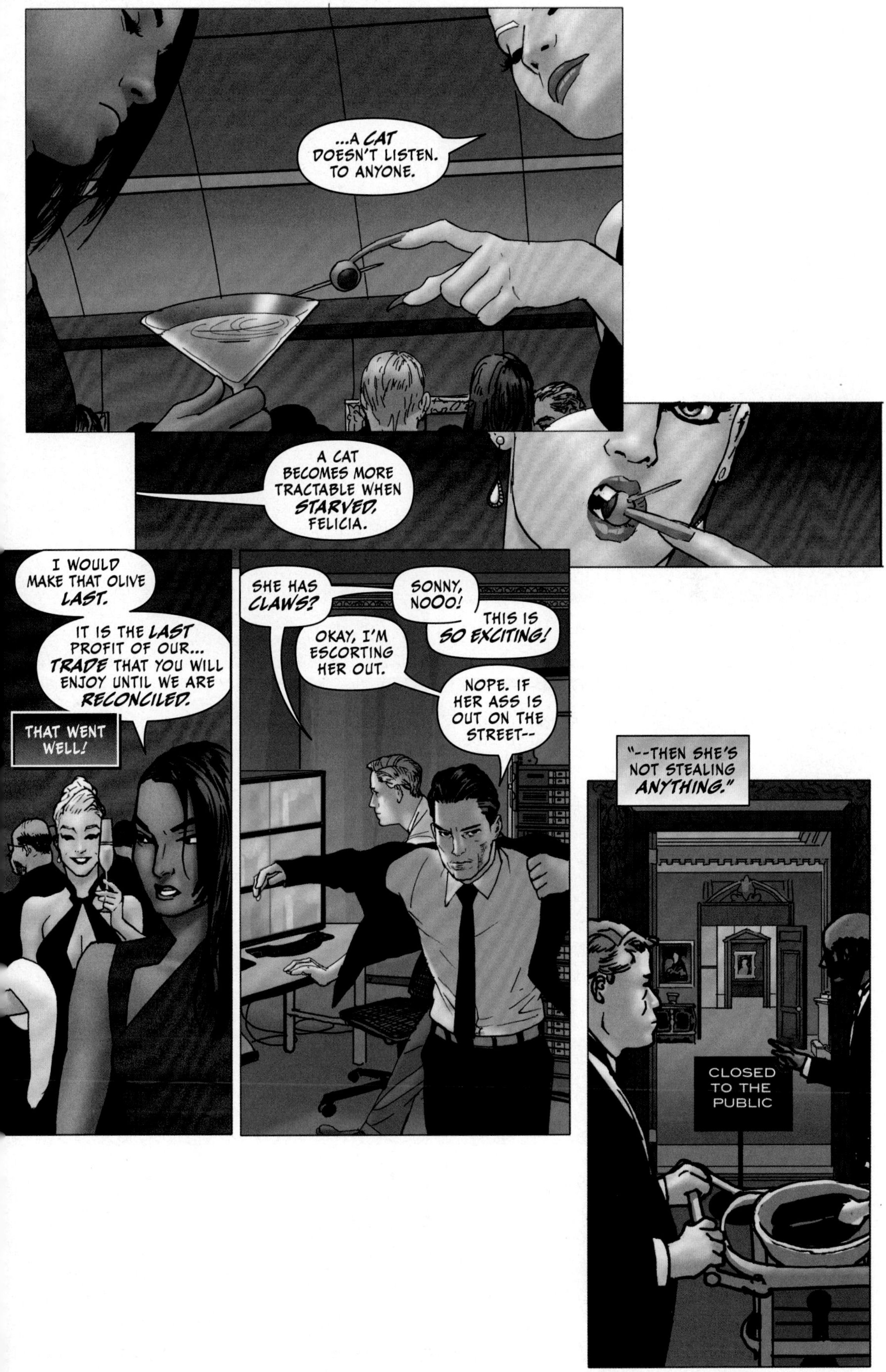
...A CAT DOESN'T LISTEN. TO ANYONE.
A CAT BECOMES MORE TRACTABLE WHEN STARVED, FELICIA.
I WOULD MAKE THAT OLIVE LAST.
IT IS THE LAST PROFIT OF OUR... TRADE THAT YOU WILL ENJOY UNTIL WE ARE RECONCILED.
THAT WENT WELL!
SHE HAS CLAWS?
SONNY, NOOO!
THIS IS SO EXCITING!
OKAY, I'M ESCORTING HER OUT.
NOPE. IF HER ASS IS OUT ON THE STREET--
"--THEN SHE'S NOT STEALING ANYTHING."
CLOSED TO THE PUBLIC

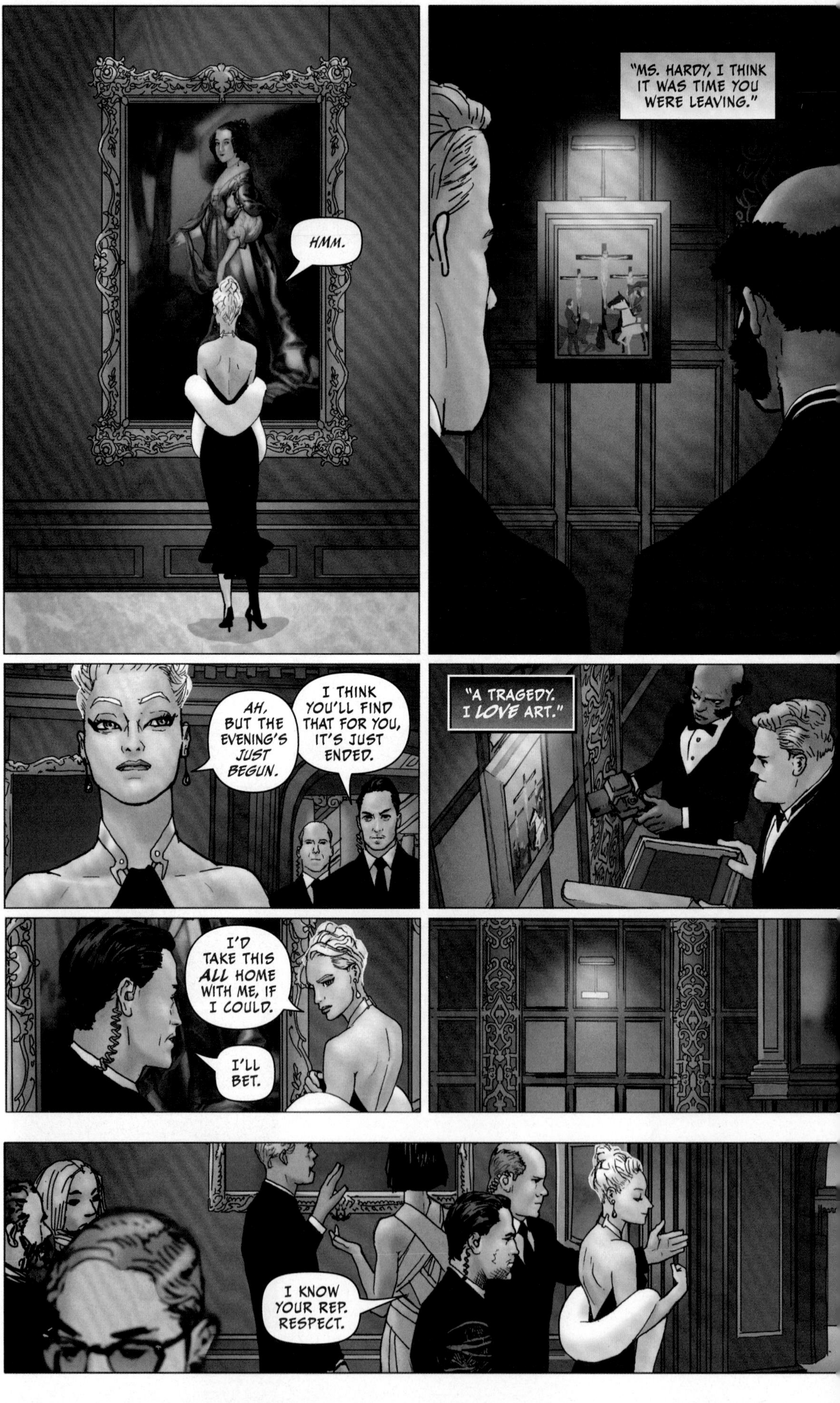
HMM.
"MS. HARDY, I THINK IT WAS TIME YOU WERE LEAVING."
AH, BUT THE EVENING'S JUST BEGUN.
I THINK YOU'LL FIND THAT FOR YOU, IT'S JUST ENDED.
"A TRAGEDY. I LOVE ART."
I'D TAKE THIS ALL HOME WITH ME, IF I COULD.
I'LL BET.
I KNOW YOUR REP. RESPECT.

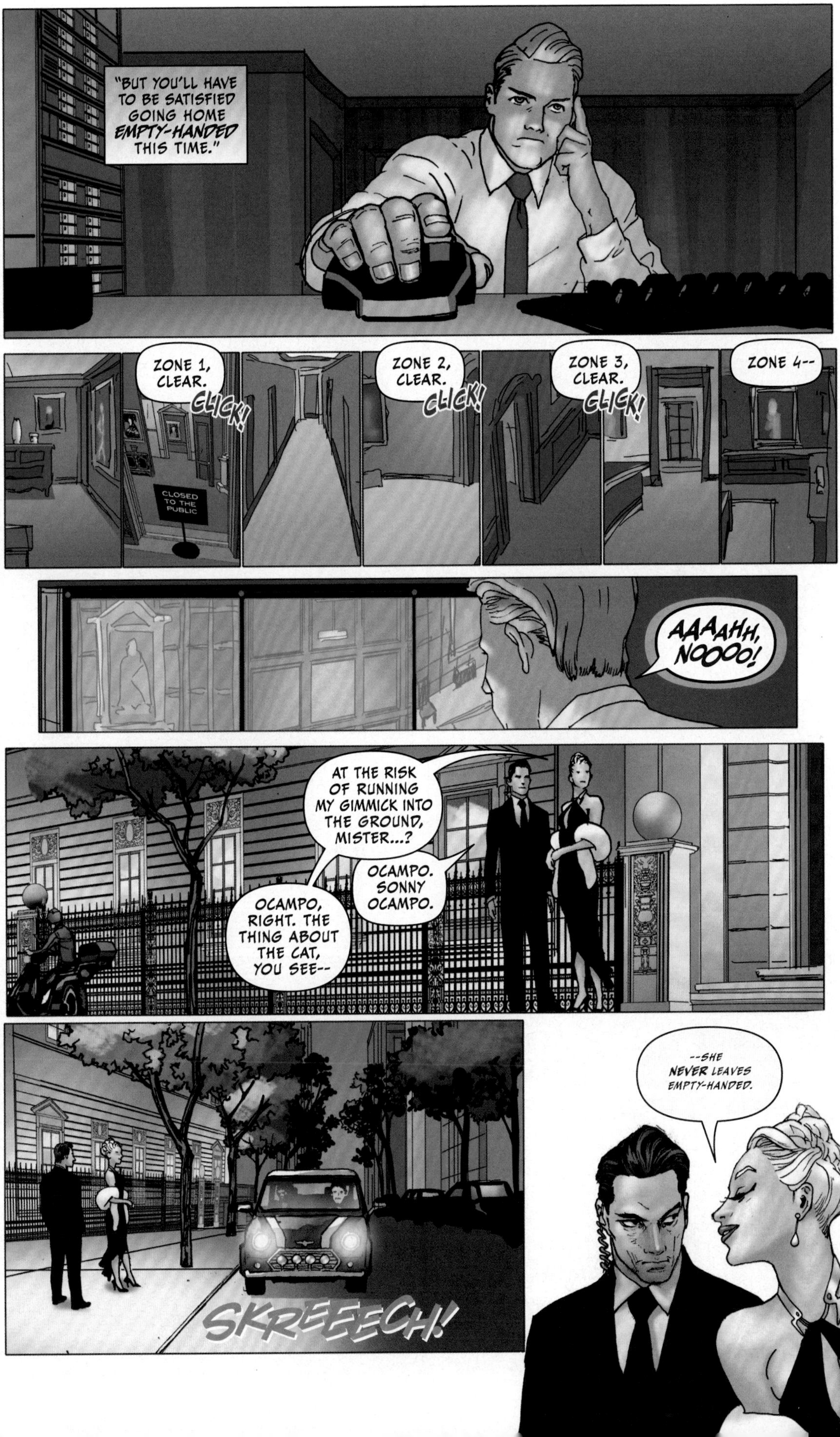
"BUT YOU'LL HAVE TO BE SATISFIED GOING HOME EMPTY-HANDED THIS TIME."
ZONE 1, CLEAR.
CLICK!
CLOSED TO THE PUBLIC
ZONE 2, CLEAR.
CLICK!
ZONE 3, CLEAR.
CLICK!
ZONE 4--
AAAAHH, NOOOO!
AT THE RISK OF RUNNING MY GIMMICK INTO THE GROUND, MISTER...?
OCAMPO. SONNY OCAMPO.
OCAMPO, RIGHT. THE THING ABOUT THE CAT, YOU SEE--
SKREEEECH!
--SHE NEVER LEAVES EMPTY-HANDED.

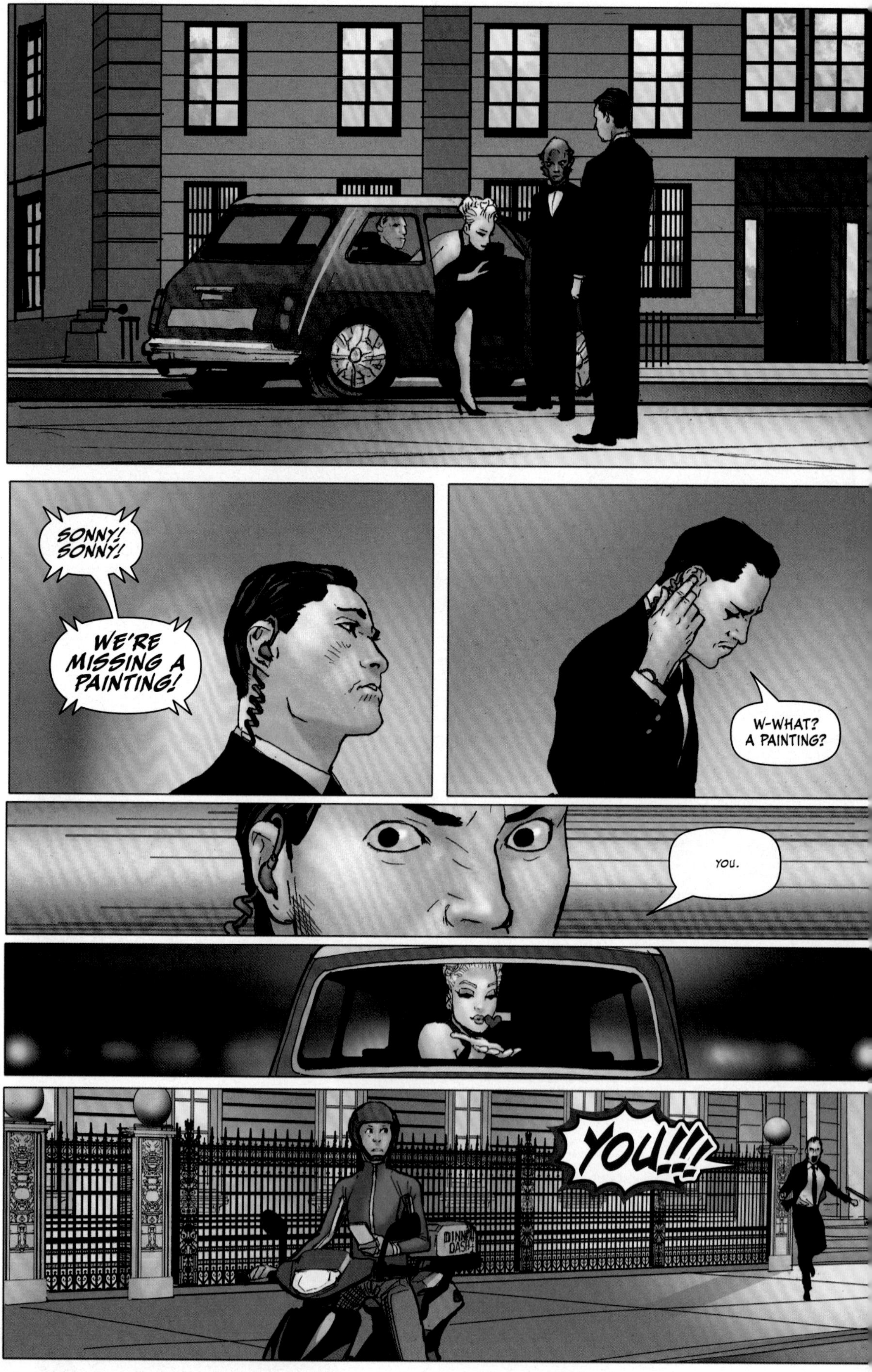
SONNY! SONNY!
WE'RE MISSING A PAINTING!
W-WHAT? A PAINTING?
YOU.
YOU!!!

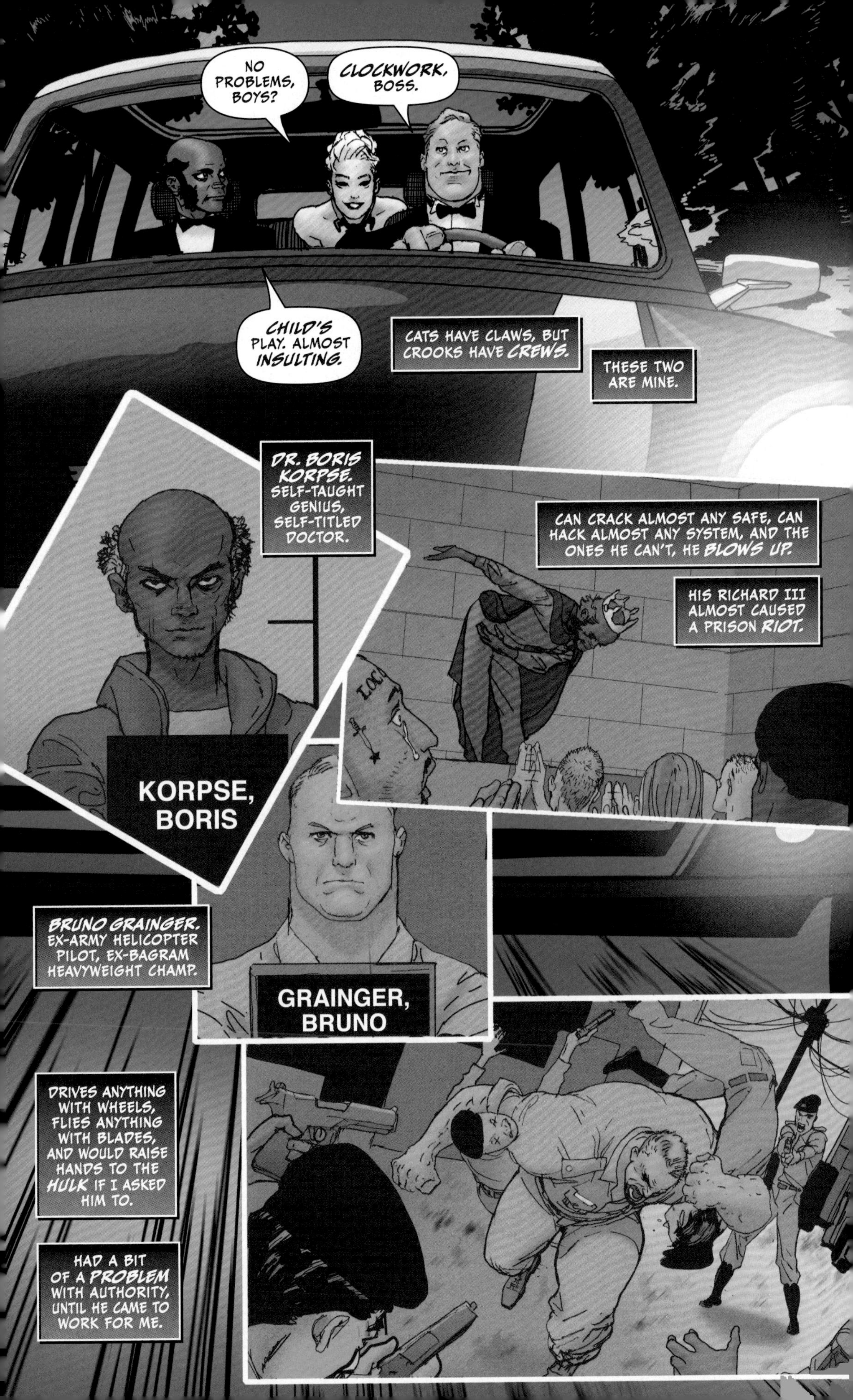
NO PROBLEMS, BOYS?
CLOCKWORK, BOSS.
CHILD'S PLAY. ALMOST INSULTING.
CATS HAVE CLAWS, BUT CROOKS HAVE CREWS.
THESE TWO ARE MINE.
DR. BORIS KORPSE. SELF-TAUGHT GENIUS, SELF-TITLED DOCTOR.
KORPSE, BORIS
CAN CRACK ALMOST ANY SAFE, CAN HACK ALMOST ANY SYSTEM, AND THE ONES HE CAN'T, HE BLOWS UP.
HIS RICHARD III ALMOST CAUSED A PRISON RIOT.
BRUNO GRAINGER. EX-ARMY HELICOPTER PILOT, EX-BAGRAM HEAVYWEIGHT CHAMP.
GRAINGER, BRUNO
DRIVES ANYTHING WITH WHEELS, FLIES ANYTHING WITH BLADES, AND WOULD RAISE HANDS TO THE HULK IF I ASKED HIM TO.
HAD A BIT OF A PROBLEM WITH AUTHORITY, UNTIL HE CAME TO WORK FOR ME.

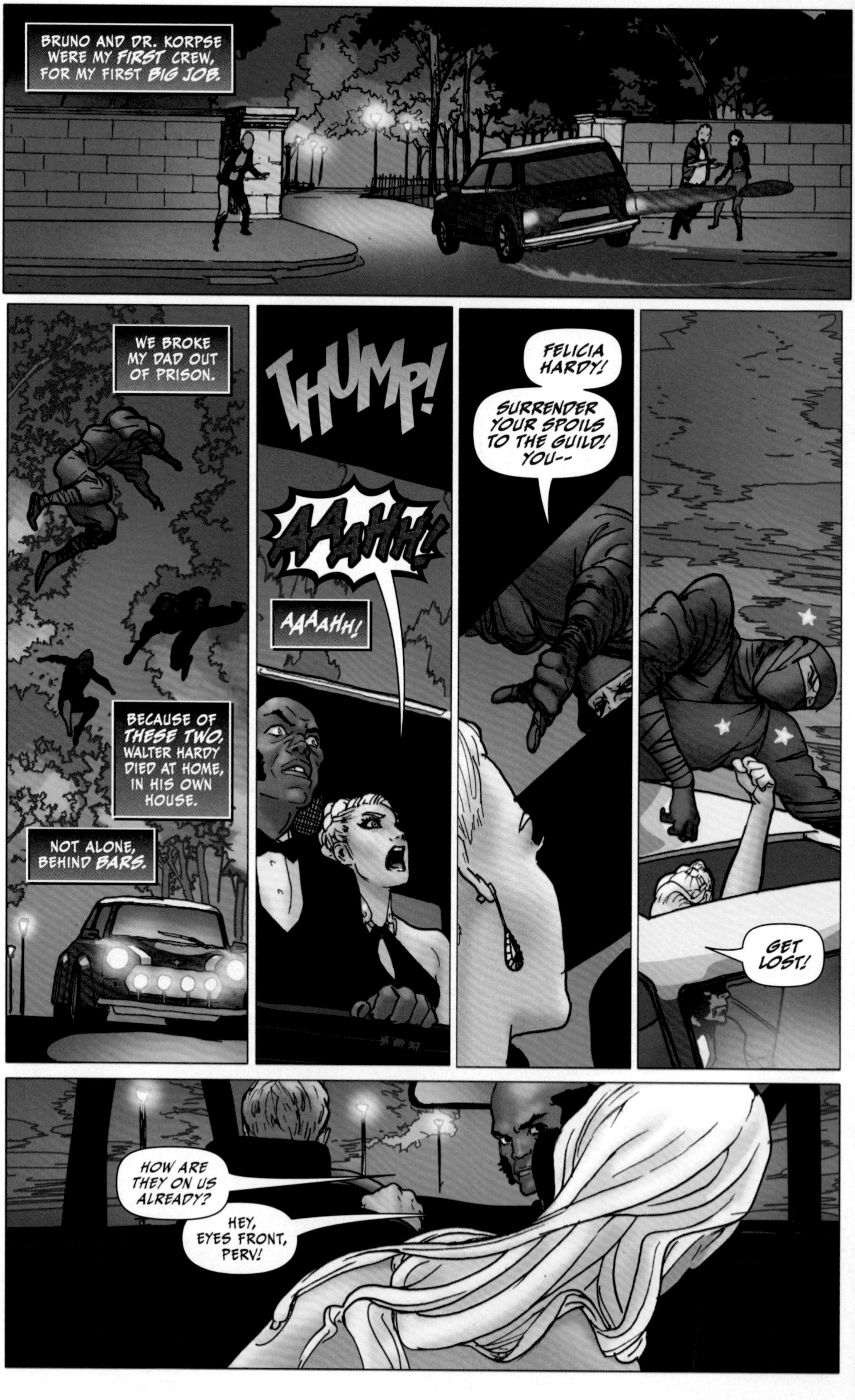
BRUNO AND DR. KORPSE WERE MY FIRST CREW, FOR MY FIRST BIG JOB.
WE BROKE MY DAD OUT OF PRISON.
BECAUSE OF THESE TWO, WALTER HARDY DIED AT HOME, IN HIS OWN HOUSE.
NOT ALONE, BEHIND BARS.
THUMP!
AAAHH!
AAAAHH!
FELICIA HARDY!
SURRENDER YOUR SPOILS TO THE GUILD! YOU--
GET LOST!
HOW ARE THEY ON US ALREADY?
HEY, EYES FRONT, PERV!

BOSS! BOSS, YOU GOT A PLAN?

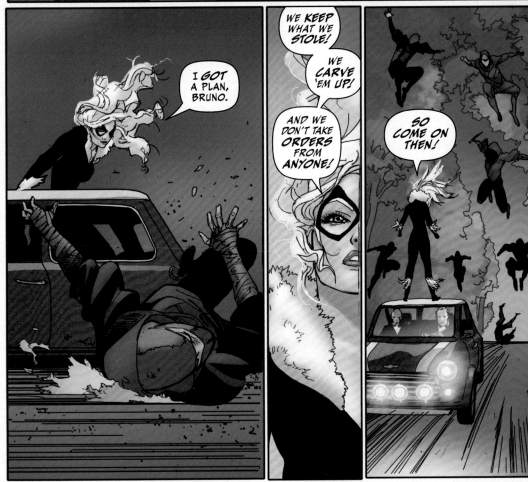

I GOT A PLAN, BRUNO.

WE KEEP WHAT WE STOLE!

WE CARVE 'EM UP!

AND WE DON'T TAKE ORDERS FROM ANYONE!

SO COME ON THEN!

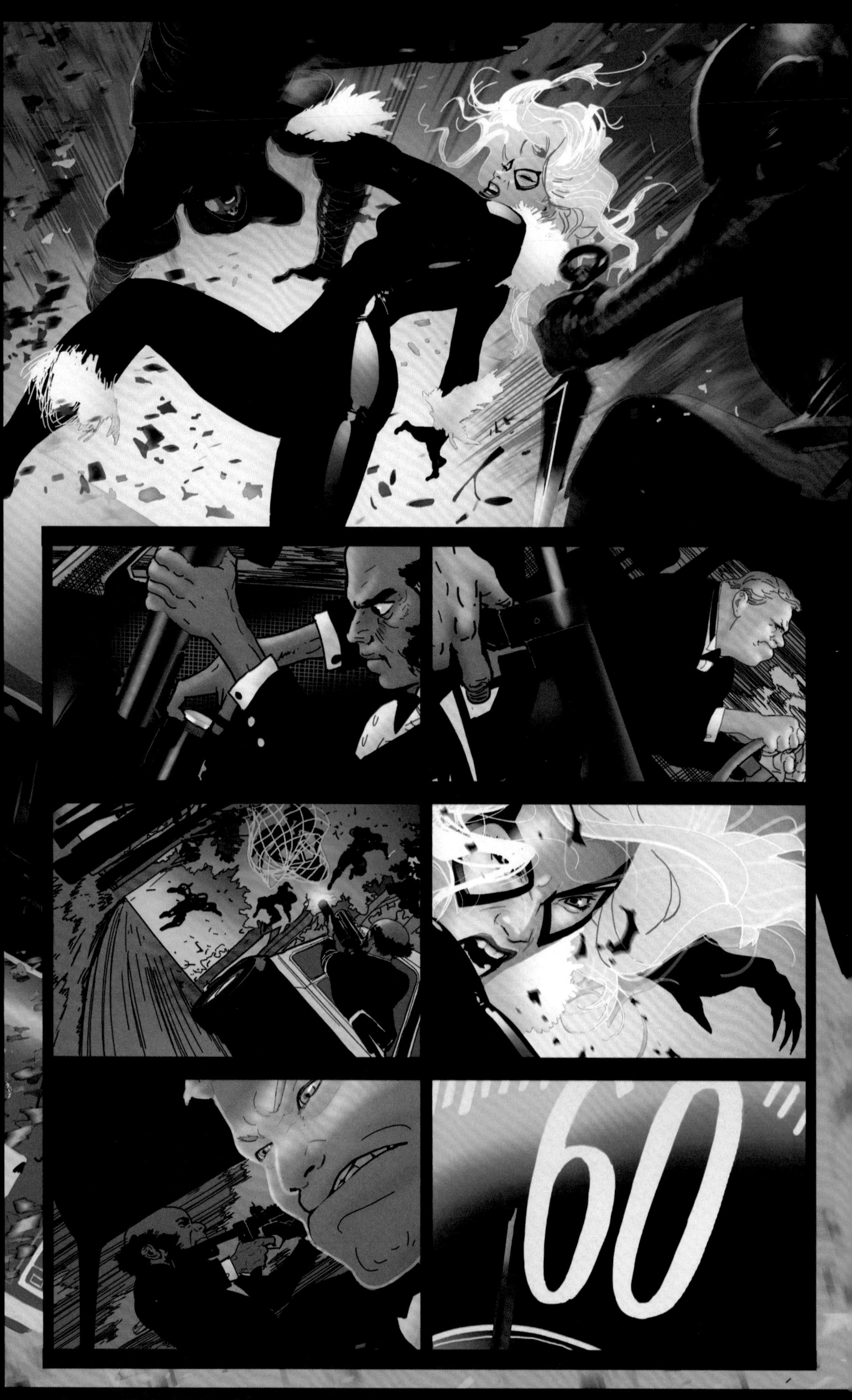

60

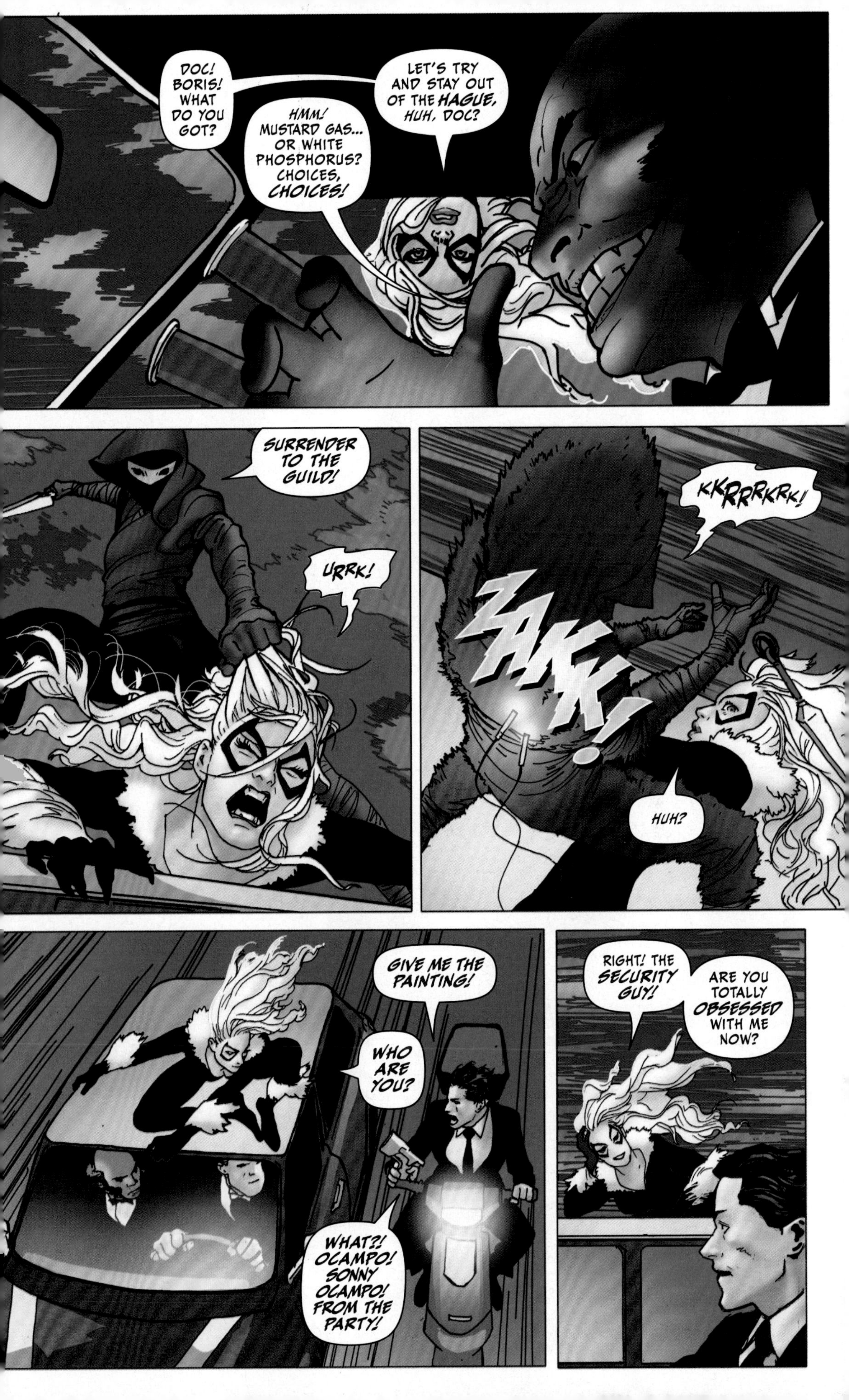
DOC! BORIS! WHAT DO YOU GOT?
LET'S TRY AND STAY OUT OF THE HAGUE, HUH, DOC?
HMM! MUSTARD GAS... OR WHITE PHOSPHORUS? CHOICES, CHOICES!
SURRENDER TO THE GUILD!
URRK!
KKRRRKRK!
ZAKK!
HUH?
GIVE ME THE PAINTING!
WHO ARE YOU?
WHAT?! OCAMPO! SONNY OCAMPO! FROM THE PARTY!
RIGHT! THE SECURITY GUY!
ARE YOU TOTALLY OBSESSED WITH ME NOW?

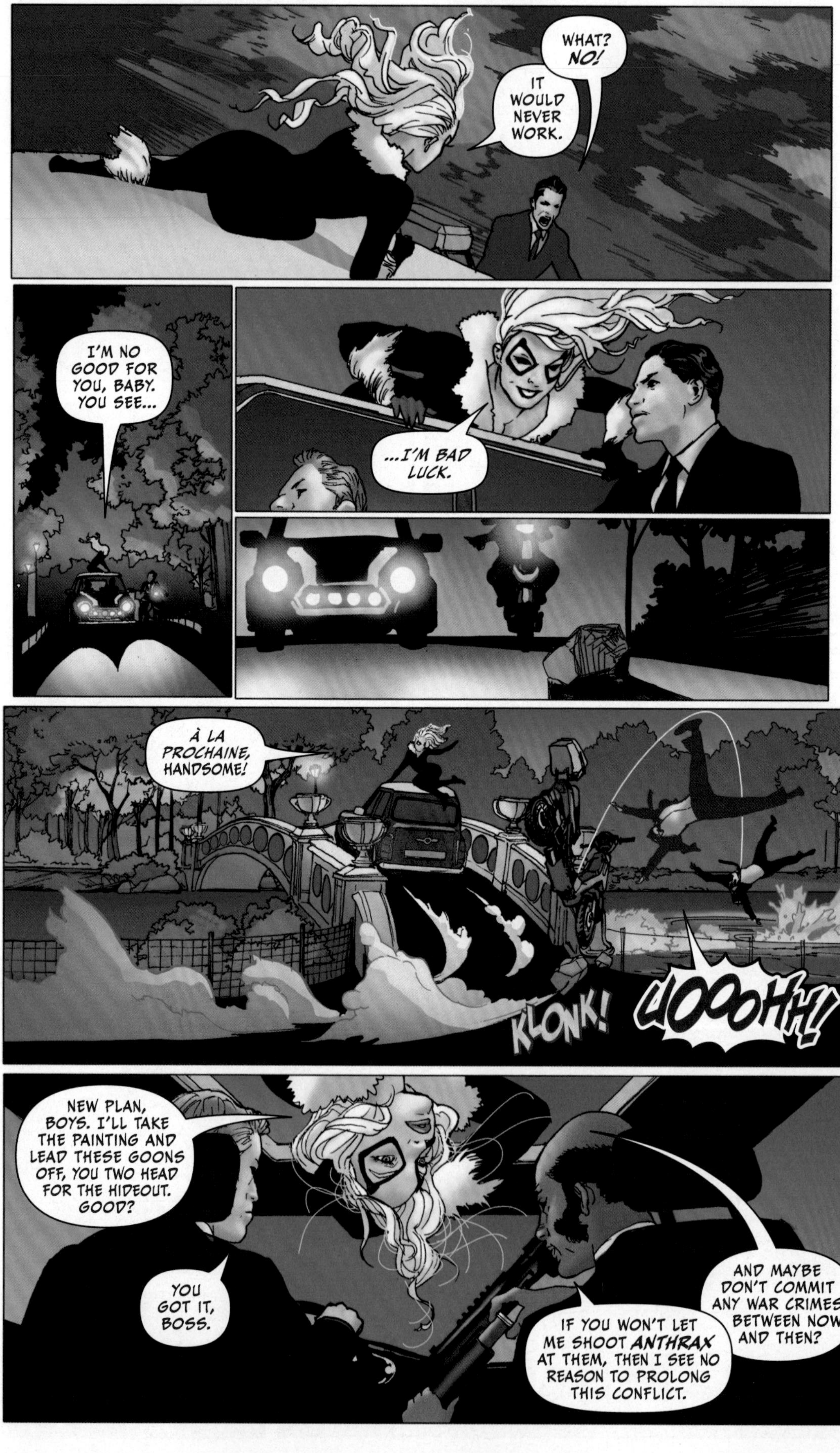
WHAT? NO!
IT WOULD NEVER WORK.
I'M NO GOOD FOR YOU, BABY. YOU SEE...
...I'M BAD LUCK.
À LA PROCHAINE, HANDSOME!
KLONK!
UOOOHH!
NEW PLAN, BOYS. I'LL TAKE THE PAINTING AND LEAD THESE GOONS OFF, YOU TWO HEAD FOR THE HIDEOUT. GOOD?
YOU GOT IT, BOSS.
IF YOU WON'T LET ME SHOOT ANTHRAX AT THEM, THEN I SEE NO REASON TO PROLONG THIS CONFLICT.
AND MAYBE DON'T COMMIT ANY WAR CRIMES BETWEEN NOW AND THEN?

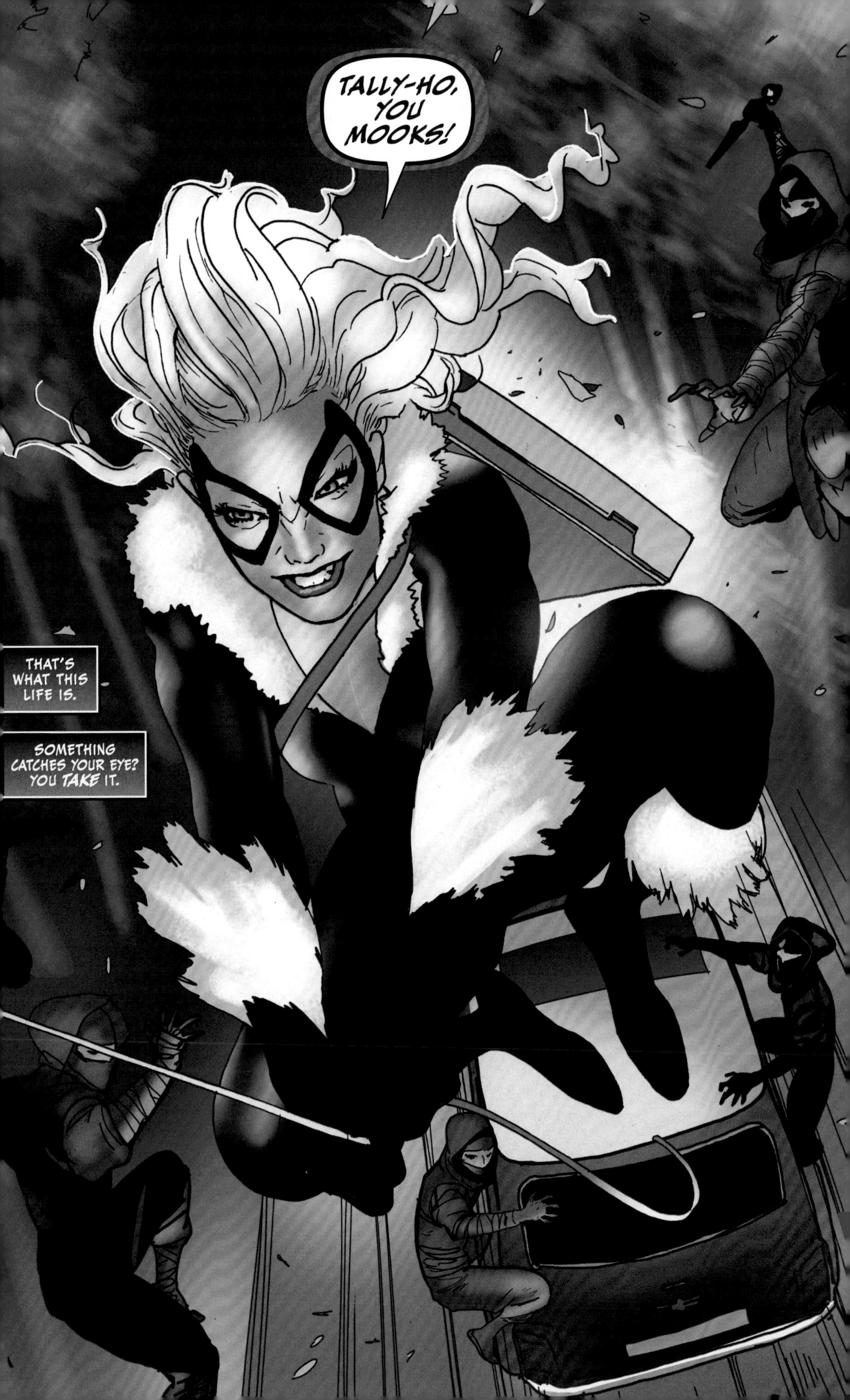
TALLY-HO, YOU MOOKS!
THAT'S WHAT THIS LIFE IS.
SOMETHING CATCHES YOUR EYE? YOU TAKE IT.

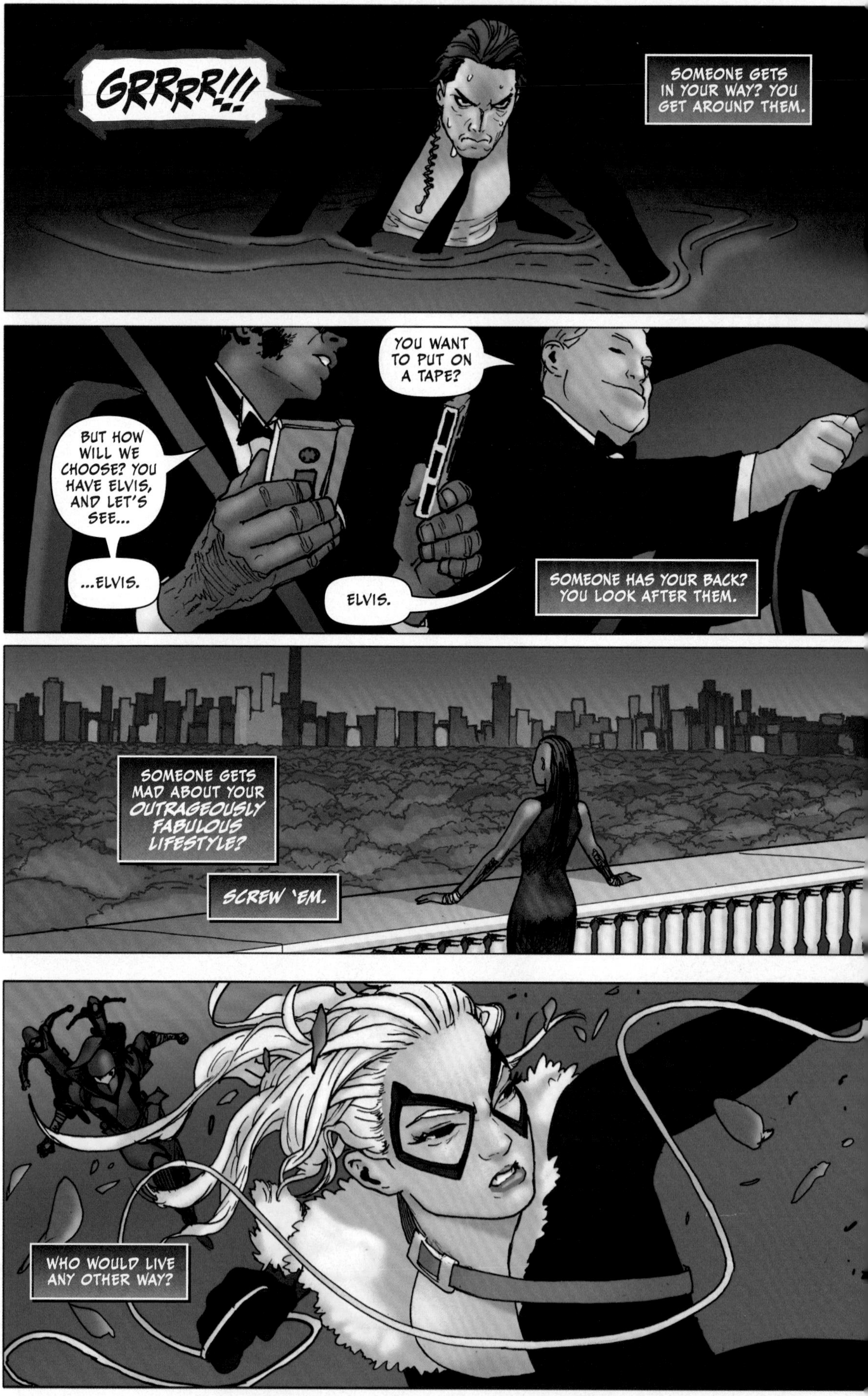
GRRRR!!!
SOMEONE GETS IN YOUR WAY? YOU GET AROUND THEM.
YOU WANT TO PUT ON A TAPE?
BUT HOW WILL WE CHOOSE? YOU HAVE ELVIS, AND LET'S SEE...
...ELVIS.
ELVIS.
SOMEONE HAS YOUR BACK? YOU LOOK AFTER THEM.
SOMEONE GETS MAD ABOUT YOUR OUTRAGEOUSLY FABULOUS LIFESTYLE?
SCREW 'EM.
WHO WOULD LIVE ANY OTHER WAY?

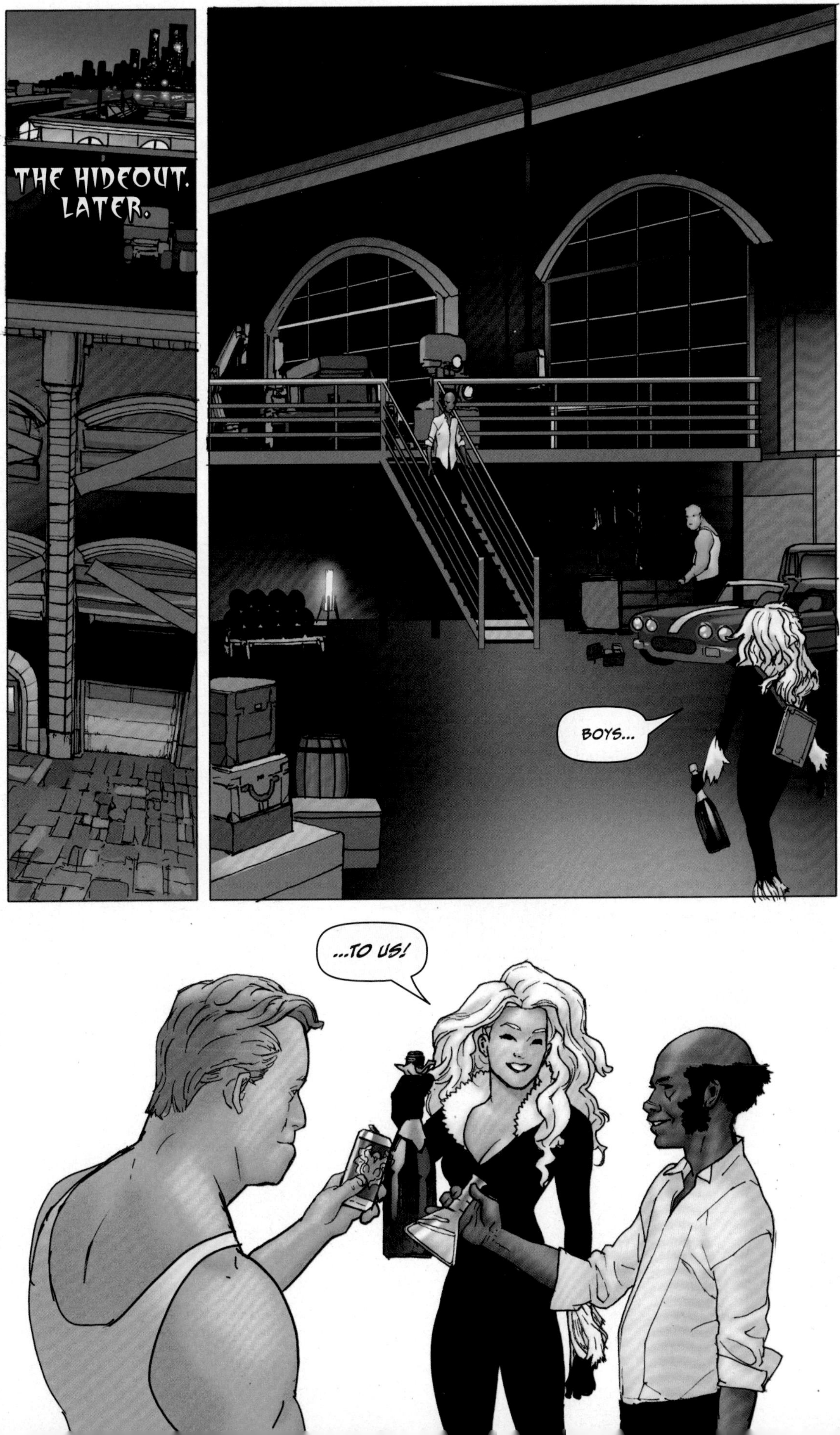
THE HIDEOUT. LATER.
BOYS...
...TO US!

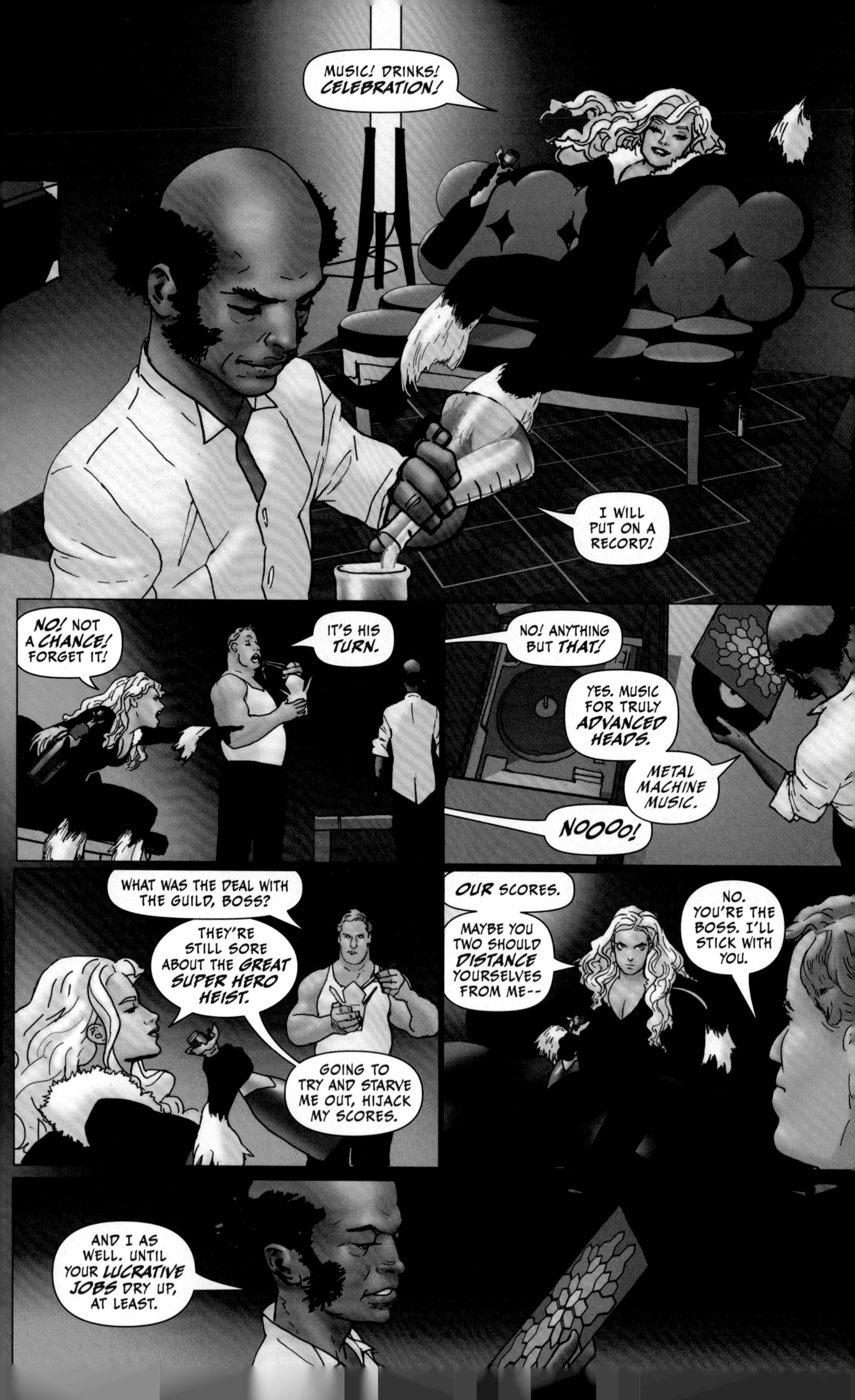
MUSIC! DRINKS! CELEBRATION!
I WILL PUT ON A RECORD!
NO! NOT A CHANCE! FORGET IT!
IT'S HIS TURN.
NO! ANYTHING BUT THAT!
YES. MUSIC FOR TRULY ADVANCED HEADS.
METAL MACHINE MUSIC.
NOOOO!
WHAT WAS THE DEAL WITH THE GUILD, BOSS?
THEY'RE STILL SORE ABOUT THE GREAT SUPER HERO HEIST.
GOING TO TRY AND STARVE ME OUT, HIJACK MY SCORES.
OUR SCORES.
MAYBE YOU TWO SHOULD DISTANCE YOURSELVES FROM ME--
NO. YOU'RE THE BOSS. I'LL STICK WITH YOU.
AND I AS WELL. UNTIL YOUR LUCRATIVE JOBS DRY UP, AT LEAST.

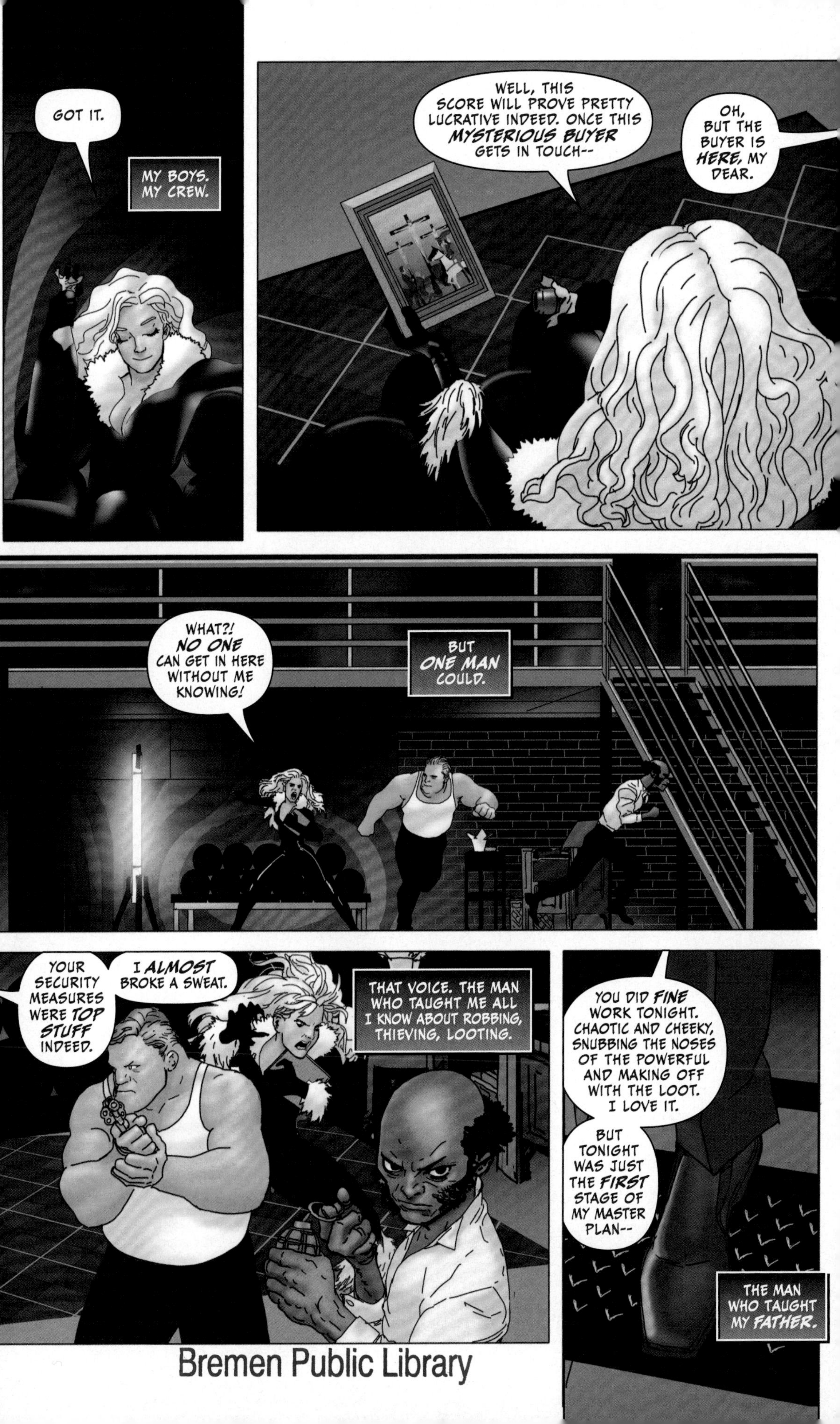
GOT IT.
MY BOYS. MY CREW.
WELL, THIS SCORE WILL PROVE PRETTY LUCRATIVE INDEED. ONCE THIS MYSTERIOUS BUYER GETS IN TOUCH--
OH, BUT THE BUYER IS HERE, MY DEAR.
WHAT?! NO ONE CAN GET IN HERE WITHOUT ME KNOWING!
BUT ONE MAN COULD.
YOUR SECURITY MEASURES WERE TOP STUFF INDEED.
I ALMOST BROKE A SWEAT.
THAT VOICE. THE MAN WHO TAUGHT ME ALL I KNOW ABOUT ROBBING, THIEVING, LOOTING.
YOU DID FINE WORK TONIGHT. CHAOTIC AND CHEEKY, SNUBBING THE NOSES OF THE POWERFUL AND MAKING OFF WITH THE LOOT. I LOVE IT.
BUT TONIGHT WAS JUST THE FIRST STAGE OF MY MASTER PLAN--
THE MAN WHO TAUGHT MY FATHER.

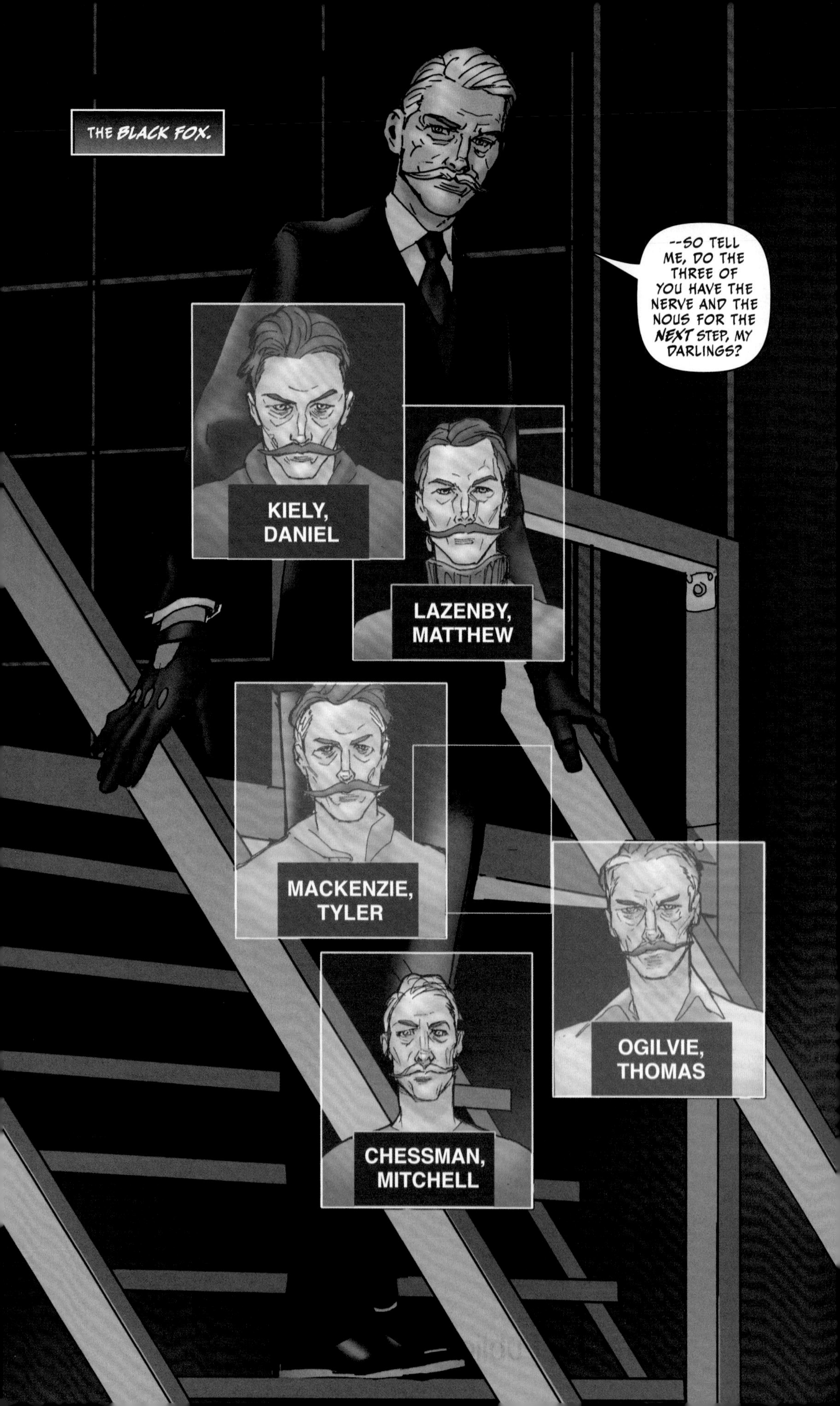
THE BLACK FOX.
--SO TELL ME, DO THE THREE OF YOU HAVE THE NERVE AND THE NOUS FOR THE NEXT STEP, MY DARLINGS?
KIELY, DANIEL
LAZENBY, MATTHEW
MACKENZIE, TYLER
OGILVIE, THOMAS
CHESSMAN, MITCHELL

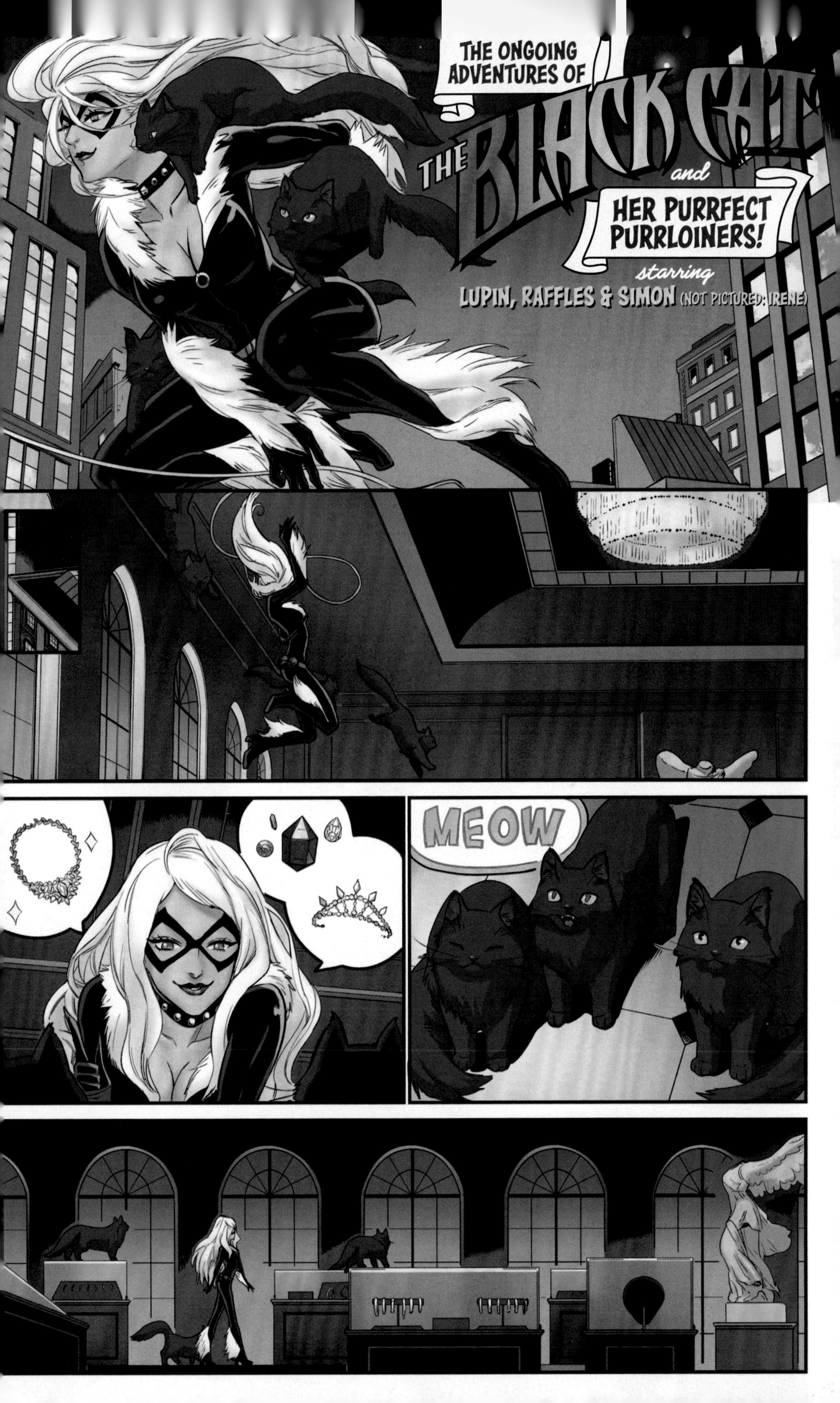
THE ONGOING ADVENTURES OF
THE BLACK CAT
and
HER PURRFECT PURRLOINERS!
starring
LUPIN, RAFFLES & SIMON (NOT PICTURED: IRENE)
MEOW

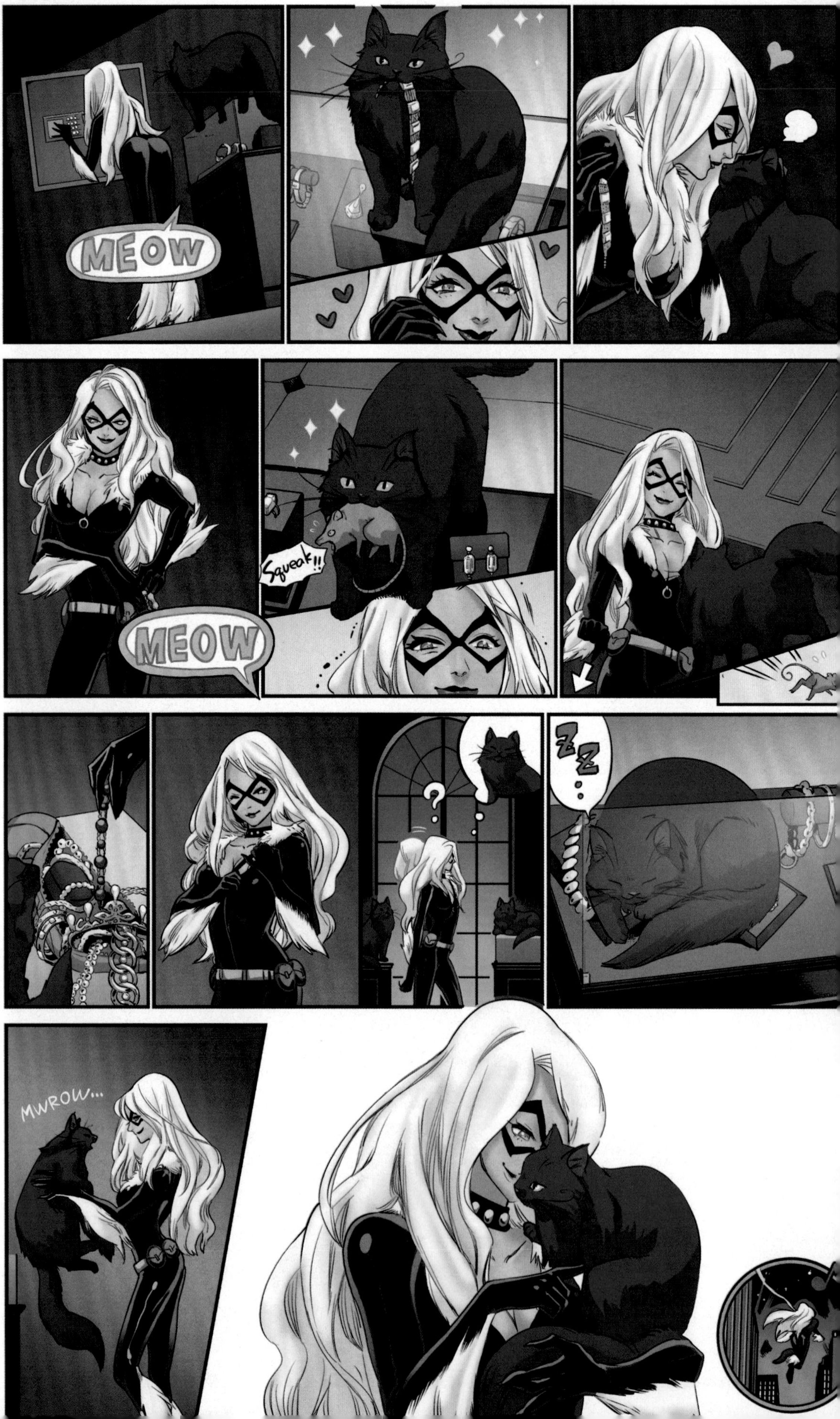
MEOW
Squeak!!
MEOW
ZZZ
MWROW...

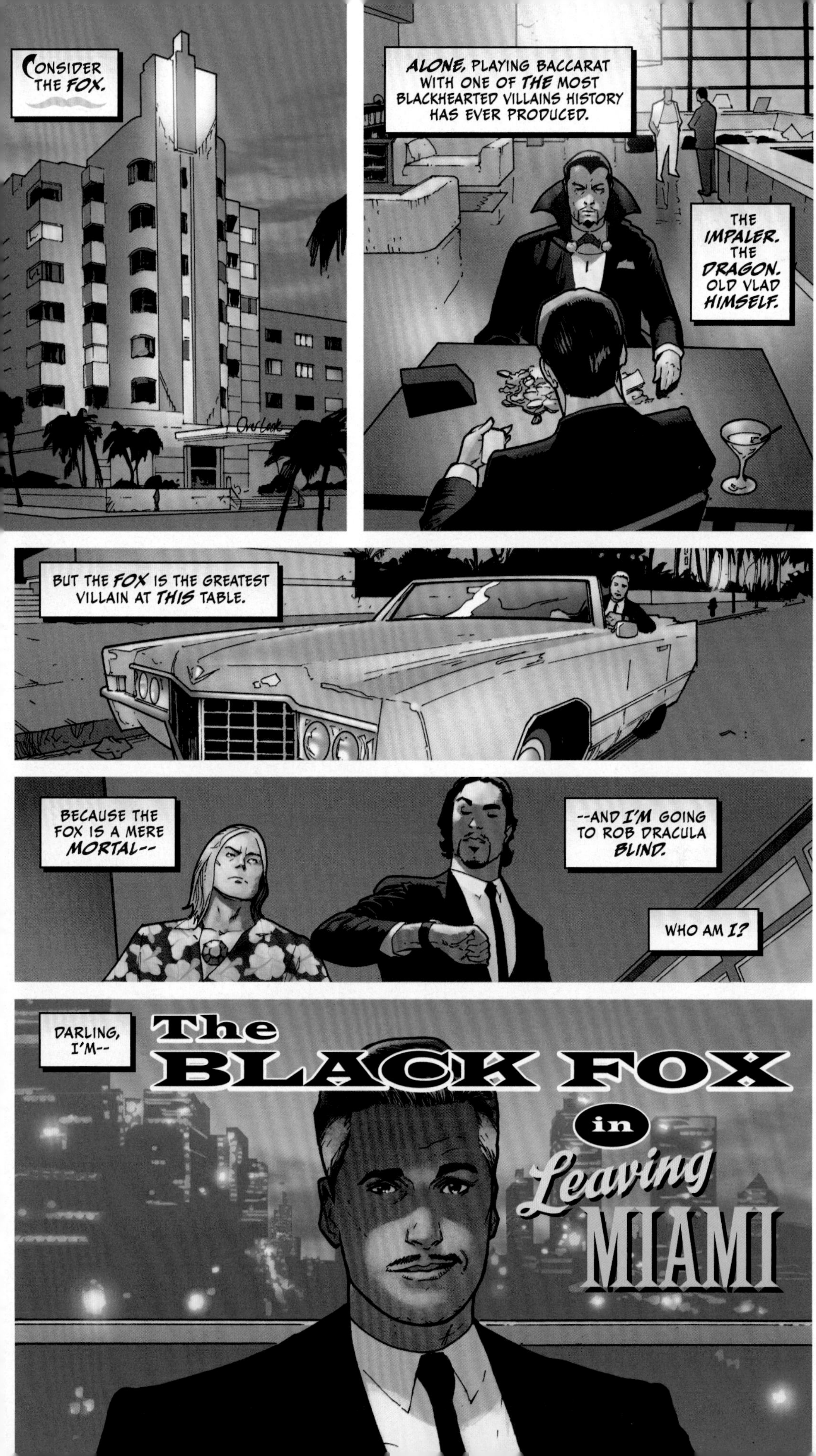
CONSIDER THE *FOX.*
ALONE, PLAYING BACCARAT WITH ONE OF *THE* MOST BLACKHEARTED VILLAINS HISTORY HAS EVER PRODUCED.
THE *IMPALER.* THE *DRAGON.* OLD VLAD *HIMSELF.*
BUT THE *FOX* IS THE GREATEST VILLAIN AT *THIS* TABLE.
BECAUSE THE FOX IS A MERE *MORTAL*--
--AND *I'M* GOING TO ROB DRACULA *BLIND.*
WHO AM *I?*
DARLING, I'M--
The BLACK FOX in Leaving MIAMI

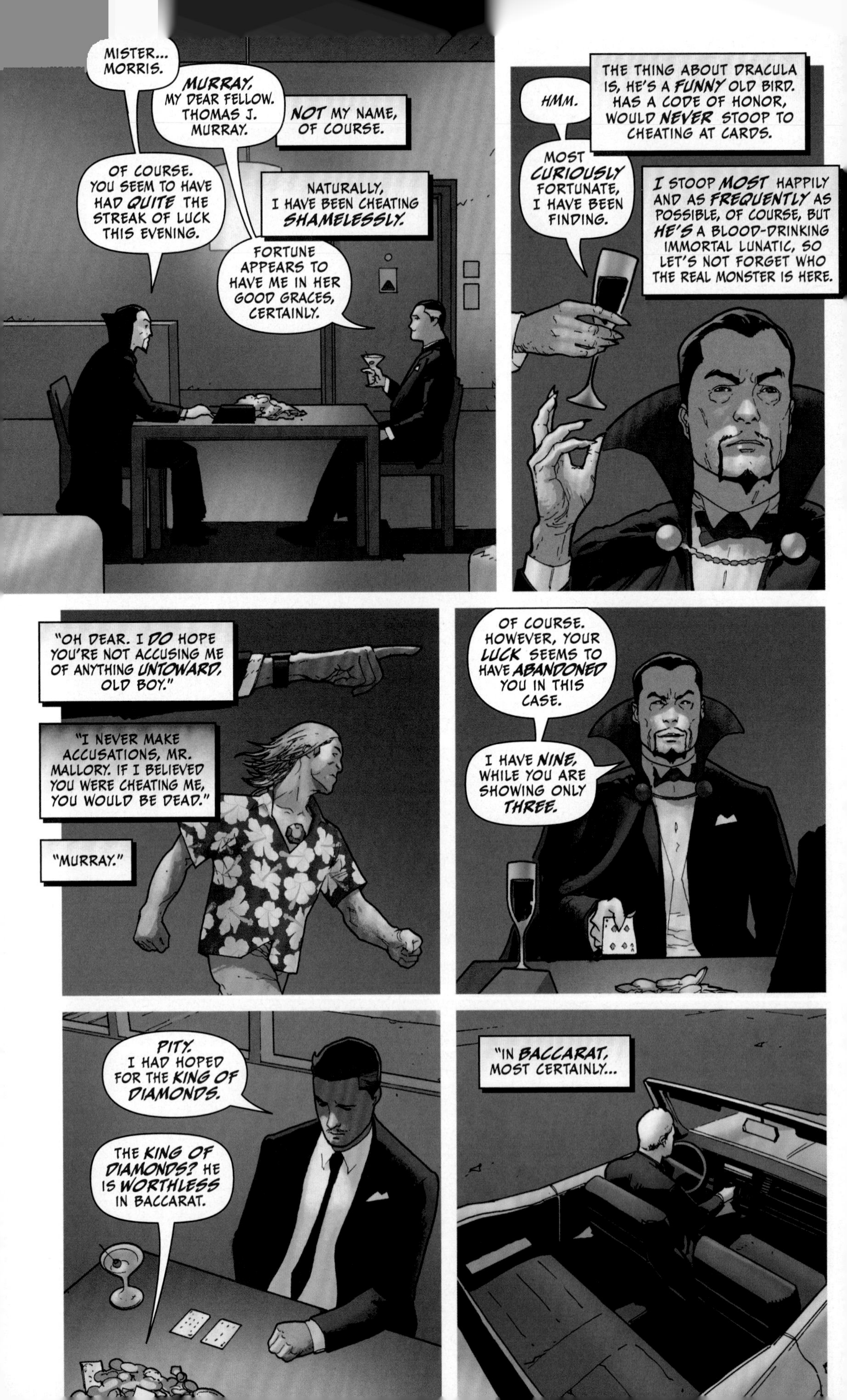
MISTER... MORRIS.
MURRAY, MY DEAR FELLOW. THOMAS J. MURRAY.
NOT MY NAME, OF COURSE.
OF COURSE. YOU SEEM TO HAVE HAD QUITE THE STREAK OF LUCK THIS EVENING.
NATURALLY, I HAVE BEEN CHEATING SHAMELESSLY.
FORTUNE APPEARS TO HAVE ME IN HER GOOD GRACES, CERTAINLY.
HMM.
THE THING ABOUT DRACULA IS, HE'S A FUNNY OLD BIRD. HAS A CODE OF HONOR, WOULD NEVER STOOP TO CHEATING AT CARDS.
MOST CURIOUSLY FORTUNATE, I HAVE BEEN FINDING.
I STOOP MOST HAPPILY AND AS FREQUENTLY AS POSSIBLE, OF COURSE, BUT HE'S A BLOOD-DRINKING IMMORTAL LUNATIC, SO LET'S NOT FORGET WHO THE REAL MONSTER IS HERE.
"OH DEAR. I DO HOPE YOU'RE NOT ACCUSING ME OF ANYTHING UNTOWARD, OLD BOY."
"I NEVER MAKE ACCUSATIONS, MR. MALLORY. IF I BELIEVED YOU WERE CHEATING ME, YOU WOULD BE DEAD."
"MURRAY."
OF COURSE. HOWEVER, YOUR LUCK SEEMS TO HAVE ABANDONED YOU IN THIS CASE.
I HAVE NINE, WHILE YOU ARE SHOWING ONLY THREE.
PITY. I HAD HOPED FOR THE KING OF DIAMONDS.
THE KING OF DIAMONDS? HE IS WORTHLESS IN BACCARAT.
"IN BACCARAT, MOST CERTAINLY...

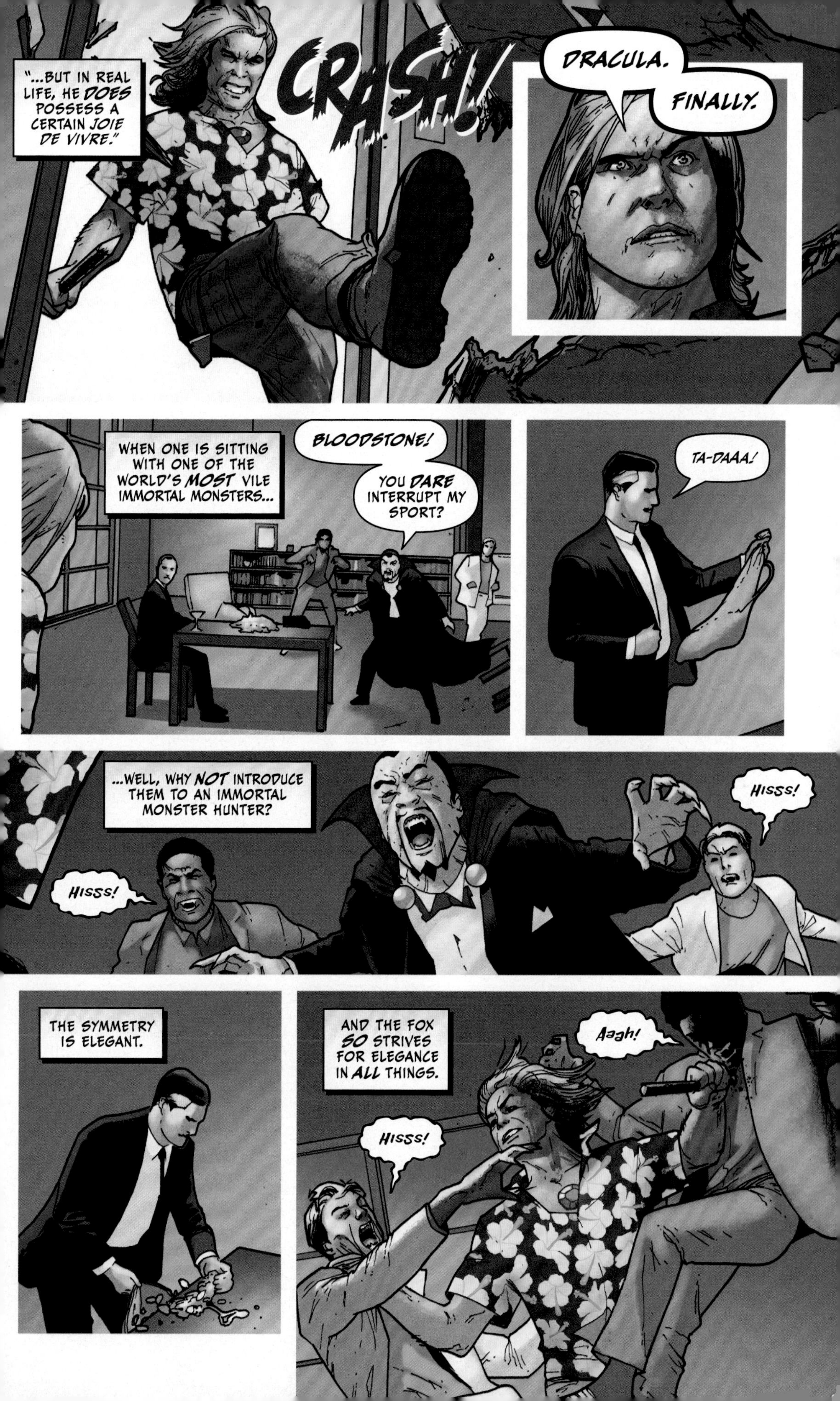
"...BUT IN REAL LIFE, HE DOES POSSESS A CERTAIN JOIE DE VIVRE."
CRASH!
DRACULA.
FINALLY.
WHEN ONE IS SITTING WITH ONE OF THE WORLD'S MOST VILE IMMORTAL MONSTERS...
BLOODSTONE!
YOU DARE INTERRUPT MY SPORT?
TA-DAAA!
...WELL, WHY NOT INTRODUCE THEM TO AN IMMORTAL MONSTER HUNTER?
HISSS!
HISSS!
THE SYMMETRY IS ELEGANT.
AND THE FOX SO STRIVES FOR ELEGANCE IN ALL THINGS.
Aagh!
HISSS!

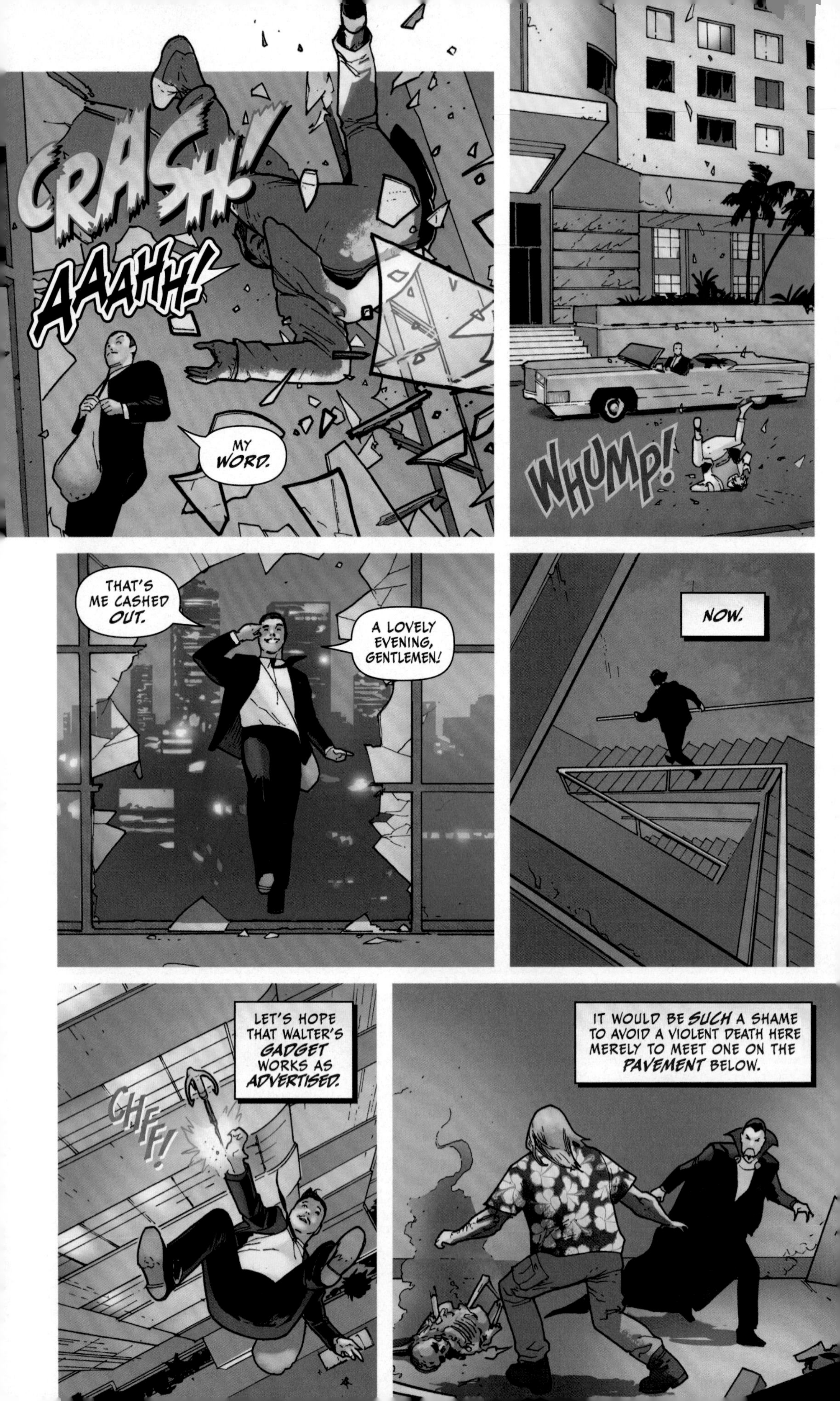
CRASH!
AAAHH!
MY WORD.
WHUMP!
THAT'S ME CASHED OUT.
A LOVELY EVENING, GENTLEMEN!
NOW.
LET'S HOPE THAT WALTER'S GADGET WORKS AS ADVERTISED.
CHFF!
IT WOULD BE SUCH A SHAME TO AVOID A VIOLENT DEATH HERE MERELY TO MEET ONE ON THE PAVEMENT BELOW.

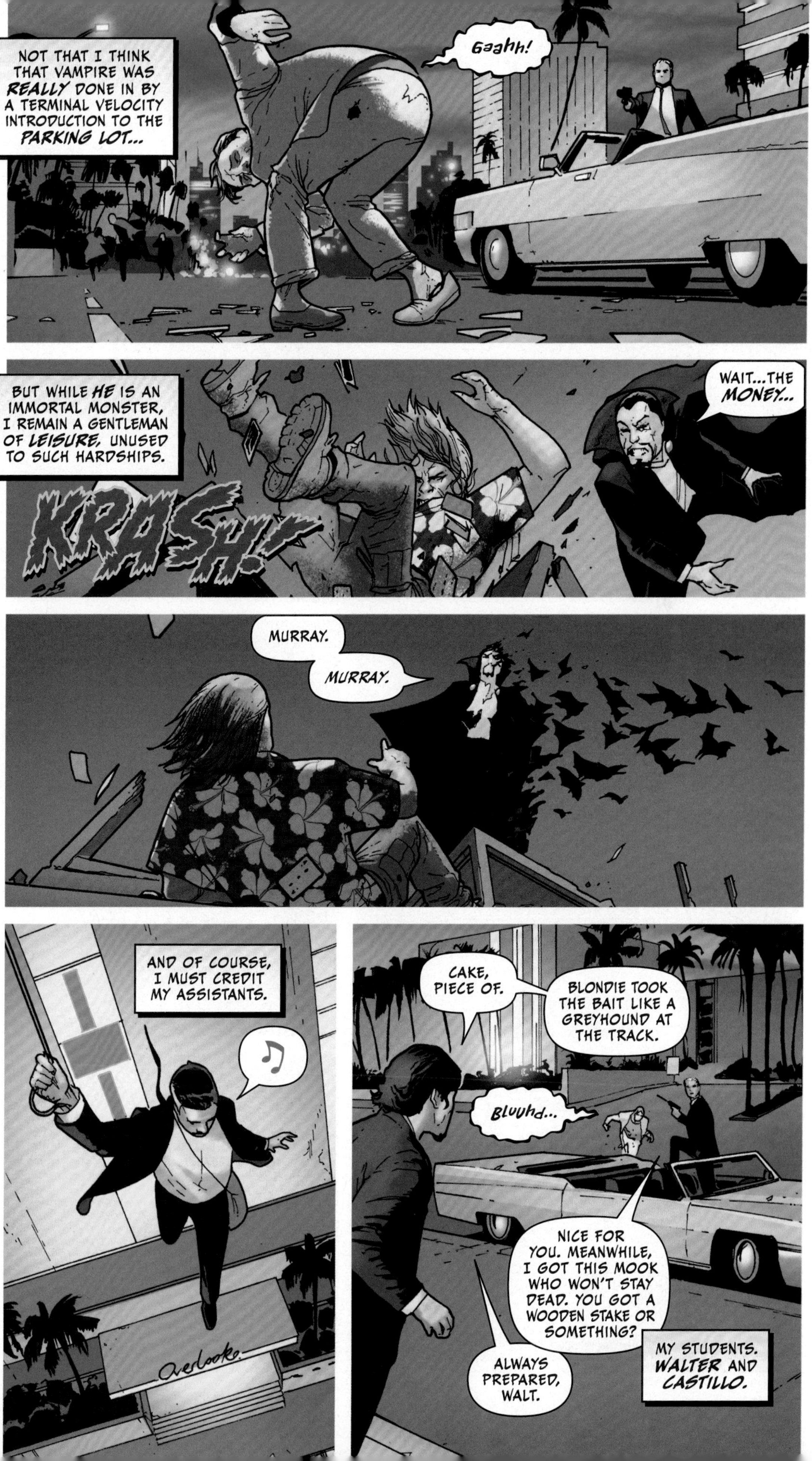
NOT THAT I THINK THAT VAMPIRE WAS REALLY DONE IN BY A TERMINAL VELOCITY INTRODUCTION TO THE PARKING LOT...
Gaahh!
BUT WHILE HE IS AN IMMORTAL MONSTER, I REMAIN A GENTLEMAN OF LEISURE, UNUSED TO SUCH HARDSHIPS.
KRASH!
WAIT...THE MONEY...
MURRAY.
MURRAY.
AND OF COURSE, I MUST CREDIT MY ASSISTANTS.
♪
Overlook
CAKE, PIECE OF.
BLONDIE TOOK THE BAIT LIKE A GREYHOUND AT THE TRACK.
Bluuhd...
NICE FOR YOU. MEANWHILE, I GOT THIS MOOK WHO WON'T STAY DEAD. YOU GOT A WOODEN STAKE OR SOMETHING?
ALWAYS PREPARED, WALT.
MY STUDENTS. WALTER AND CASTILLO.

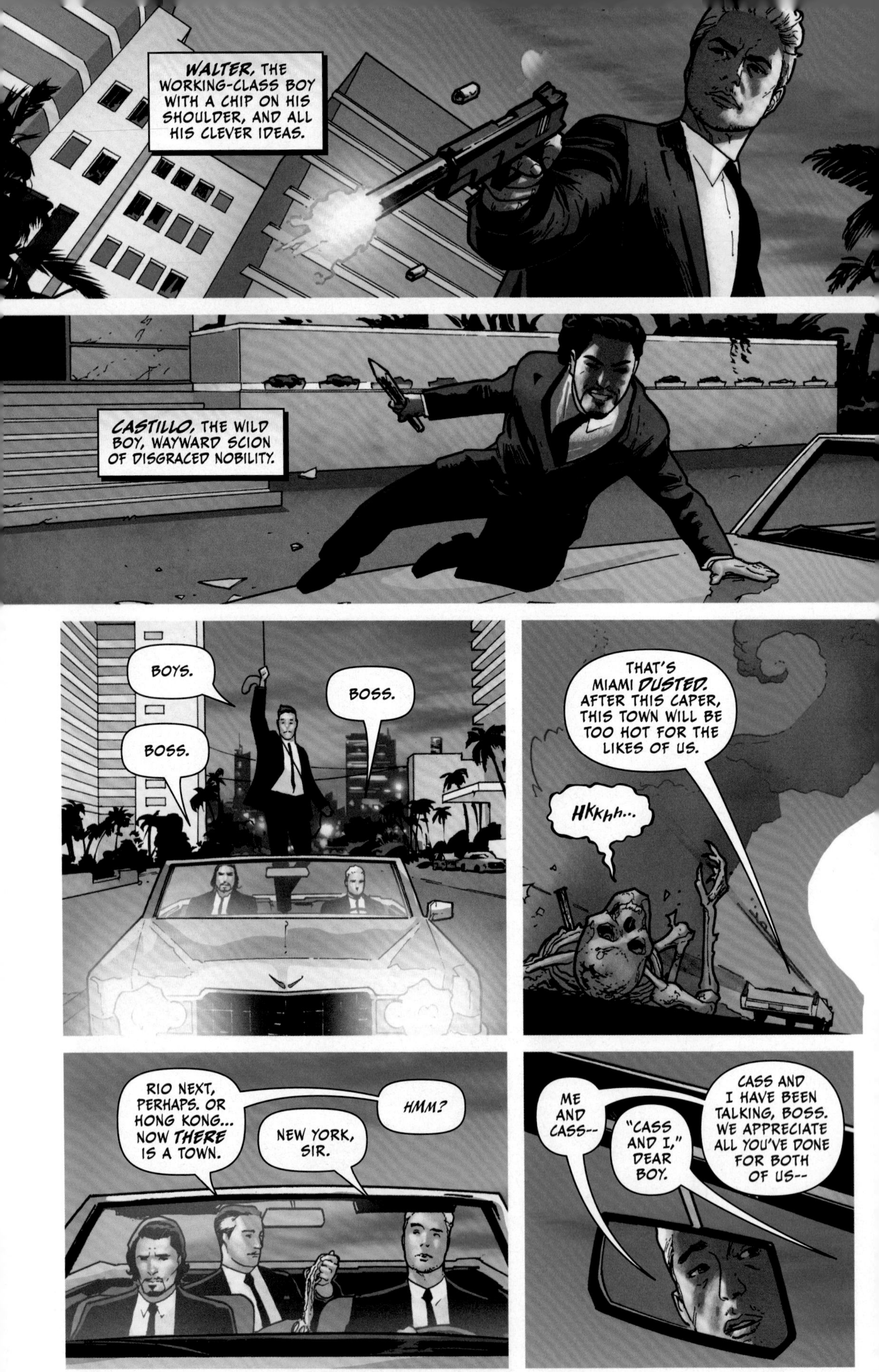
WALTER, THE WORKING-CLASS BOY WITH A CHIP ON HIS SHOULDER, AND ALL HIS CLEVER IDEAS.
CASTILLO, THE WILD BOY, WAYWARD SCION OF DISGRACED NOBILITY.
BOYS.
BOSS.
BOSS.
THAT'S MIAMI DUSTED. AFTER THIS CAPER, THIS TOWN WILL BE TOO HOT FOR THE LIKES OF US.
HKkhh...
RIO NEXT, PERHAPS. OR HONG KONG... NOW THERE IS A TOWN.
HMM?
NEW YORK, SIR.
CASS AND I HAVE BEEN TALKING, BOSS. WE APPRECIATE ALL YOU'VE DONE FOR BOTH OF US--
ME AND CASS--
"CASS AND I," DEAR BOY.

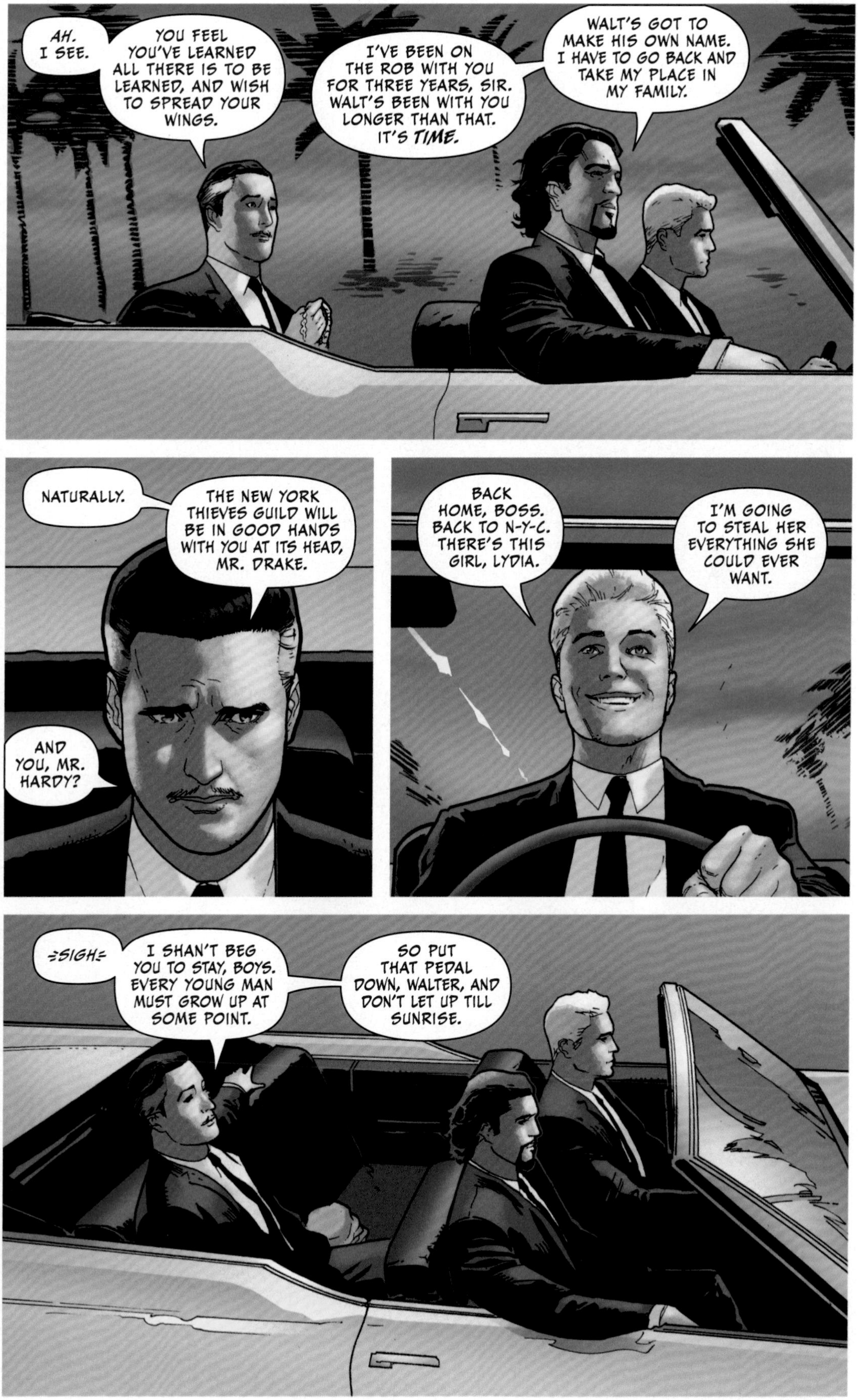
AH. I SEE.
YOU FEEL YOU'VE LEARNED ALL THERE IS TO BE LEARNED, AND WISH TO SPREAD YOUR WINGS.
I'VE BEEN ON THE ROB WITH YOU FOR THREE YEARS, SIR. WALT'S BEEN WITH YOU LONGER THAN THAT. IT'S TIME.
WALT'S GOT TO MAKE HIS OWN NAME. I HAVE TO GO BACK AND TAKE MY PLACE IN MY FAMILY.
NATURALLY.
THE NEW YORK THIEVES GUILD WILL BE IN GOOD HANDS WITH YOU AT ITS HEAD, MR. DRAKE.
AND YOU, MR. HARDY?
BACK HOME, BOSS. BACK TO N-Y-C. THERE'S THIS GIRL, LYDIA.
I'M GOING TO STEAL HER EVERYTHING SHE COULD EVER WANT.
=SIGH=
I SHAN'T BEG YOU TO STAY, BOYS. EVERY YOUNG MAN MUST GROW UP AT SOME POINT.
SO PUT THAT PEDAL DOWN, WALTER, AND DON'T LET UP TILL SUNRISE.

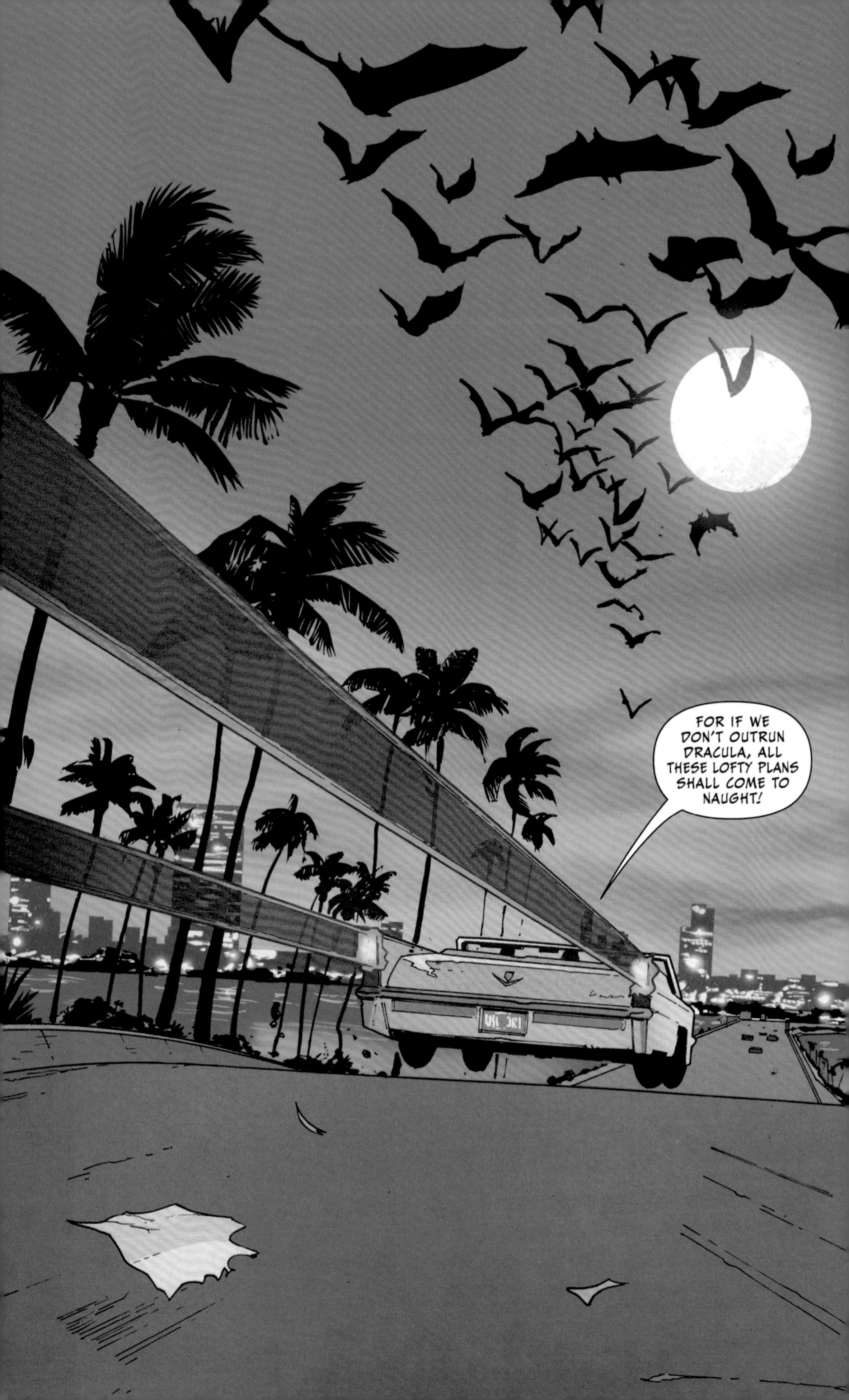
FOR IF WE DON'T OUTRUN DRACULA, ALL THESE LOFTY PLANS SHALL COME TO NAUGHT!

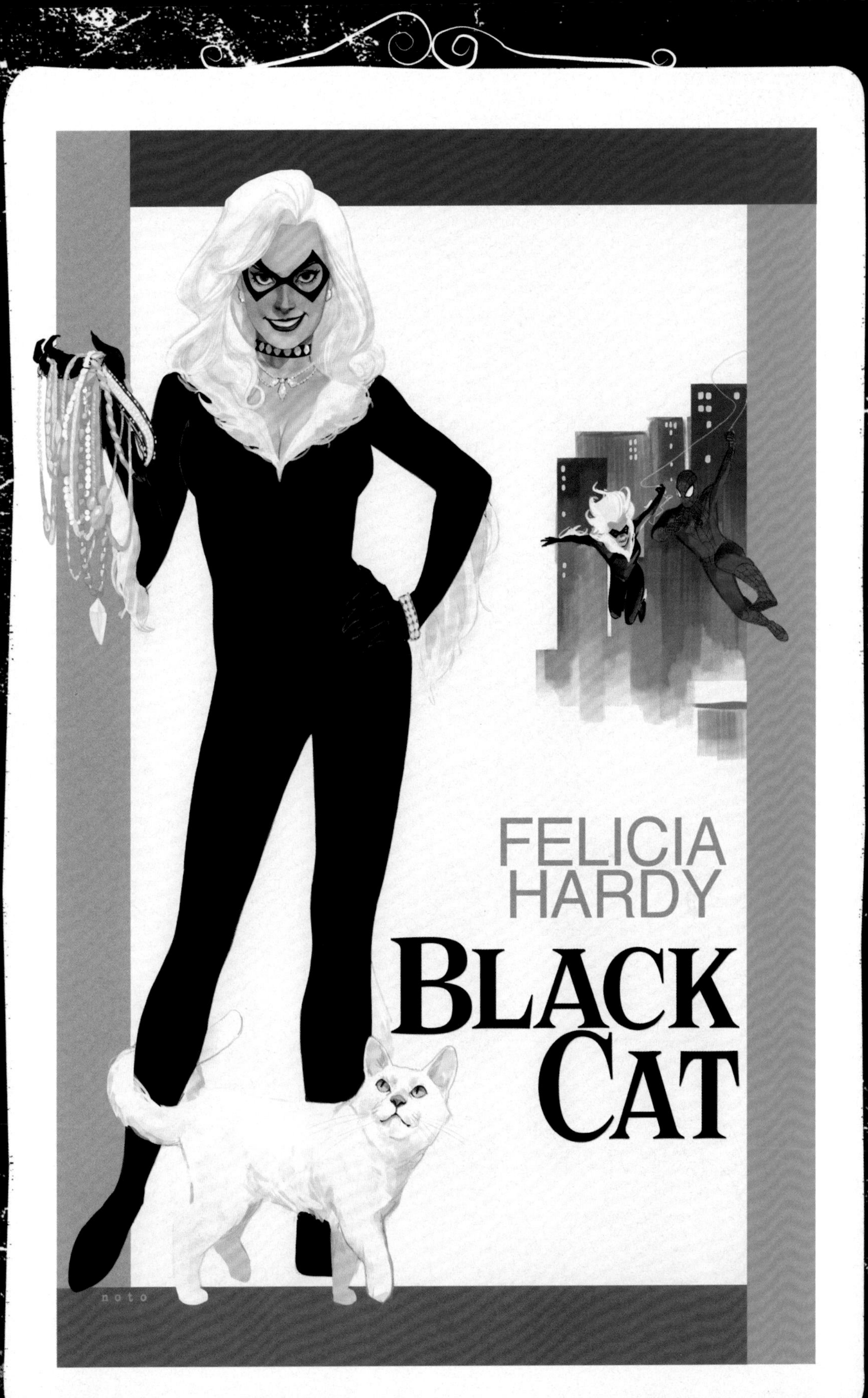
FELICIA
HARDY
BLACK
CAT
noto

#1 variant by **PHIL NOTO**

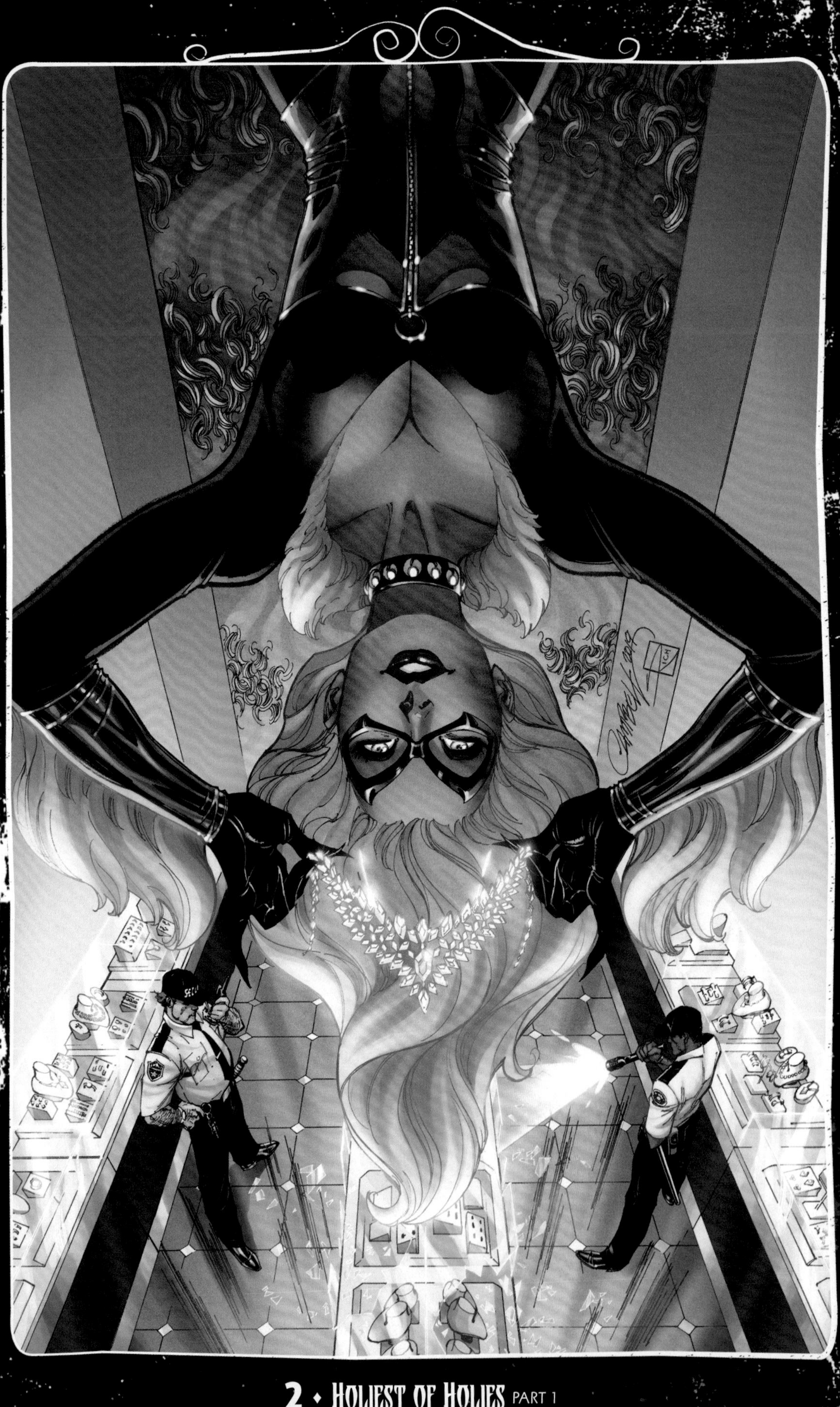

2 • HOLIEST OF HOLIES PART 1

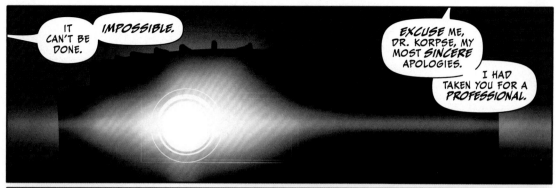

IT CAN'T BE DONE.

IMPOSSIBLE.

EXCUSE ME, DR. KORPSE, MY MOST *SINCERE* APOLOGIES.

I HAD TAKEN YOU FOR A *PROFESSIONAL*.

AND I HAD TAKEN *YOU* FOR SOMEONE WITHOUT *DEMENTIA*.

TELL ME, WAS IT ALL THOSE TIMES *SPIDER-MAN* HIT YOU ON THE HEAD? OR JUST OLD *AGE*?

Heh.

SPIDER-MAN?

LET ME TELL YOU ABOUT *SPIDER-MAN*, YOU LITTLE *PUNK--*

THAT WALL-CRAWLER?

Pah, WE TOOK DOWN SPIDER-MAN!

Hey!

IT'S *TRUE.**

*AMAZING SPIDER-MAN VOL. 1 #196!

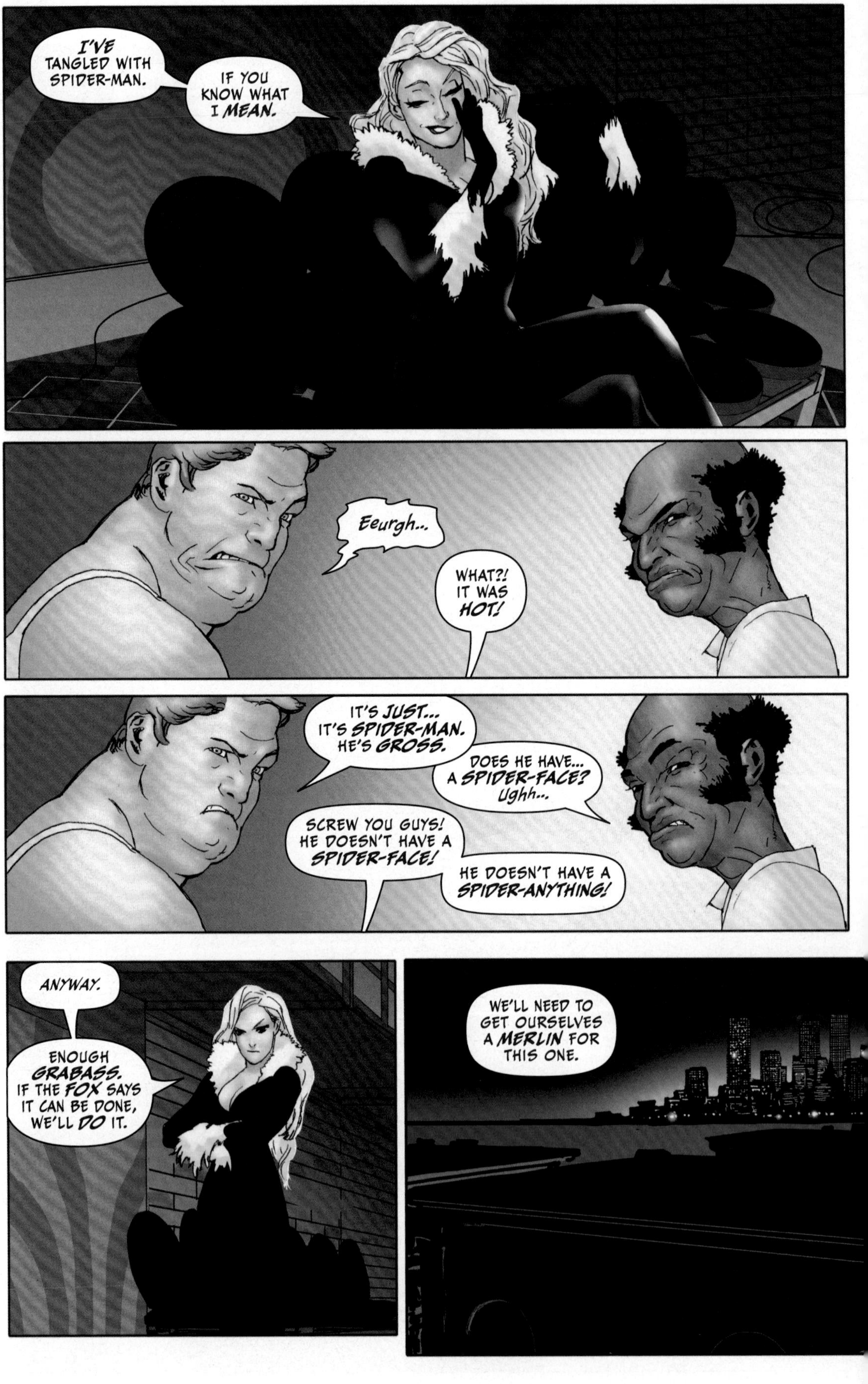
I'VE TANGLED WITH SPIDER-MAN.
IF YOU KNOW WHAT I MEAN.
Eeurgh...
WHAT?! IT WAS HOT!
IT'S JUST... IT'S SPIDER-MAN. HE'S GROSS.
DOES HE HAVE... A SPIDER-FACE? Ughh...
SCREW YOU GUYS! HE DOESN'T HAVE A SPIDER-FACE!
HE DOESN'T HAVE A SPIDER-ANYTHING!
ANYWAY.
ENOUGH GRABASS. IF THE FOX SAYS IT CAN BE DONE, WE'LL DO IT.
WE'LL NEED TO GET OURSELVES A MERLIN FOR THIS ONE.

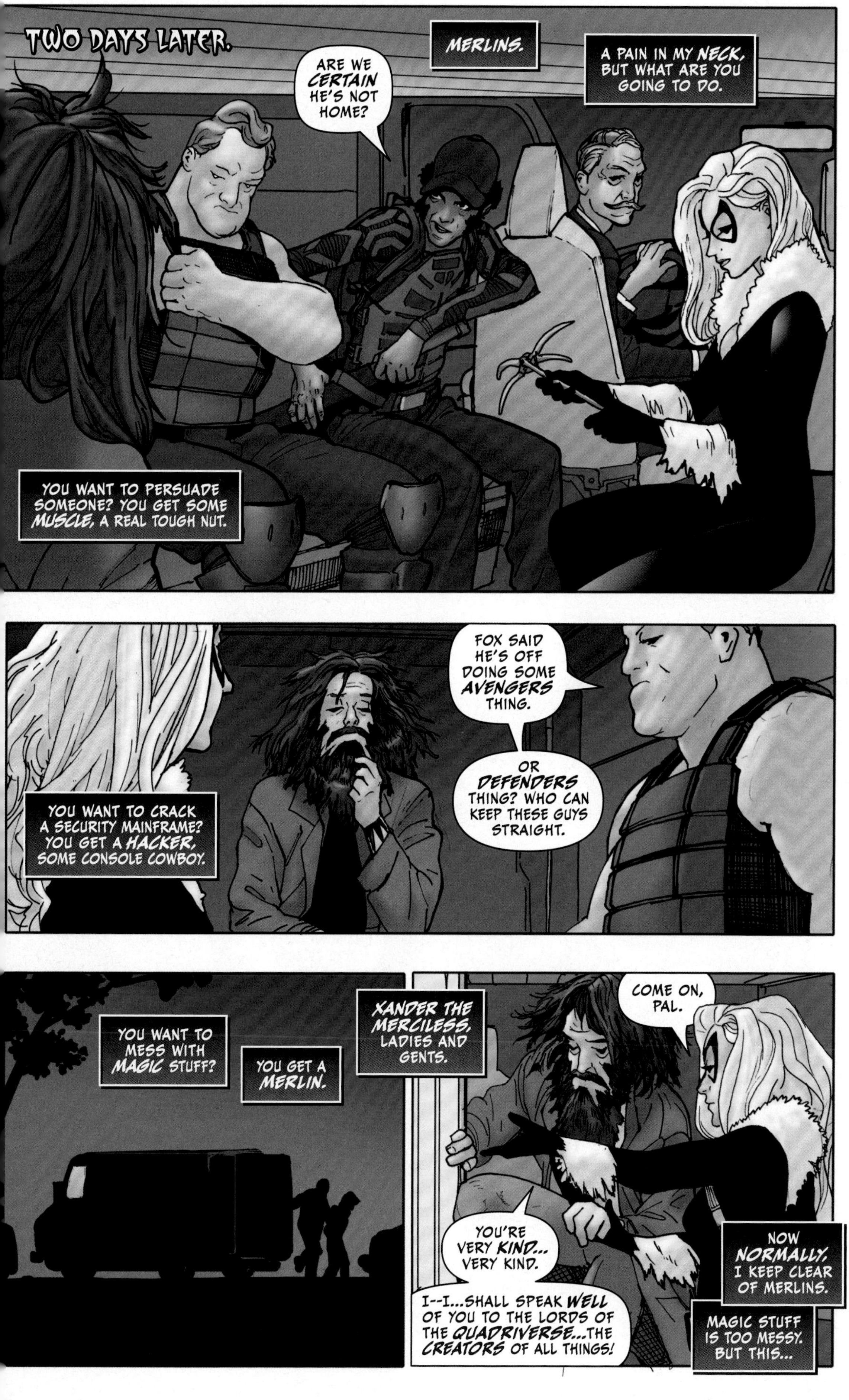

TWO DAYS LATER.
ARE WE CERTAIN HE'S NOT HOME?
MERLINS.
A PAIN IN MY NECK, BUT WHAT ARE YOU GOING TO DO.
YOU WANT TO PERSUADE SOMEONE? YOU GET SOME MUSCLE, A REAL TOUGH NUT.
YOU WANT TO CRACK A SECURITY MAINFRAME? YOU GET A HACKER, SOME CONSOLE COWBOY.
FOX SAID HE'S OFF DOING SOME AVENGERS THING.
OR DEFENDERS THING? WHO CAN KEEP THESE GUYS STRAIGHT.
YOU WANT TO MESS WITH MAGIC STUFF?
YOU GET A MERLIN.
XANDER THE MERCILESS, LADIES AND GENTS.
COME ON, PAL.
YOU'RE VERY KIND... VERY KIND.
I--I...SHALL SPEAK WELL OF YOU TO THE LORDS OF THE QUADRIVERSE...THE CREATORS OF ALL THINGS!
NOW NORMALLY, I KEEP CLEAR OF MERLINS.
MAGIC STUFF IS TOO MESSY. BUT THIS...

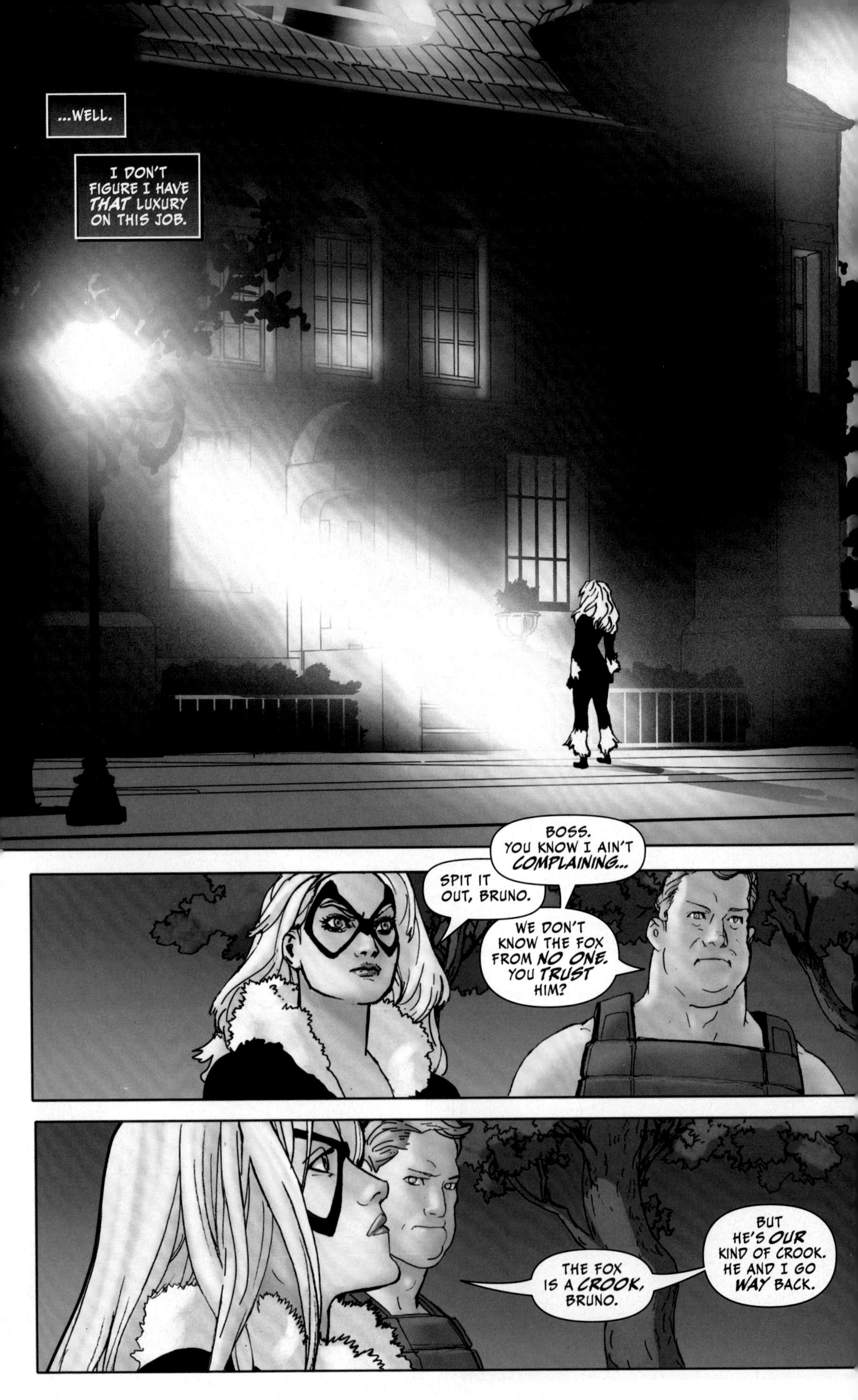
...WELL.
I DON'T FIGURE I HAVE THAT LUXURY ON THIS JOB.
BOSS. YOU KNOW I AIN'T COMPLAINING...
SPIT IT OUT, BRUNO.
WE DON'T KNOW THE FOX FROM NO ONE. YOU TRUST HIM?
THE FOX IS A CROOK, BRUNO.
BUT HE'S OUR KIND OF CROOK. HE AND I GO WAY BACK.

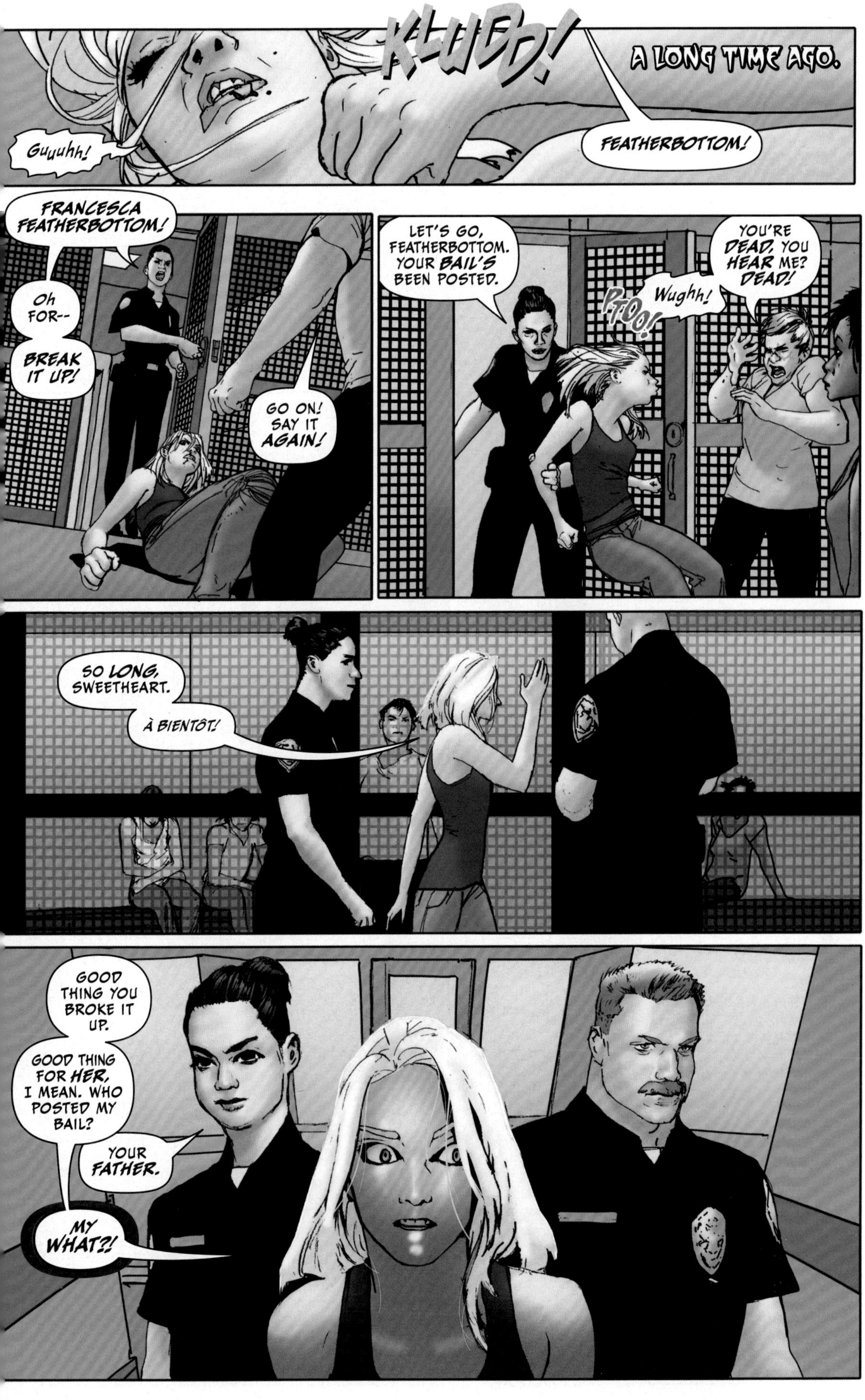
KLUDD!
A LONG TIME AGO.
Guuuhh!
FEATHERBOTTOM!
FRANCESCA FEATHERBOTTOM!
Oh FOR--
BREAK IT UP!
GO ON! SAY IT AGAIN!
LET'S GO, FEATHERBOTTOM. YOUR BAIL'S BEEN POSTED.
PTOO!
Wughh!
YOU'RE DEAD, YOU HEAR ME? DEAD!
SO LONG, SWEETHEART.
À BIENTÔT!
GOOD THING YOU BROKE IT UP.
GOOD THING FOR HER, I MEAN. WHO POSTED MY BAIL?
YOUR FATHER.
MY WHAT?!

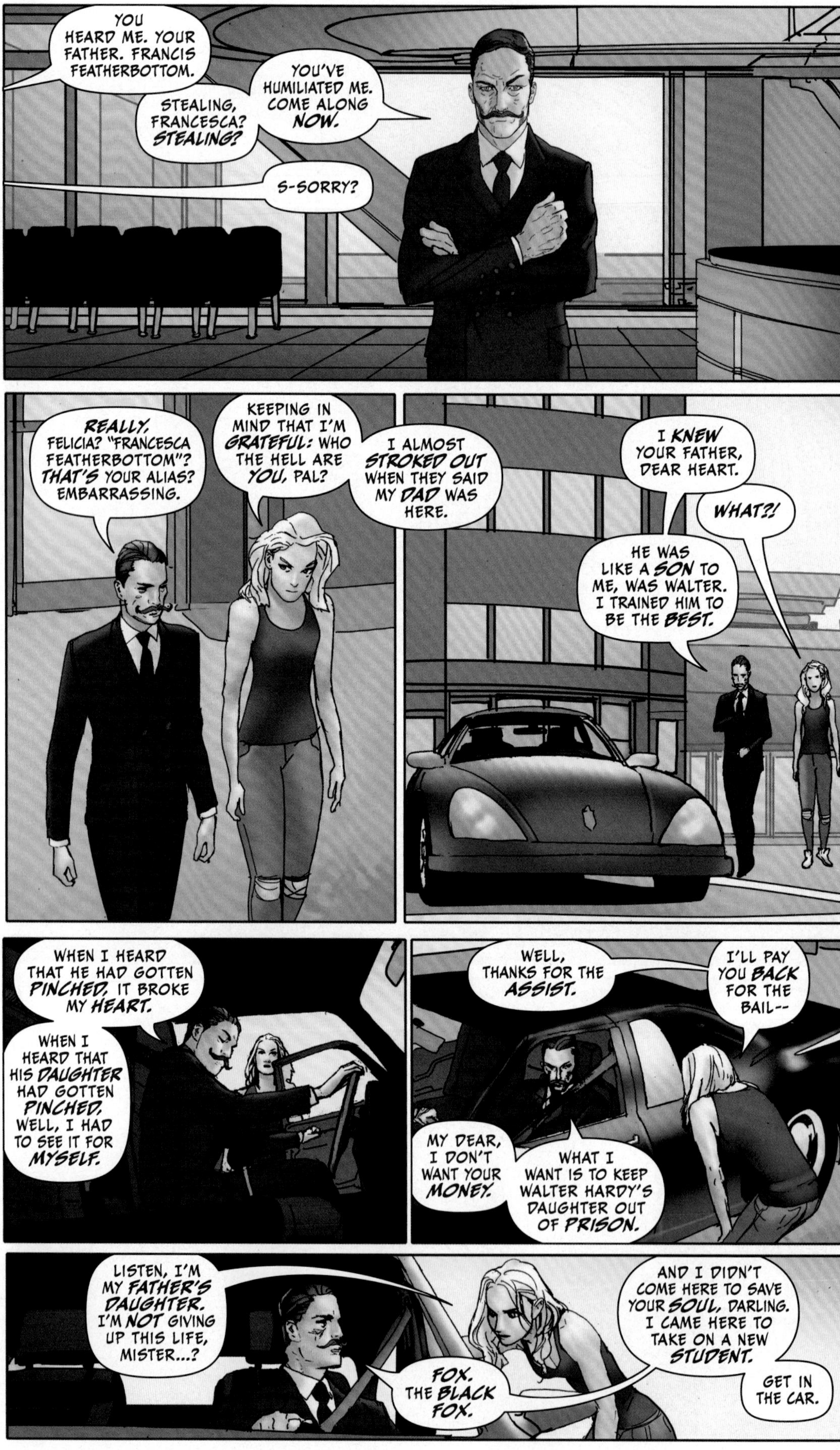
YOU HEARD ME. YOUR FATHER. FRANCIS FEATHERBOTTOM.
STEALING, FRANCESCA? STEALING?
YOU'VE HUMILIATED ME. COME ALONG NOW.
S-SORRY?
REALLY, FELICIA? "FRANCESCA FEATHERBOTTOM"? THAT'S YOUR ALIAS? EMBARRASSING.
KEEPING IN MIND THAT I'M GRATEFUL: WHO THE HELL ARE YOU, PAL?
I ALMOST STROKED OUT WHEN THEY SAID MY DAD WAS HERE.
I KNEW YOUR FATHER, DEAR HEART.
WHAT?!
HE WAS LIKE A SON TO ME, WAS WALTER. I TRAINED HIM TO BE THE BEST.
WHEN I HEARD THAT HE HAD GOTTEN PINCHED, IT BROKE MY HEART.
WHEN I HEARD THAT HIS DAUGHTER HAD GOTTEN PINCHED, WELL, I HAD TO SEE IT FOR MYSELF.
WELL, THANKS FOR THE ASSIST.
I'LL PAY YOU BACK FOR THE BAIL--
MY DEAR, I DON'T WANT YOUR MONEY.
WHAT I WANT IS TO KEEP WALTER HARDY'S DAUGHTER OUT OF PRISON.
LISTEN, I'M MY FATHER'S DAUGHTER. I'M NOT GIVING UP THIS LIFE, MISTER...?
FOX. THE BLACK FOX.
AND I DIDN'T COME HERE TO SAVE YOUR SOUL, DARLING. I CAME HERE TO TAKE ON A NEW STUDENT.
GET IN THE CAR.

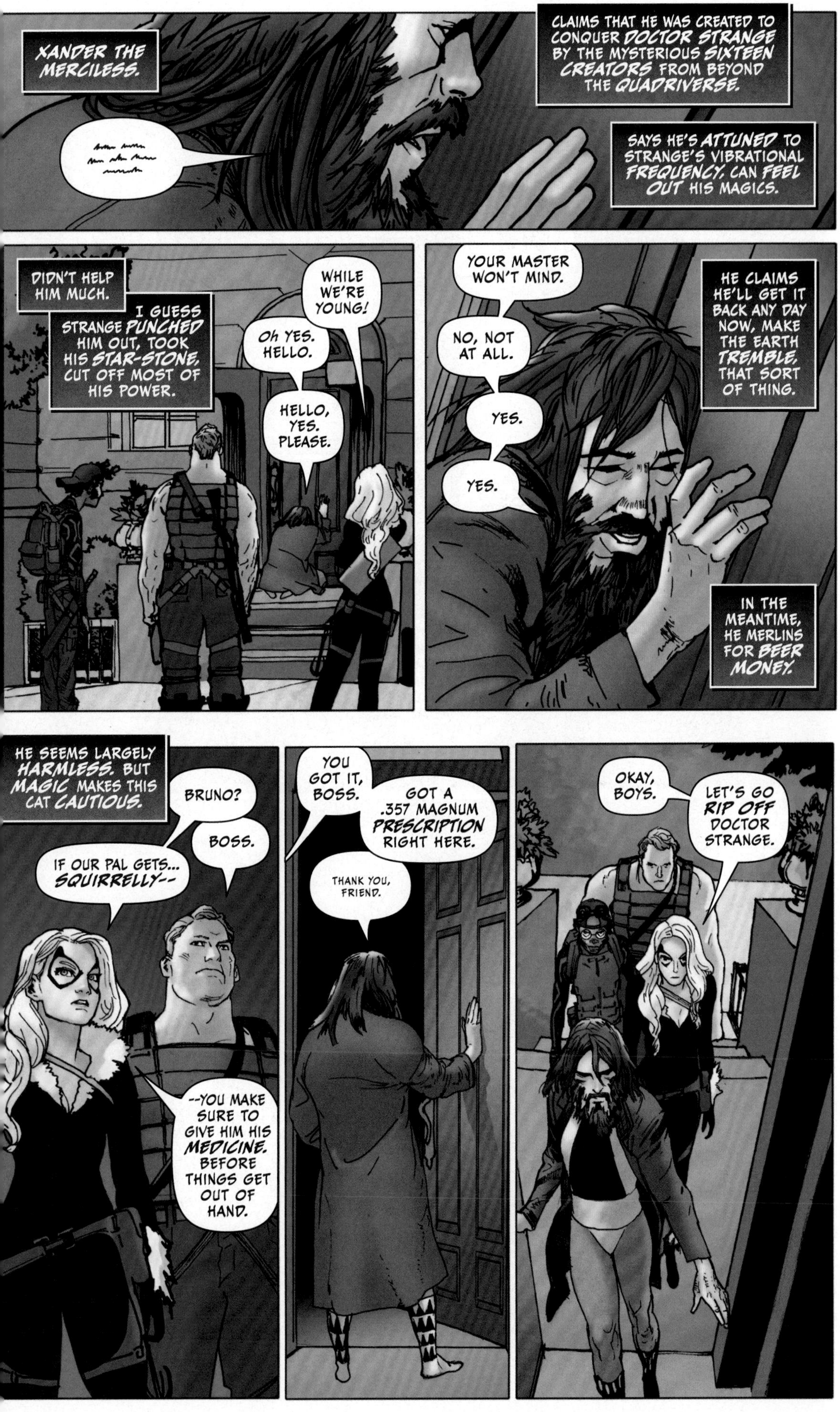

XANDER THE MERCILESS.
CLAIMS THAT HE WAS CREATED TO CONQUER DOCTOR STRANGE BY THE MYSTERIOUS SIXTEEN CREATORS FROM BEYOND THE QUADRIVERSE.
SAYS HE'S ATTUNED TO STRANGE'S VIBRATIONAL FREQUENCY, CAN FEEL OUT HIS MAGICS.
DIDN'T HELP HIM MUCH.
I GUESS STRANGE PUNCHED HIM OUT, TOOK HIS STAR-STONE, CUT OFF MOST OF HIS POWER.
WHILE WE'RE YOUNG!
Oh YES. HELLO.
HELLO, YES. PLEASE.
YOUR MASTER WON'T MIND.
NO, NOT AT ALL.
YES.
YES.
HE CLAIMS HE'LL GET IT BACK ANY DAY NOW, MAKE THE EARTH TREMBLE, THAT SORT OF THING.
IN THE MEANTIME, HE MERLINS FOR BEER MONEY.
HE SEEMS LARGELY HARMLESS. BUT MAGIC MAKES THIS CAT CAUTIOUS.
BRUNO?
BOSS.
IF OUR PAL GETS... SQUIRRELLY--
--YOU MAKE SURE TO GIVE HIM HIS MEDICINE. BEFORE THINGS GET OUT OF HAND.
YOU GOT IT, BOSS.
GOT A .357 MAGNUM PRESCRIPTION RIGHT HERE.
THANK YOU, FRIEND.
OKAY, BOYS.
LET'S GO RIP OFF DOCTOR STRANGE.

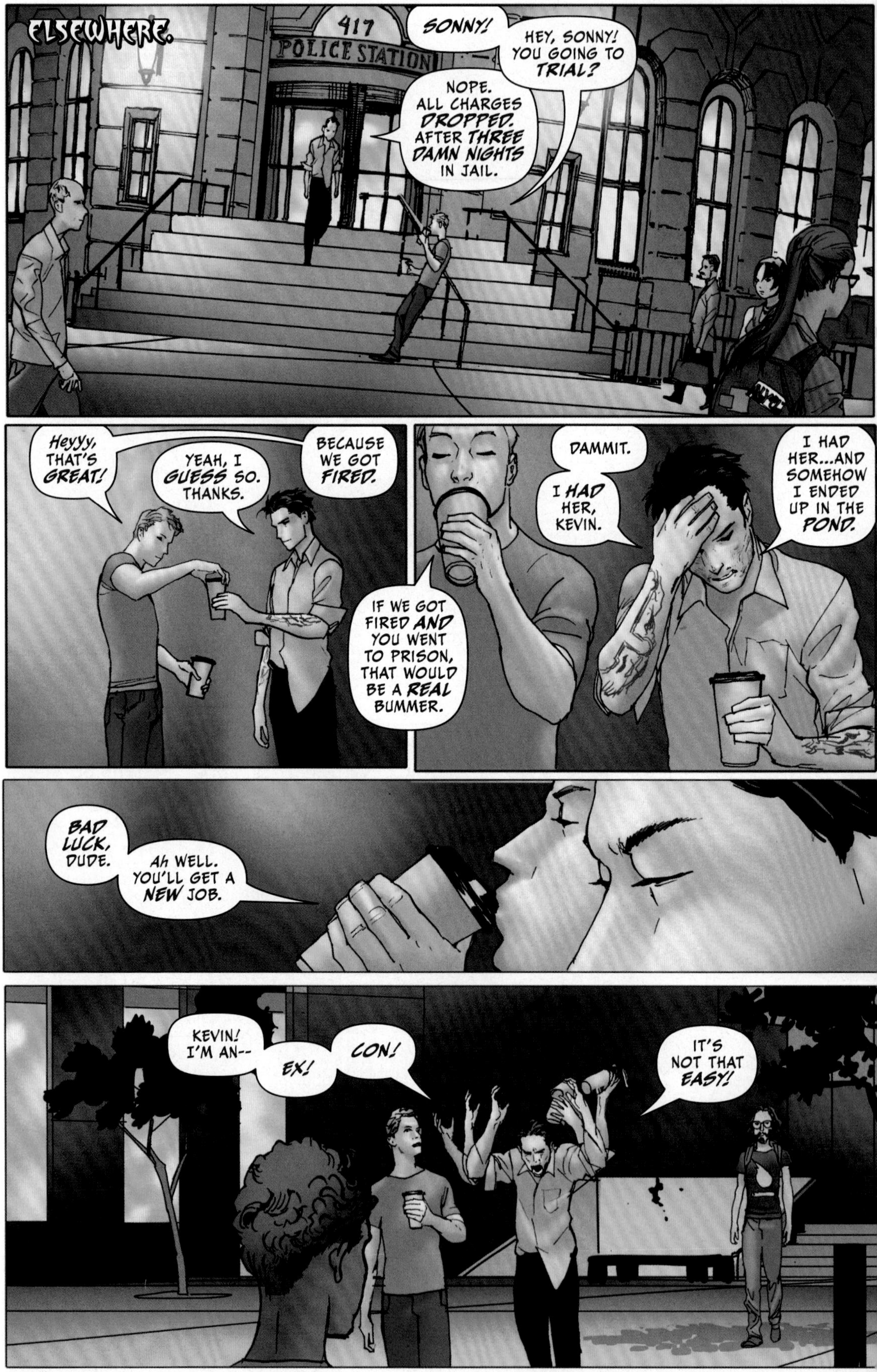
ELSEWHERE.
417
POLICE STATION
SONNY!
HEY, SONNY! YOU GOING TO TRIAL?
NOPE. ALL CHARGES DROPPED. AFTER THREE DAMN NIGHTS IN JAIL.
Heyyy, THAT'S GREAT!
YEAH, I GUESS SO. THANKS.
BECAUSE WE GOT FIRED.
DAMMIT.
I HAD HER, KEVIN.
I HAD HER...AND SOMEHOW I ENDED UP IN THE POND.
IF WE GOT FIRED AND YOU WENT TO PRISON, THAT WOULD BE A REAL BUMMER.
BAD LUCK, DUDE.
Ah WELL. YOU'LL GET A NEW JOB.
KEVIN! I'M AN--
EX!
CON!
IT'S NOT THAT EASY!

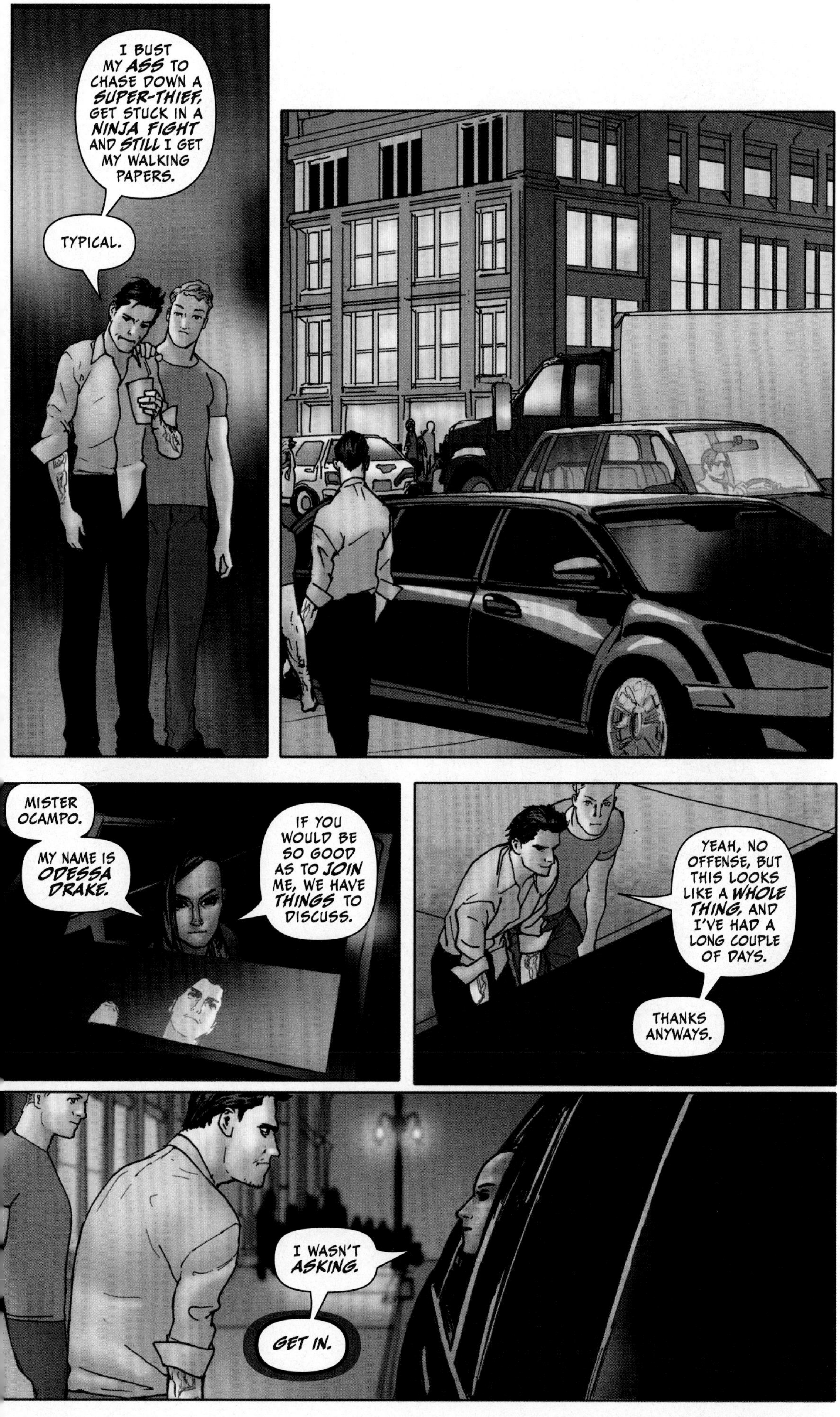
I BUST MY ASS TO CHASE DOWN A SUPER-THIEF, GET STUCK IN A NINJA FIGHT AND STILL I GET MY WALKING PAPERS.
TYPICAL.
MISTER OCAMPO.
MY NAME IS ODESSA DRAKE.
IF YOU WOULD BE SO GOOD AS TO JOIN ME, WE HAVE THINGS TO DISCUSS.
YEAH, NO OFFENSE, BUT THIS LOOKS LIKE A WHOLE THING, AND I'VE HAD A LONG COUPLE OF DAYS.
THANKS ANYWAYS.
I WASN'T ASKING.
GET IN.

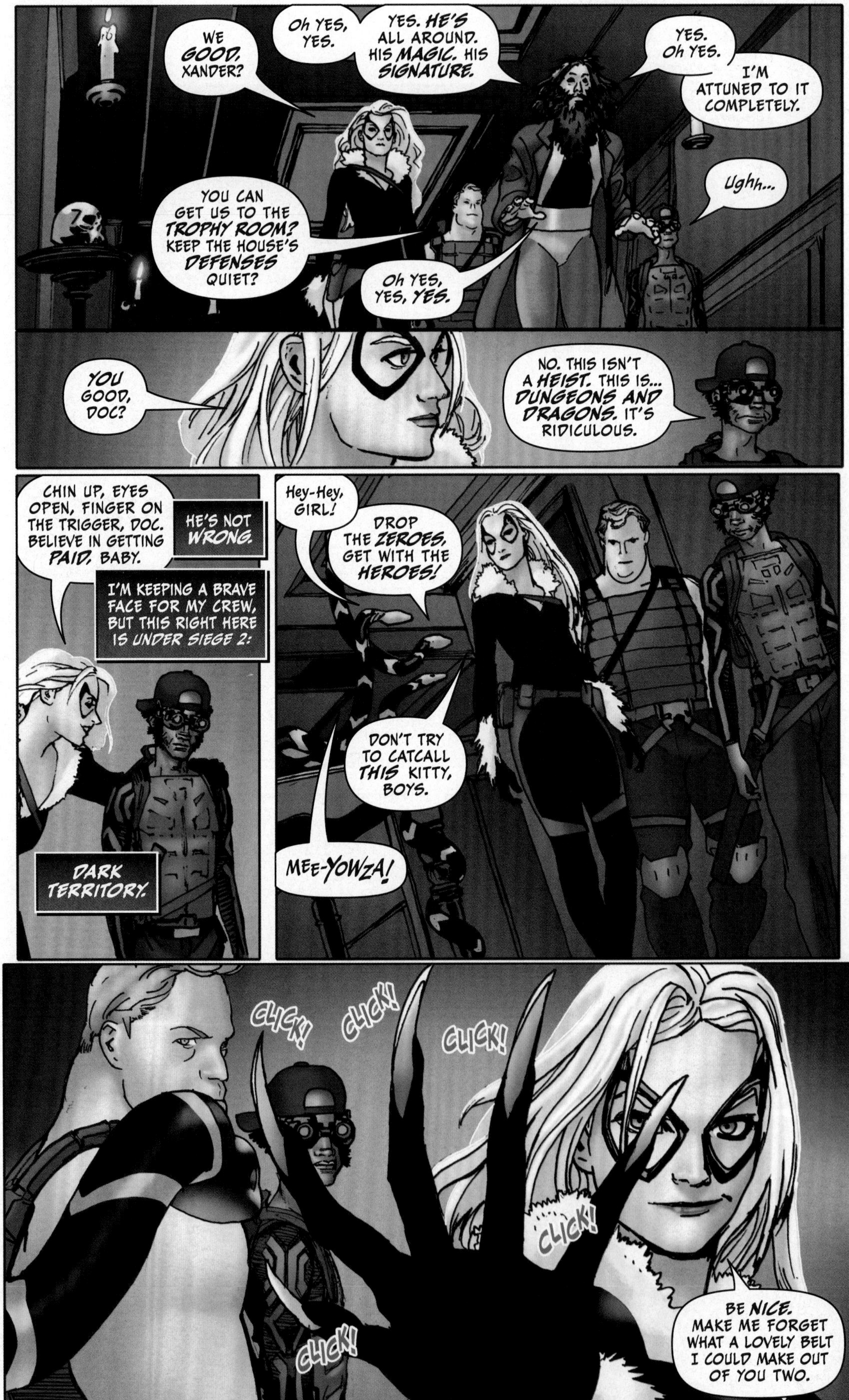

WE GOOD, XANDER?
Oh YES, YES.
YES. HE'S ALL AROUND. HIS MAGIC. HIS SIGNATURE.
YES. Oh YES.
I'M ATTUNED TO IT COMPLETELY.
YOU CAN GET US TO THE TROPHY ROOM? KEEP THE HOUSE'S DEFENSES QUIET?
Oh YES, YES, YES.
Ughh...
YOU GOOD, DOC?
NO. THIS ISN'T A HEIST. THIS IS... DUNGEONS AND DRAGONS. IT'S RIDICULOUS.
CHIN UP, EYES OPEN, FINGER ON THE TRIGGER, DOC. BELIEVE IN GETTING PAID, BABY.
HE'S NOT WRONG.
I'M KEEPING A BRAVE FACE FOR MY CREW, BUT THIS RIGHT HERE IS UNDER SIEGE 2:
DARK TERRITORY.
Hey-Hey, GIRL!
DROP THE ZEROES, GET WITH THE HEROES!
DON'T TRY TO CATCALL THIS KITTY, BOYS.
MEE-YOWZA!
CLICK!
CLICK!
CLICK!
CLICK!
CLICK!
BE NICE. MAKE ME FORGET WHAT A LOVELY BELT I COULD MAKE OUT OF YOU TWO.

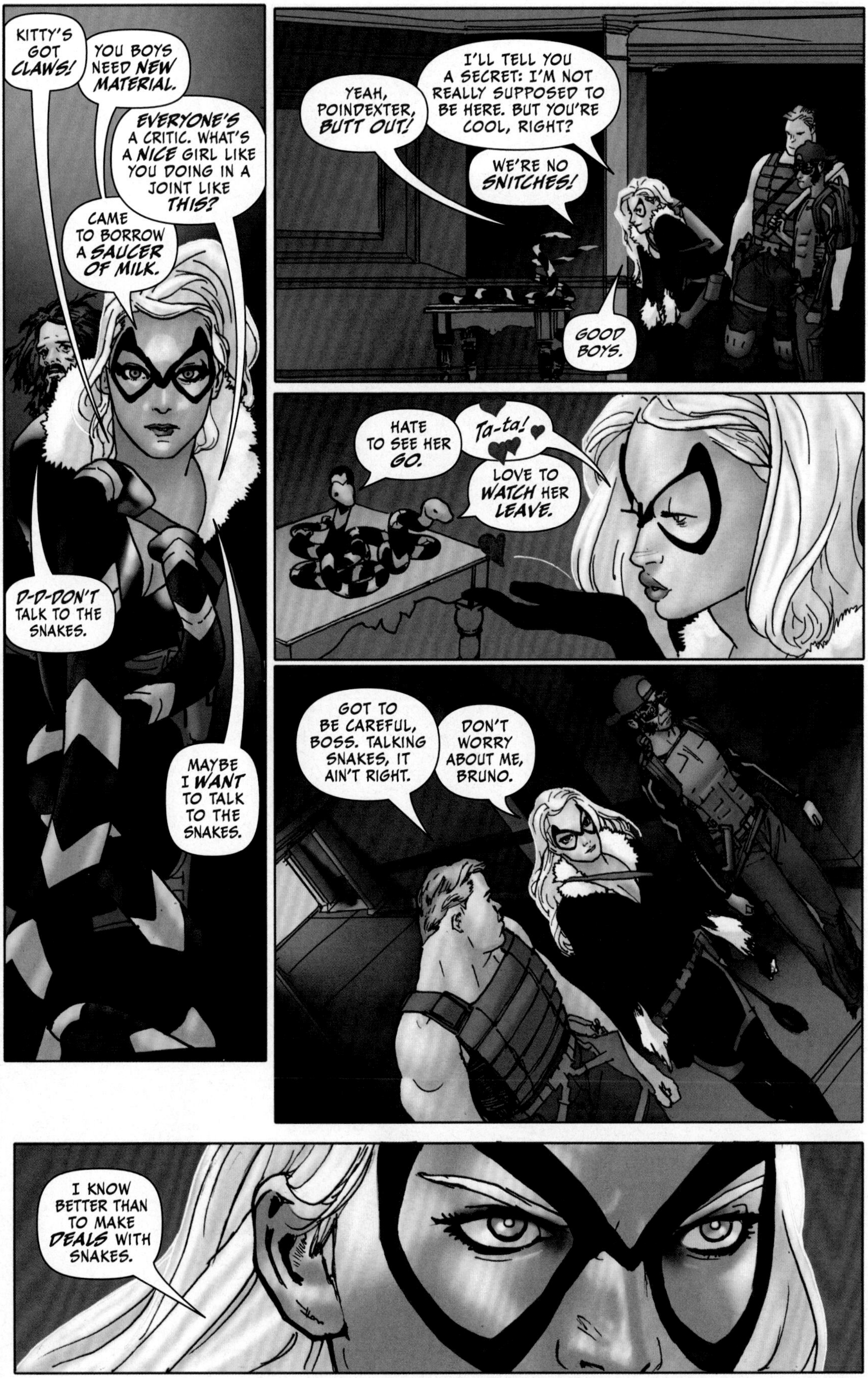
KITTY'S GOT CLAWS!
YOU BOYS NEED NEW MATERIAL.
EVERYONE'S A CRITIC. WHAT'S A NICE GIRL LIKE YOU DOING IN A JOINT LIKE THIS?
CAME TO BORROW A SAUCER OF MILK.
D-D-DON'T TALK TO THE SNAKES.
MAYBE I WANT TO TALK TO THE SNAKES.
I'LL TELL YOU A SECRET: I'M NOT REALLY SUPPOSED TO BE HERE. BUT YOU'RE COOL, RIGHT?
YEAH, POINDEXTER, BUTT OUT!
WE'RE NO SNITCHES!
GOOD BOYS.
Ta-ta!
HATE TO SEE HER GO.
LOVE TO WATCH HER LEAVE.
GOT TO BE CAREFUL, BOSS. TALKING SNAKES, IT AIN'T RIGHT.
DON'T WORRY ABOUT ME, BRUNO.
I KNOW BETTER THAN TO MAKE DEALS WITH SNAKES.

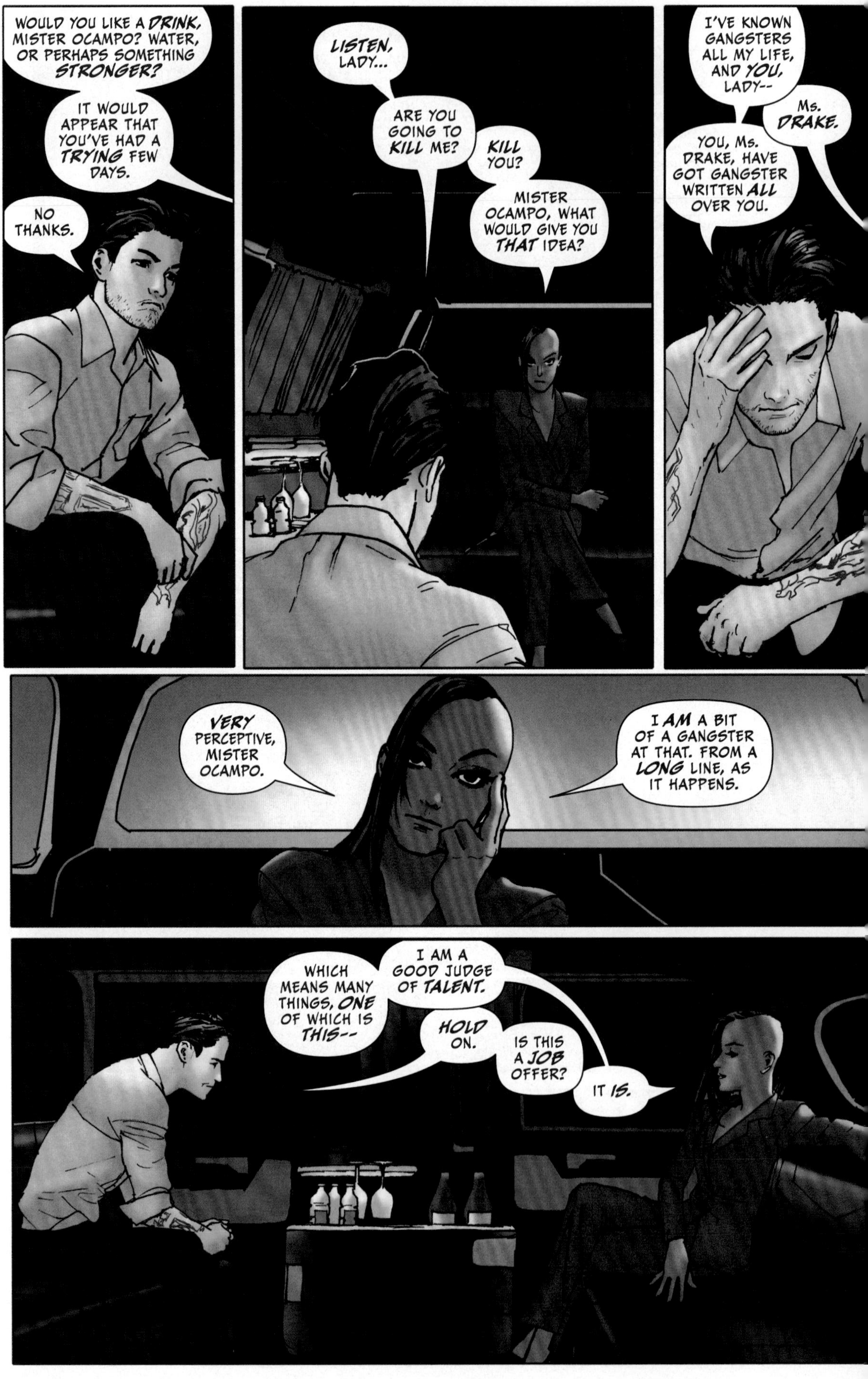
WOULD YOU LIKE A DRINK, MISTER OCAMPO? WATER, OR PERHAPS SOMETHING STRONGER?
IT WOULD APPEAR THAT YOU'VE HAD A TRYING FEW DAYS.
NO THANKS.
LISTEN, LADY...
ARE YOU GOING TO KILL ME?
KILL YOU?
MISTER OCAMPO, WHAT WOULD GIVE YOU THAT IDEA?
I'VE KNOWN GANGSTERS ALL MY LIFE, AND YOU, LADY--
Ms. DRAKE.
YOU, Ms. DRAKE, HAVE GOT GANGSTER WRITTEN ALL OVER YOU.
VERY PERCEPTIVE, MISTER OCAMPO.
I AM A BIT OF A GANGSTER AT THAT. FROM A LONG LINE, AS IT HAPPENS.
I AM A GOOD JUDGE OF TALENT.
WHICH MEANS MANY THINGS, ONE OF WHICH IS THIS--
HOLD ON.
IS THIS A JOB OFFER?
IT IS.

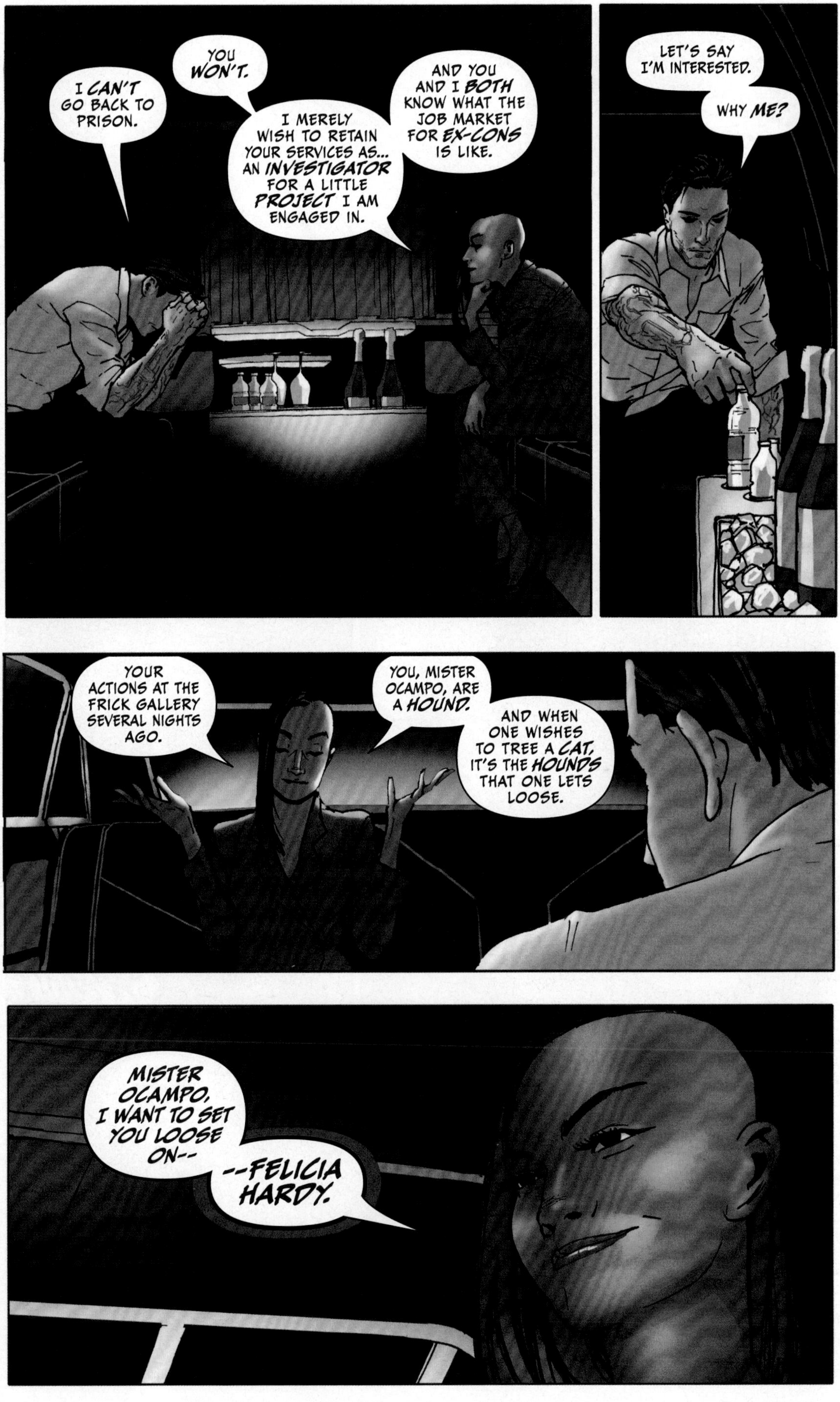
I CAN'T GO BACK TO PRISON.
YOU WON'T.
I MERELY WISH TO RETAIN YOUR SERVICES AS... AN INVESTIGATOR FOR A LITTLE PROJECT I AM ENGAGED IN.
AND YOU AND I BOTH KNOW WHAT THE JOB MARKET FOR EX-CONS IS LIKE.
LET'S SAY I'M INTERESTED.
WHY ME?
YOUR ACTIONS AT THE FRICK GALLERY SEVERAL NIGHTS AGO.
YOU, MISTER OCAMPO, ARE A HOUND.
AND WHEN ONE WISHES TO TREE A CAT, IT'S THE HOUNDS THAT ONE LETS LOOSE.
MISTER OCAMPO, I WANT TO SET YOU LOOSE ON--
--FELICIA HARDY.

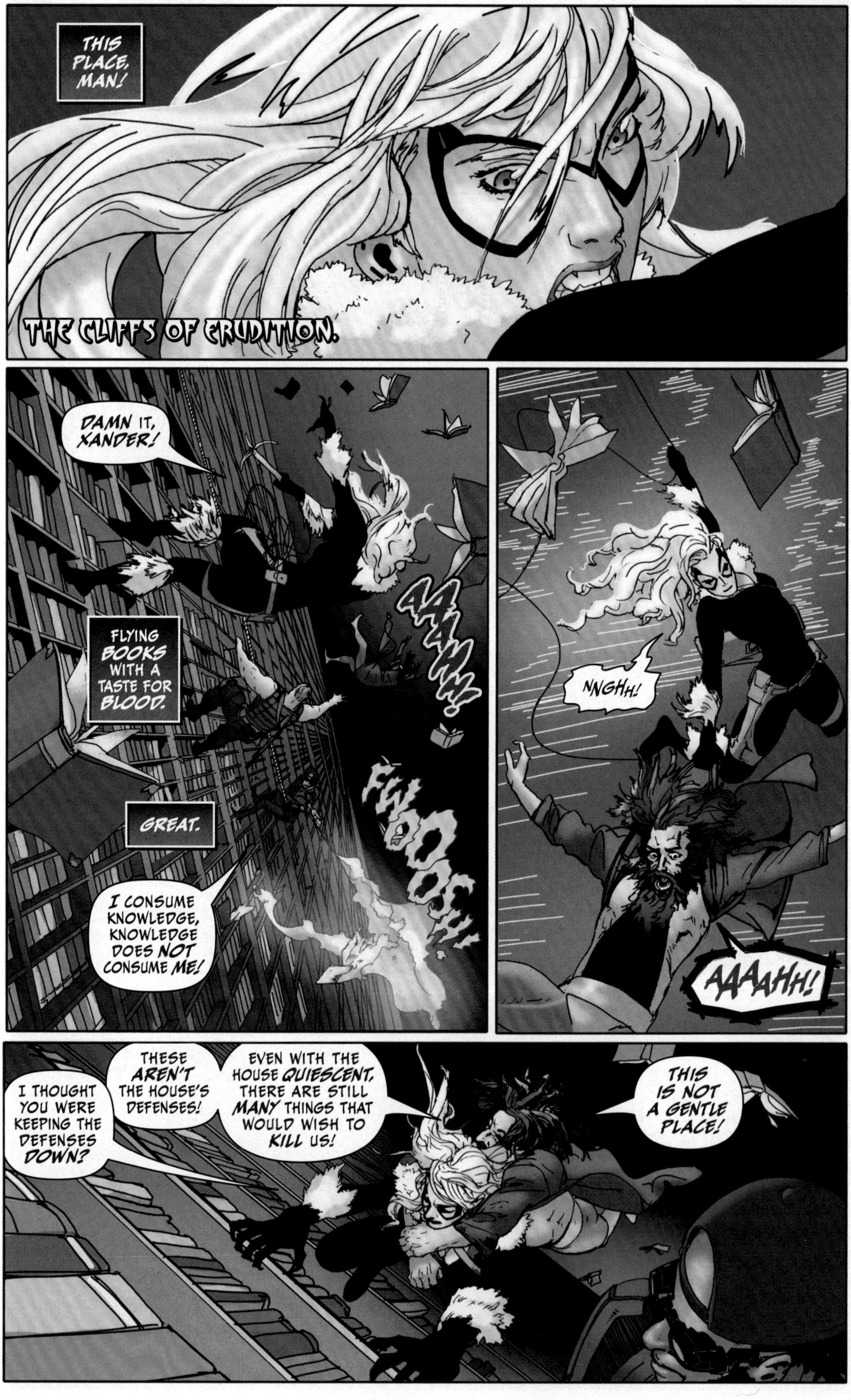
THIS PLACE, MAN!
THE CLIFFS OF ERUDITION.
DAMN IT, XANDER!
AAAAHH!
FLYING BOOKS WITH A TASTE FOR BLOOD.
GREAT.
FWOOOSH!
I CONSUME KNOWLEDGE, KNOWLEDGE DOES NOT CONSUME ME!
NNGHH!
AAAAHH!
I THOUGHT YOU WERE KEEPING THE DEFENSES DOWN?
THESE AREN'T THE HOUSE'S DEFENSES!
EVEN WITH THE HOUSE QUIESCENT, THERE ARE STILL MANY THINGS THAT WOULD WISH TO KILL US!
THIS IS NOT A GENTLE PLACE!

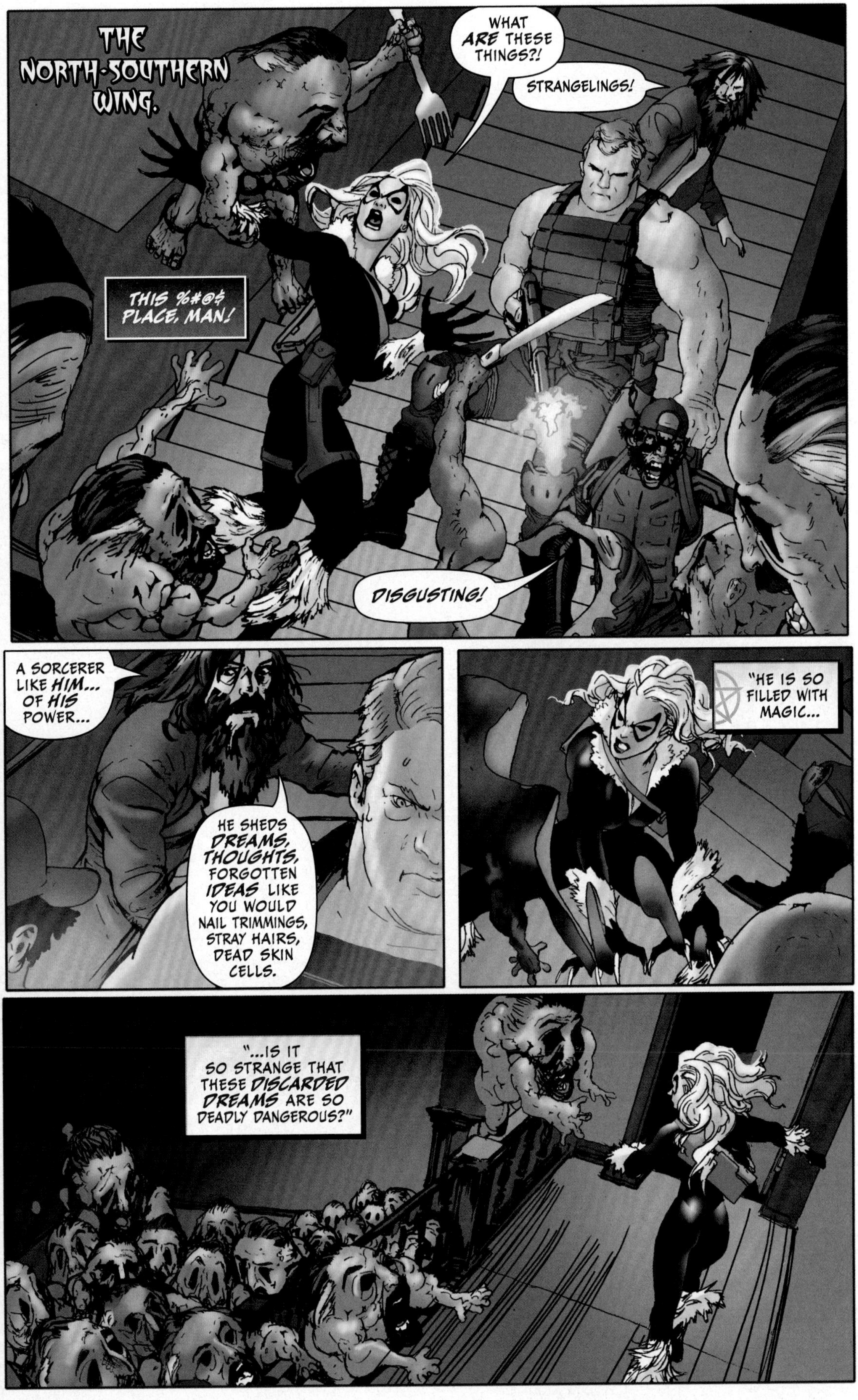
THE NORTH-SOUTHERN WING.
WHAT ARE THESE THINGS?!
STRANGELINGS!
THIS %#@$ PLACE, MAN!
DISGUSTING!
A SORCERER LIKE HIM... OF HIS POWER...
HE SHEDS DREAMS, THOUGHTS, FORGOTTEN IDEAS LIKE YOU WOULD NAIL TRIMMINGS, STRAY HAIRS, DEAD SKIN CELLS.
"HE IS SO FILLED WITH MAGIC...
"...IS IT SO STRANGE THAT THESE DISCARDED DREAMS ARE SO DEADLY DANGEROUS?"

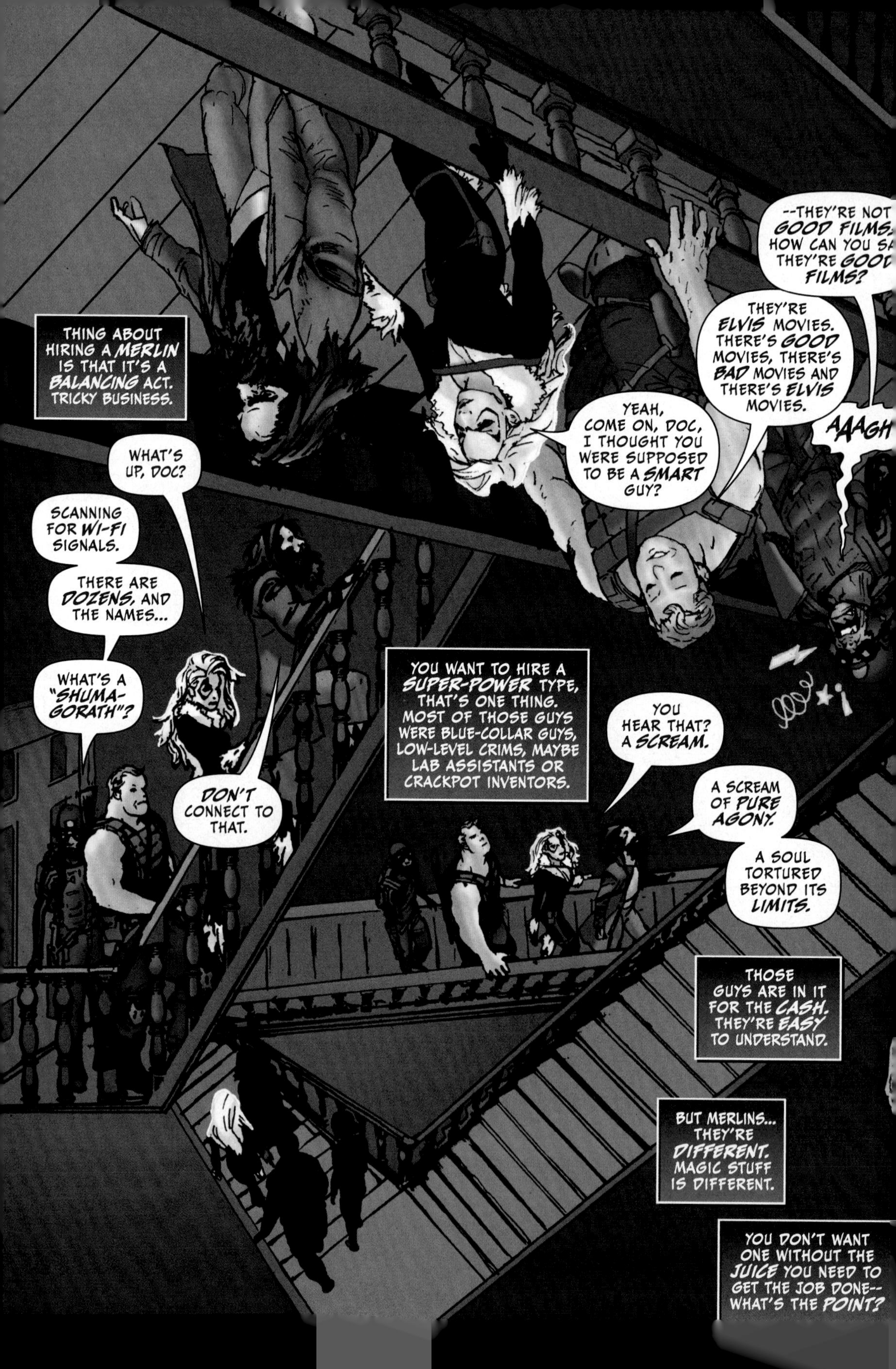

THING ABOUT HIRING A MERLIN IS THAT IT'S A BALANCING ACT. TRICKY BUSINESS.
YEAH, COME ON, DOC, I THOUGHT YOU WERE SUPPOSED TO BE A SMART GUY?
THEY'RE ELVIS MOVIES. THERE'S GOOD MOVIES, THERE'S BAD MOVIES AND THERE'S ELVIS MOVIES.
--THEY'RE NOT GOOD FILMS. HOW CAN YOU SA THEY'RE GOOD FILMS?
AAAGH
WHAT'S UP, DOC?
SCANNING FOR WI-FI SIGNALS.
THERE ARE DOZENS, AND THE NAMES...
WHAT'S A "SHUMA-GORATH"?
DON'T CONNECT TO THAT.
YOU WANT TO HIRE A SUPER-POWER TYPE, THAT'S ONE THING. MOST OF THOSE GUYS WERE BLUE-COLLAR GUYS, LOW-LEVEL CRIMS, MAYBE LAB ASSISTANTS OR CRACKPOT INVENTORS.
YOU HEAR THAT? A SCREAM.
A SCREAM OF PURE AGONY.
A SOUL TORTURED BEYOND ITS LIMITS.
THOSE GUYS ARE IN IT FOR THE CASH. THEY'RE EASY TO UNDERSTAND.
BUT MERLINS... THEY'RE DIFFERENT. MAGIC STUFF IS DIFFERENT.
YOU DON'T WANT ONE WITHOUT THE JUICE YOU NEED TO GET THE JOB DONE--WHAT'S THE POINT?

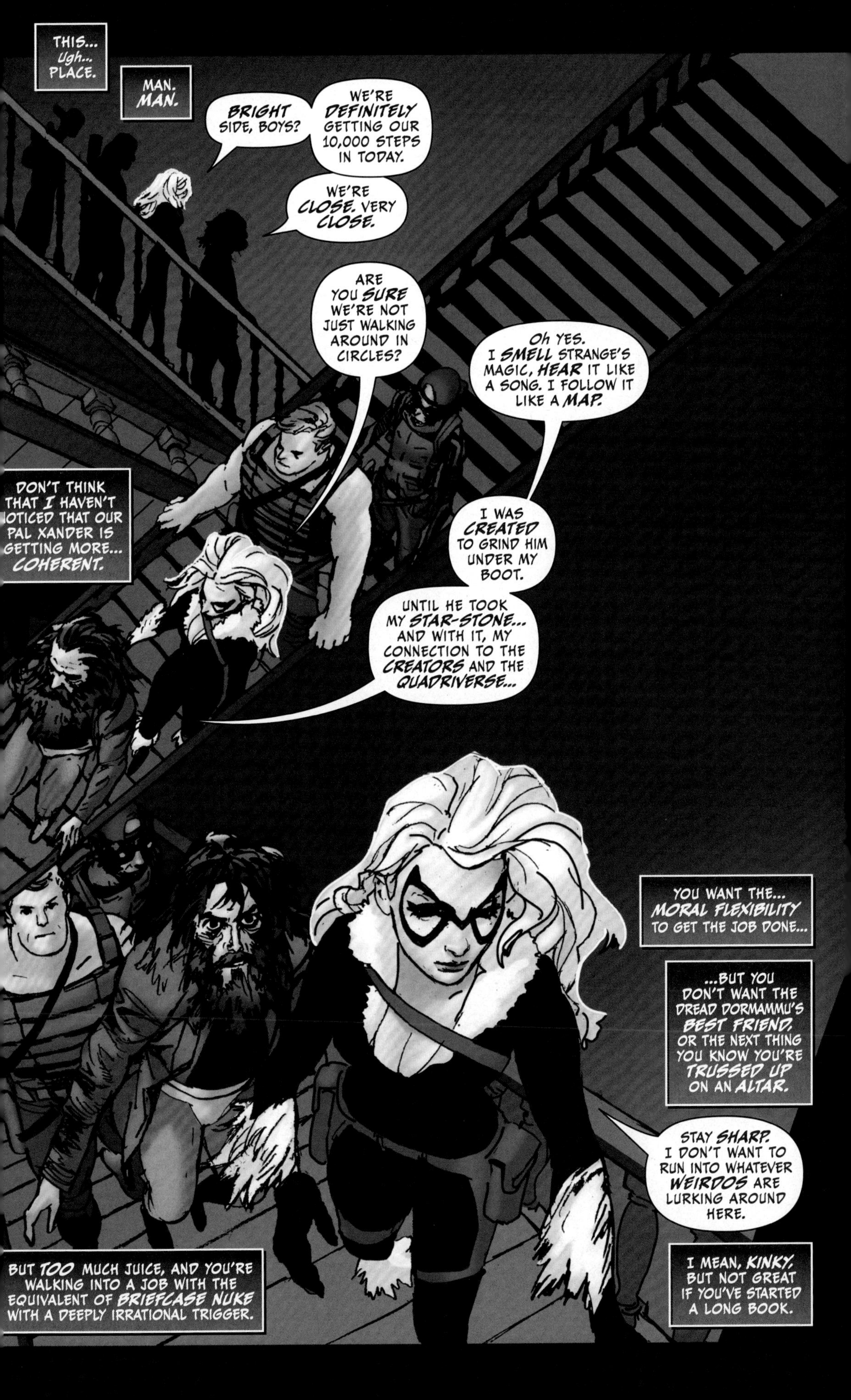
THIS... Ugh... PLACE.
MAN. MAN.
BRIGHT SIDE, BOYS?
WE'RE DEFINITELY GETTING OUR 10,000 STEPS IN TODAY.
WE'RE CLOSE. VERY CLOSE.
ARE YOU SURE WE'RE NOT JUST WALKING AROUND IN CIRCLES?
Oh YES. I SMELL STRANGE'S MAGIC, HEAR IT LIKE A SONG. I FOLLOW IT LIKE A MAP.
DON'T THINK THAT I HAVEN'T NOTICED THAT OUR PAL XANDER IS GETTING MORE... COHERENT.
I WAS CREATED TO GRIND HIM UNDER MY BOOT.
UNTIL HE TOOK MY STAR-STONE... AND WITH IT, MY CONNECTION TO THE CREATORS AND THE QUADRIVERSE...
YOU WANT THE... MORAL FLEXIBILITY TO GET THE JOB DONE...
...BUT YOU DON'T WANT THE DREAD DORMAMMU'S BEST FRIEND, OR THE NEXT THING YOU KNOW YOU'RE TRUSSED UP ON AN ALTAR.
STAY SHARP. I DON'T WANT TO RUN INTO WHATEVER WEIRDOS ARE LURKING AROUND HERE.
BUT TOO MUCH JUICE, AND YOU'RE WALKING INTO A JOB WITH THE EQUIVALENT OF BRIEFCASE NUKE WITH A DEEPLY IRRATIONAL TRIGGER.
I MEAN, KINKY, BUT NOT GREAT IF YOU'VE STARTED A LONG BOOK.

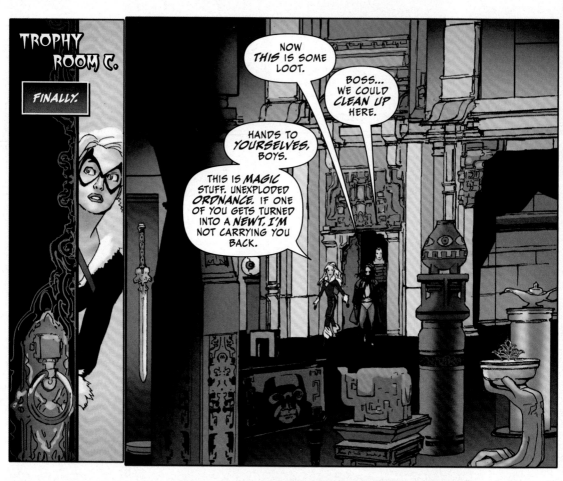

TROPHY ROOM C.

FINALLY.

NOW *THIS* IS SOME LOOT.

BOSS... WE COULD *CLEAN UP* HERE.

HANDS TO *YOURSELVES*, BOYS.

THIS IS *MAGIC* STUFF. UNEXPLODED *ORDNANCE*. IF ONE OF YOU GETS TURNED INTO A *NEWT*, I'M NOT CARRYING YOU BACK.

Faugh! DON'T TREAT *ME* LIKE SOME CREDULOUS *BUMPKIN*, HARDY!

MAGIC, *PLEASE*.

YOU SERIOUSLY *STILL* DON'T BELIEVE IN MAGIC STUFF? *DAMN*, DOC.

WHERE *IS* IT? WHERE IS IT *HIDDEN*?

ALL JUST *SCIENTIFIC PHENOMENONA* THAT IS YET TO BE UNDERSTOOD.

YOU *SUPERSTITIOUS RUBES* WOULD PROBABLY HAVE BURNED *REED RICHARDS* AT THE *STAKE* A CENTURY AGO.

WHERE?

Oh, *Boyyys...*

I GOT IT.

IMPOSSIBLE. NO.

YES.

IT'S NOT--

IT IS!

THERE. FINALLY. THERE. FINALLY.

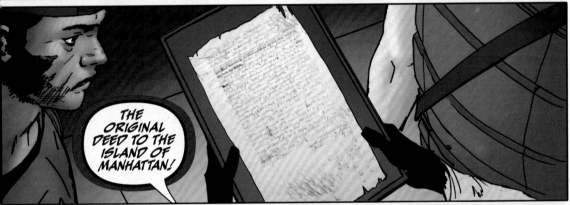

THE ORIGINAL DEED TO THE ISLAND OF MANHATTAN!

THINGS BEGIN TO HAPPEN QUICKLY.

...THE SSSTAR-SSSTONE...

THINGS BEGIN TO GO WRONG.

WAIT, WHERE DID XANDER GET TO--

BRUNO!

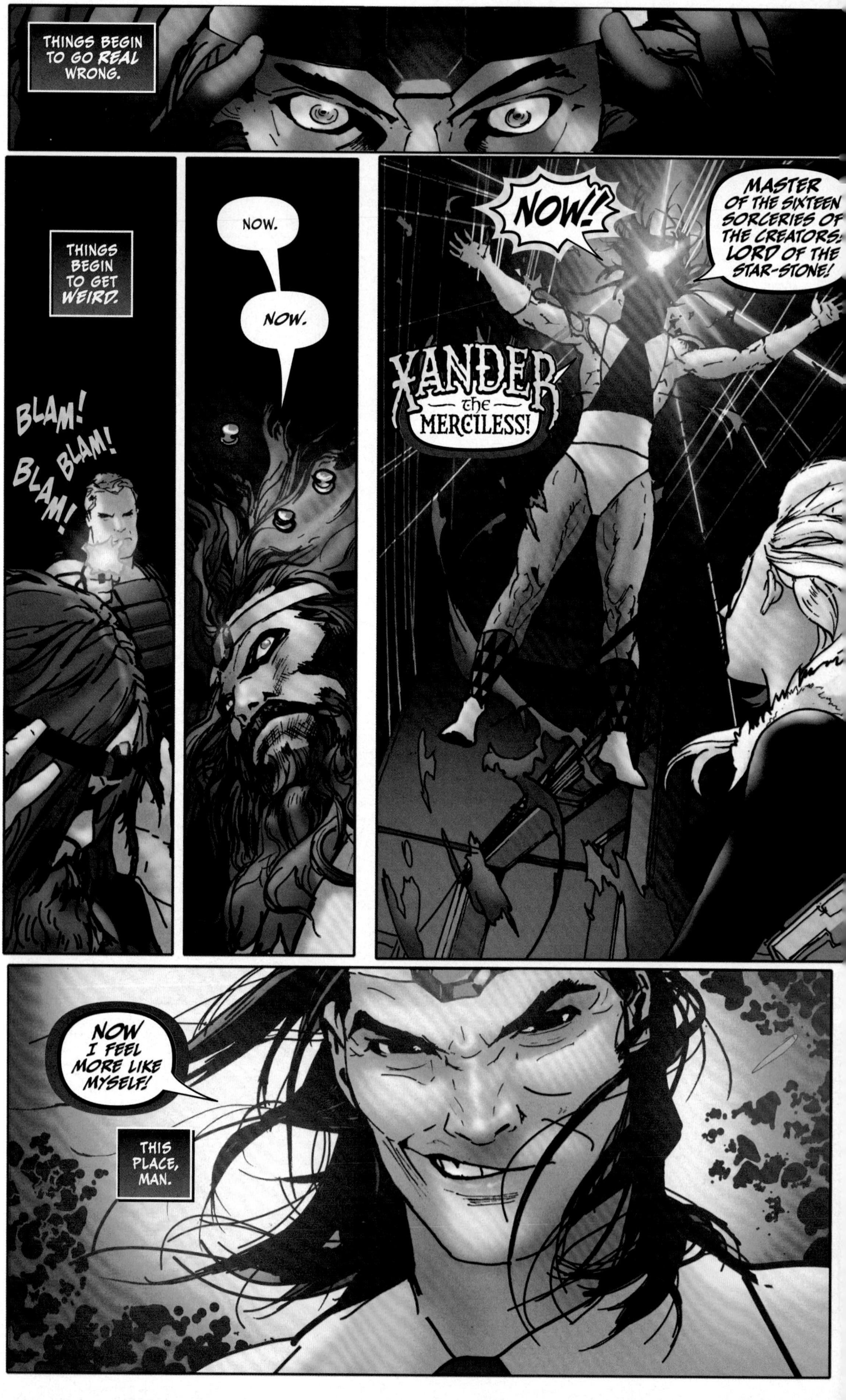
THINGS BEGIN TO GO REAL WRONG.
THINGS BEGIN TO GET WEIRD.
BLAM! BLAM! BLAM!
NOW.
NOW.
NOW!!
MASTER OF THE SIXTEEN SORCERIES OF THE CREATORS! LORD OF THE STAR-STONE!
XANDER the MERCILESS!
NOW I FEEL MORE LIKE MYSELF!
THIS PLACE, MAN.

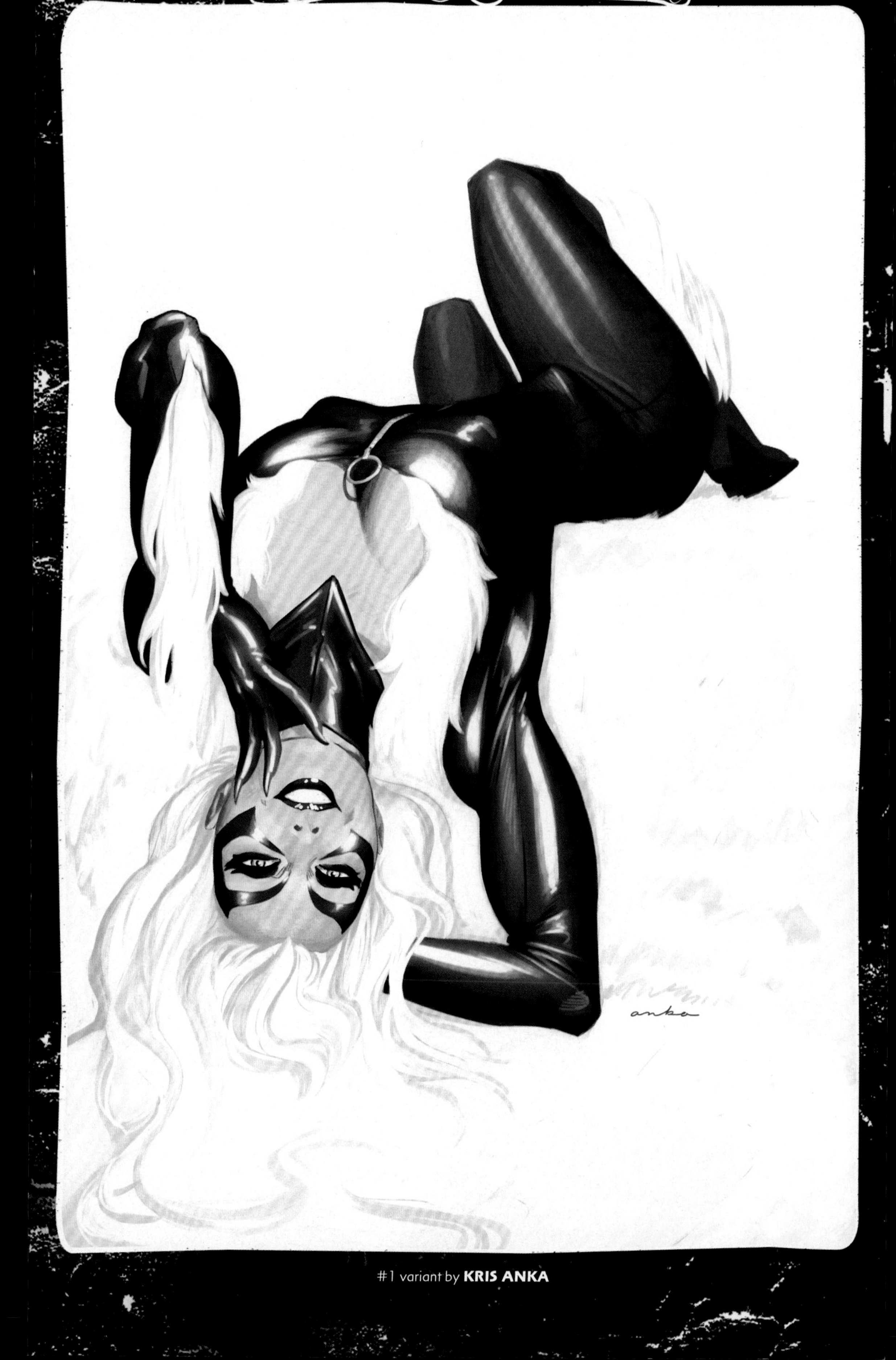
anka

#1 variant by **KRIS ANKA**

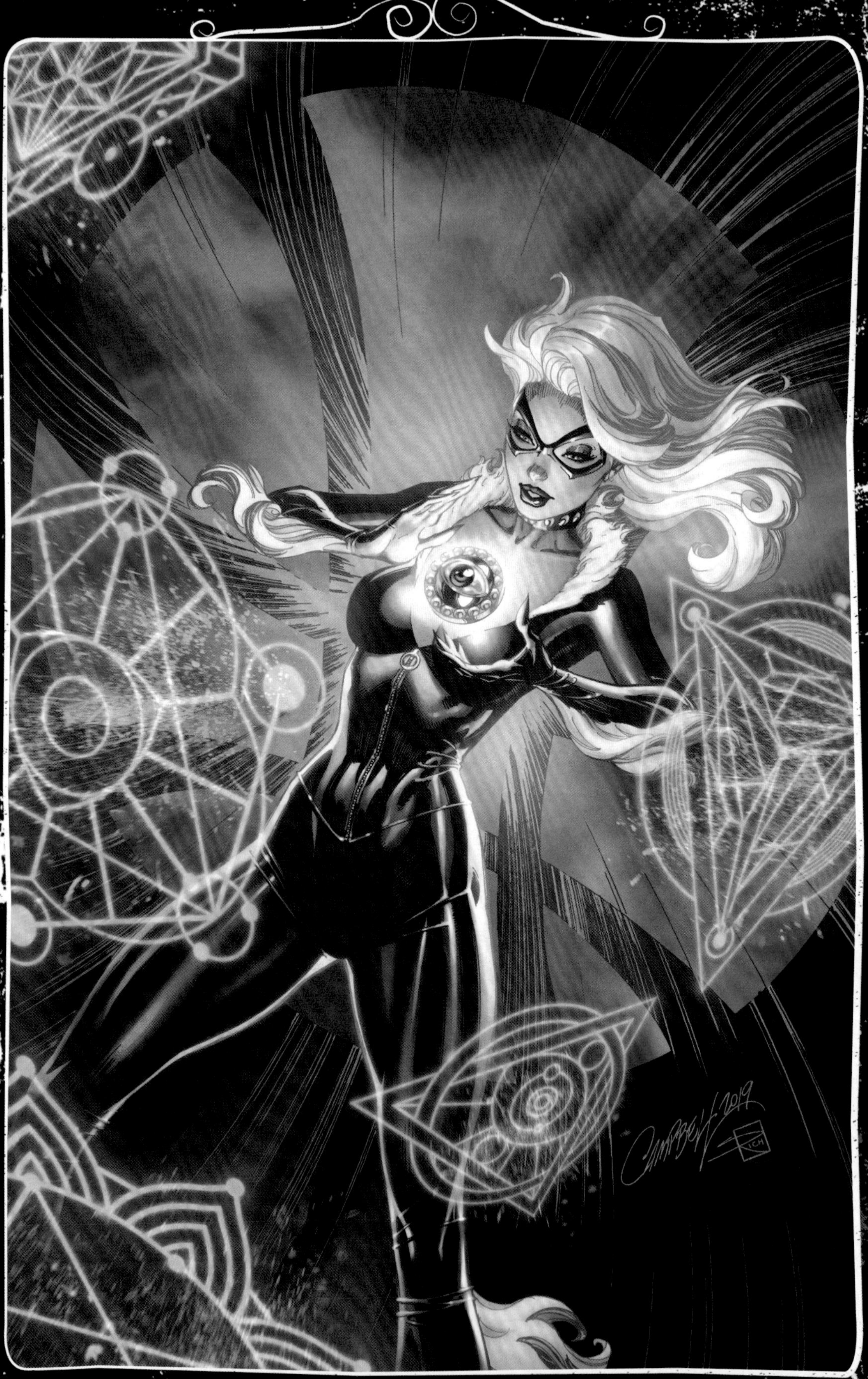

3 • Holiest of Holies PART 2

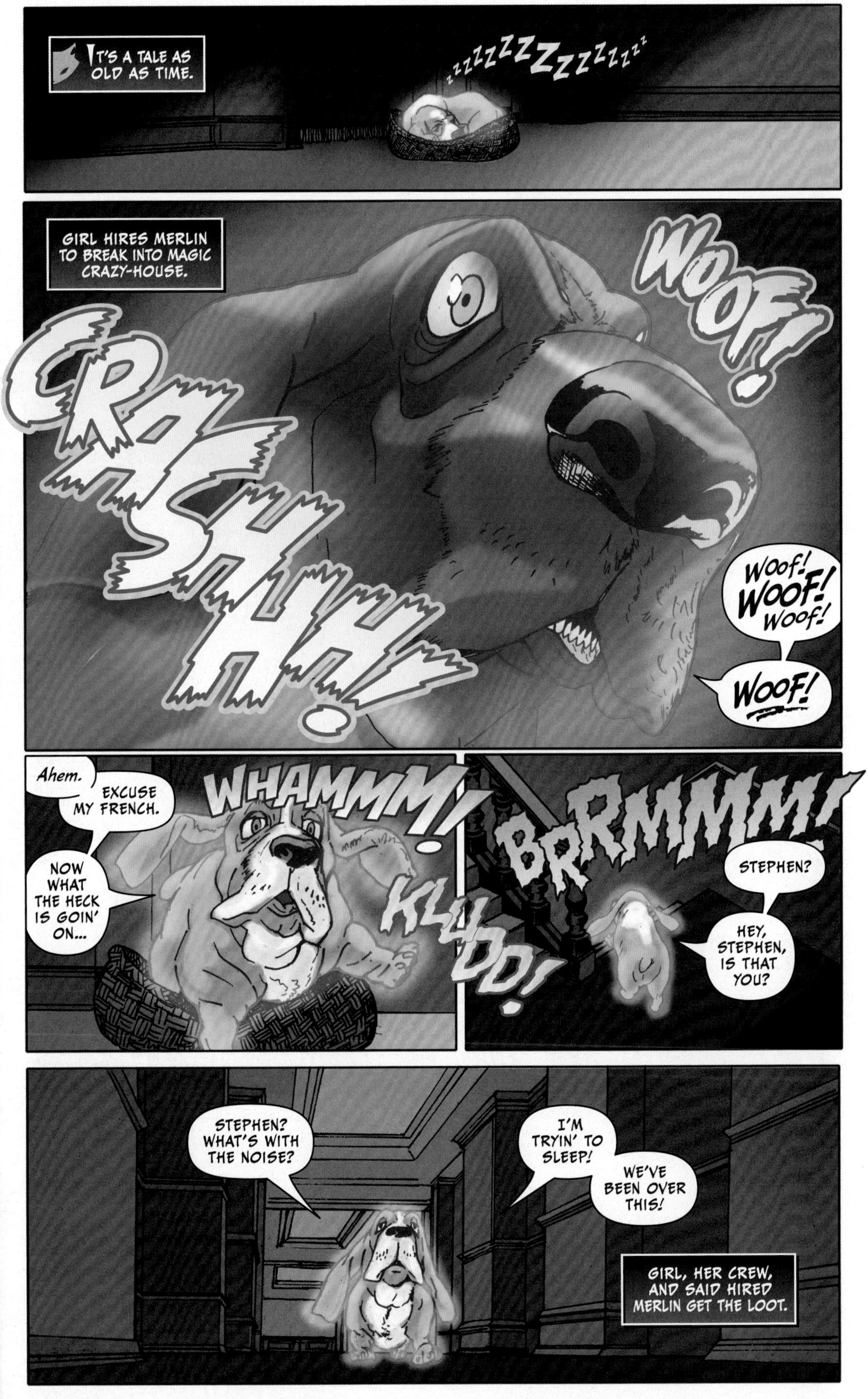
IT'S A TALE AS OLD AS TIME.
ZZZZZZZZZZZZZZZZ
GIRL HIRES MERLIN TO BREAK INTO MAGIC CRAZY-HOUSE.
WOOF!
CRASHH!
WOOF! WOOF! WOOF!
WOOF!
Ahem.
EXCUSE MY FRENCH.
NOW WHAT THE HECK IS GOIN' ON...
WHAMMM!
KLUDD!
BRRMMM!
STEPHEN?
HEY, STEPHEN, IS THAT YOU?
STEPHEN? WHAT'S WITH THE NOISE?
I'M TRYIN' TO SLEEP!
WE'VE BEEN OVER THIS!
GIRL, HER CREW, AND SAID HIRED MERLIN GET THE LOOT.

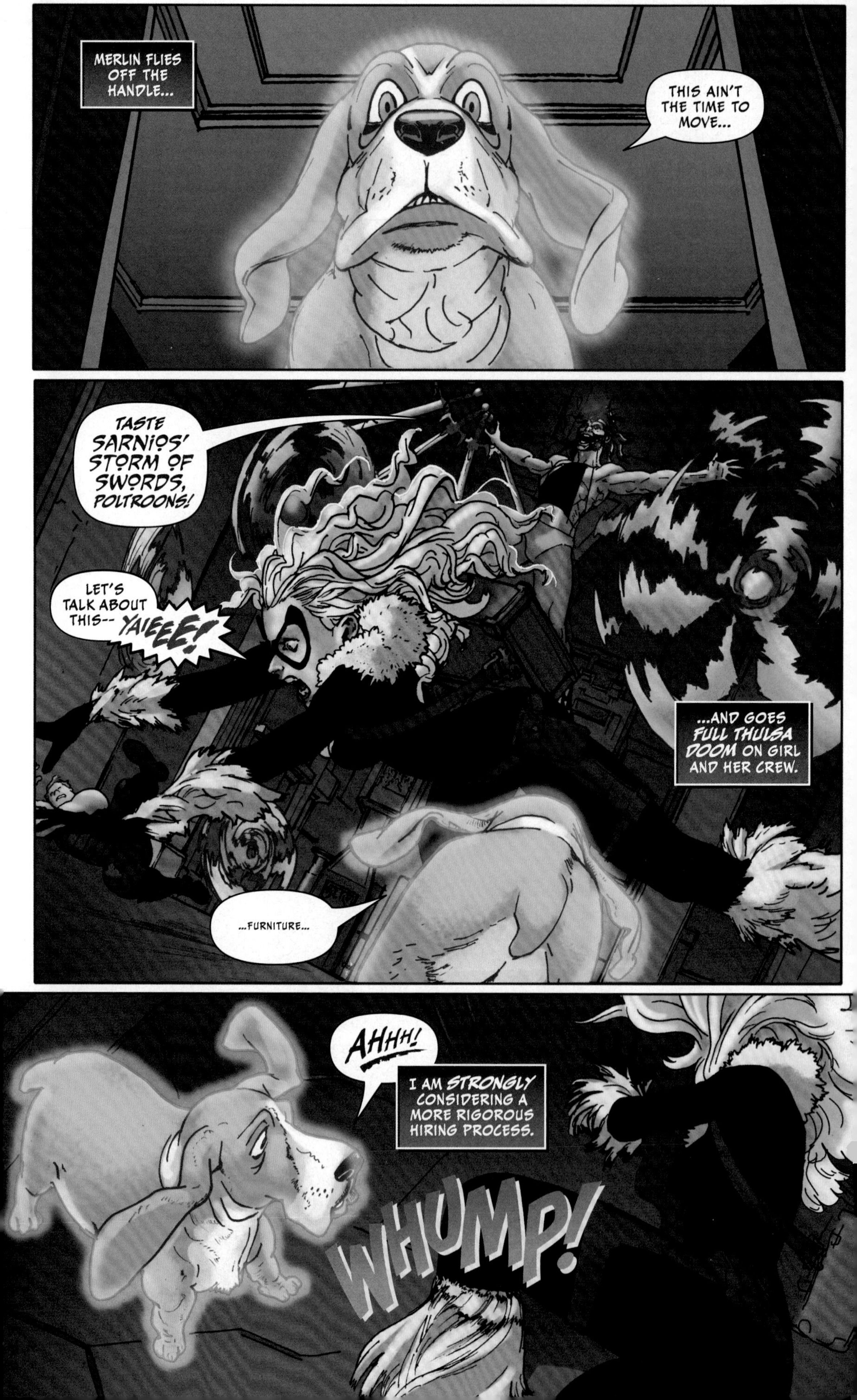
MERLIN FLIES OFF THE HANDLE...
THIS AIN'T THE TIME TO MOVE...
TASTE SARNIOS' STORM OF SWORDS, POLTROONS!
LET'S TALK ABOUT THIS-- YAIEEE!
...AND GOES FULL THULSA DOOM ON GIRL AND HER CREW.
...FURNITURE...
AHHH!
I AM STRONGLY CONSIDERING A MORE RIGOROUS HIRING PROCESS.
WHUMP!

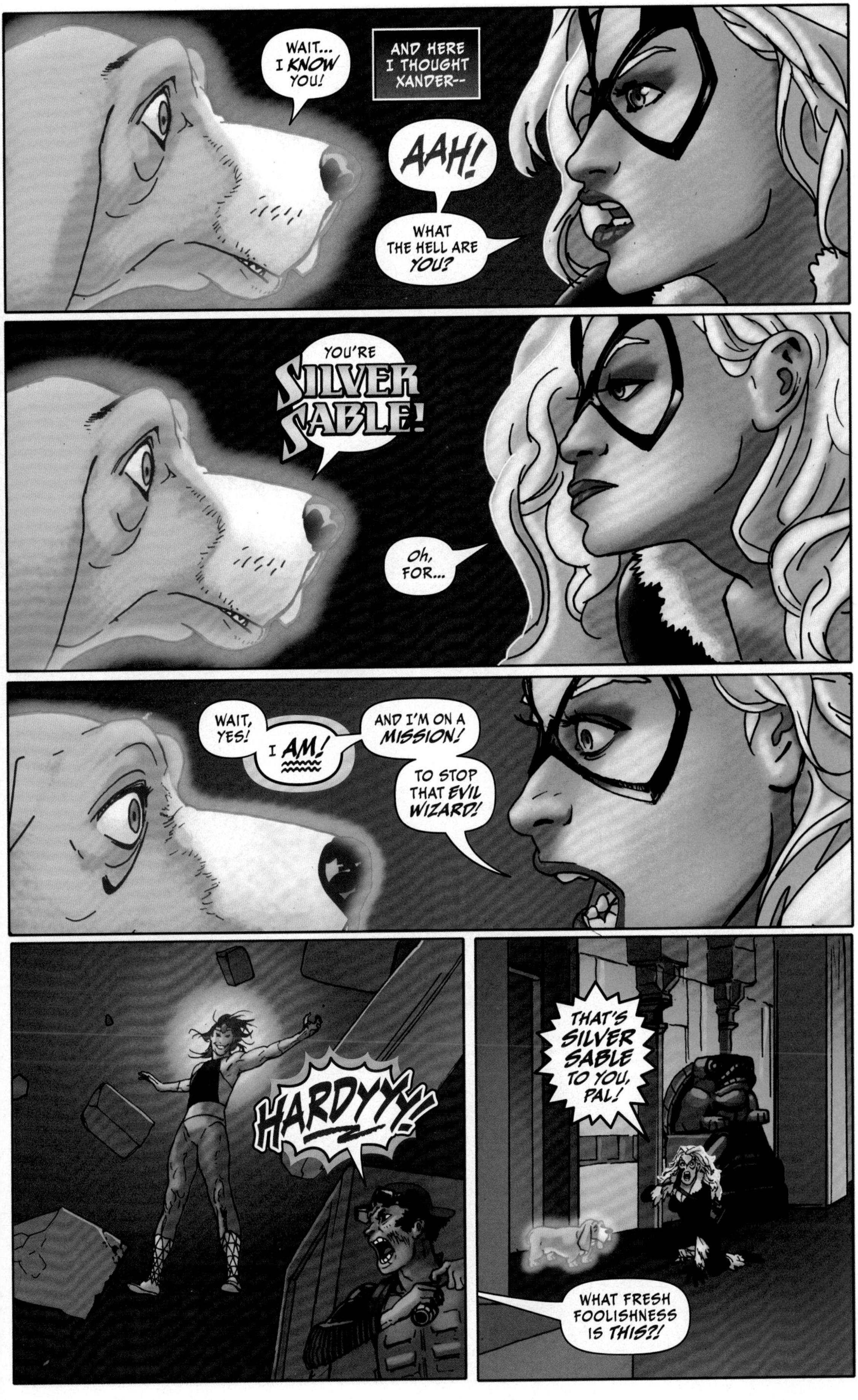
WAIT... I KNOW YOU!
AND HERE I THOUGHT XANDER--
AAH!
WHAT THE HELL ARE YOU?
YOU'RE SILVER SABLE!
Oh, FOR...
WAIT, YES!
I AM!
AND I'M ON A MISSION!
TO STOP THAT EVIL WIZARD!
HARDYYY!
THAT'S SILVER SABLE TO YOU, PAL!
WHAT FRESH FOOLISHNESS IS THIS?!

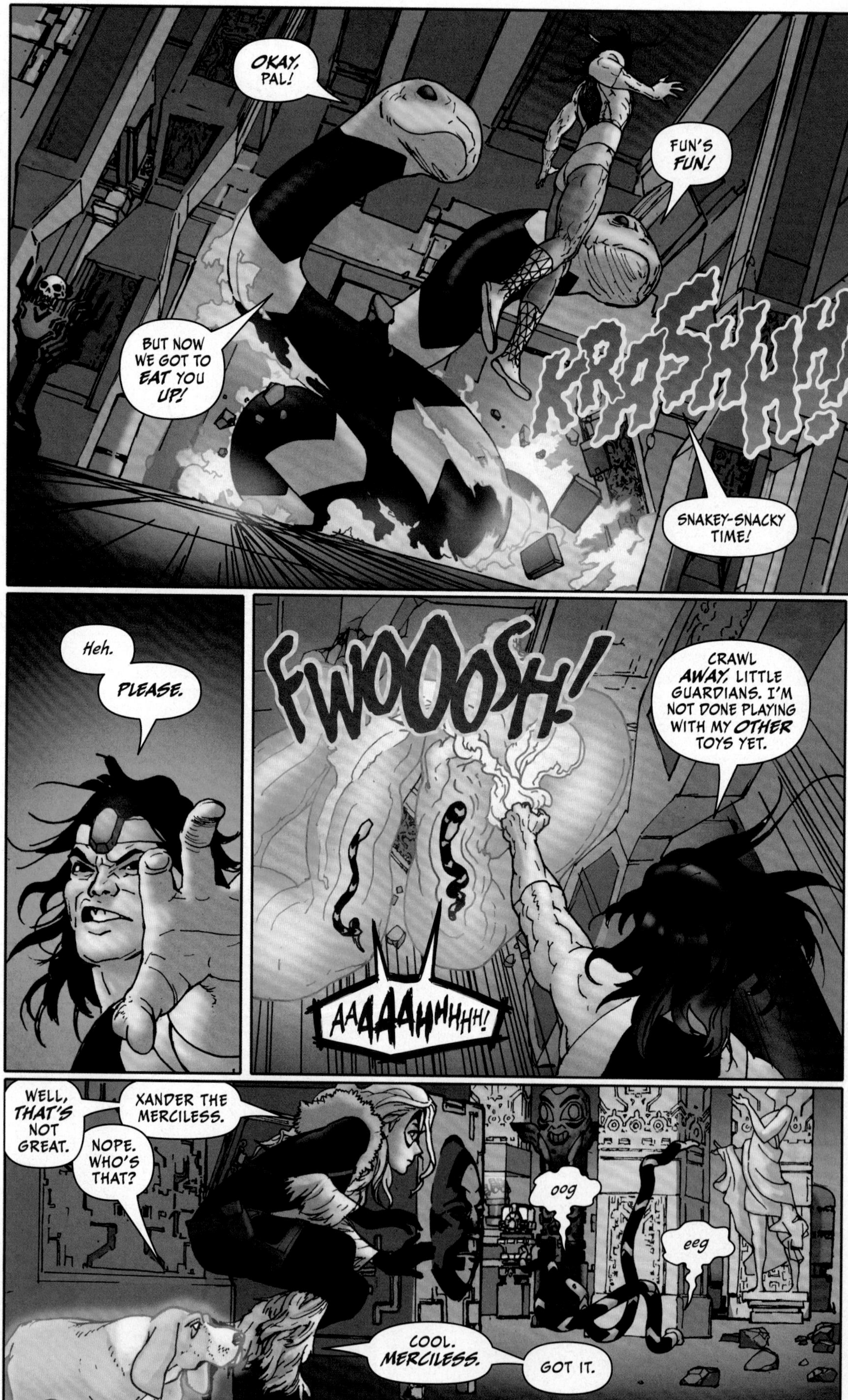
OKAY, PAL!
FUN'S FUN!
BUT NOW WE GOT TO EAT YOU UP!
KRASHH!
SNAKEY-SNACKY TIME!
Heh.
PLEASE.
FWOOOSH!
CRAWL AWAY, LITTLE GUARDIANS. I'M NOT DONE PLAYING WITH MY OTHER TOYS YET.
AAAAAHHHHH!
WELL, THAT'S NOT GREAT.
XANDER THE MERCILESS.
NOPE. WHO'S THAT?
oog
eeg
COOL. MERCILESS.
GOT IT.

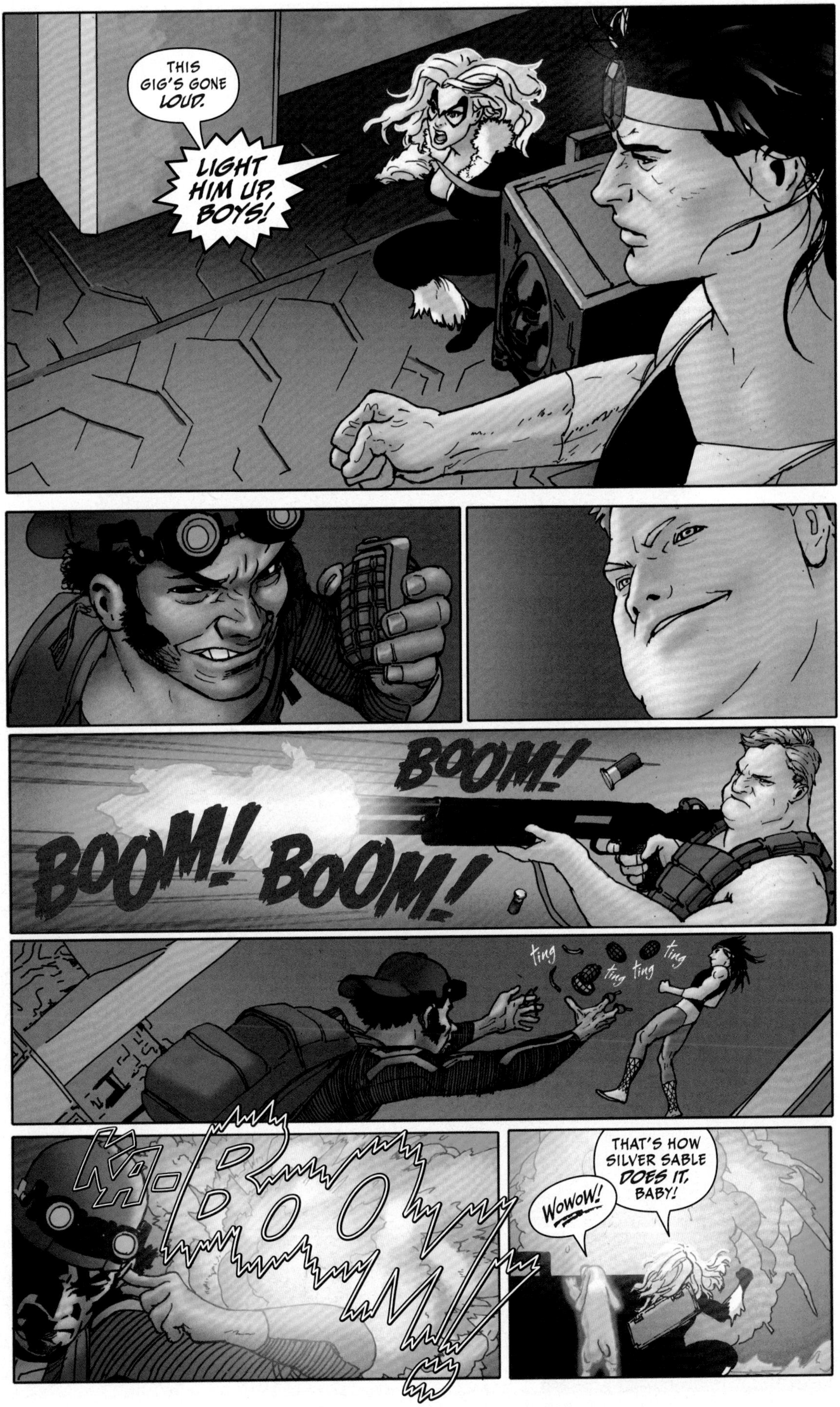
THIS GIG'S GONE LOUD.
LIGHT HIM UP, BOYS!
BOOM!
BOOM! BOOM!
ting
ting
ting
ting
WOWOW!
THAT'S HOW SILVER SABLE DOES IT, BABY!

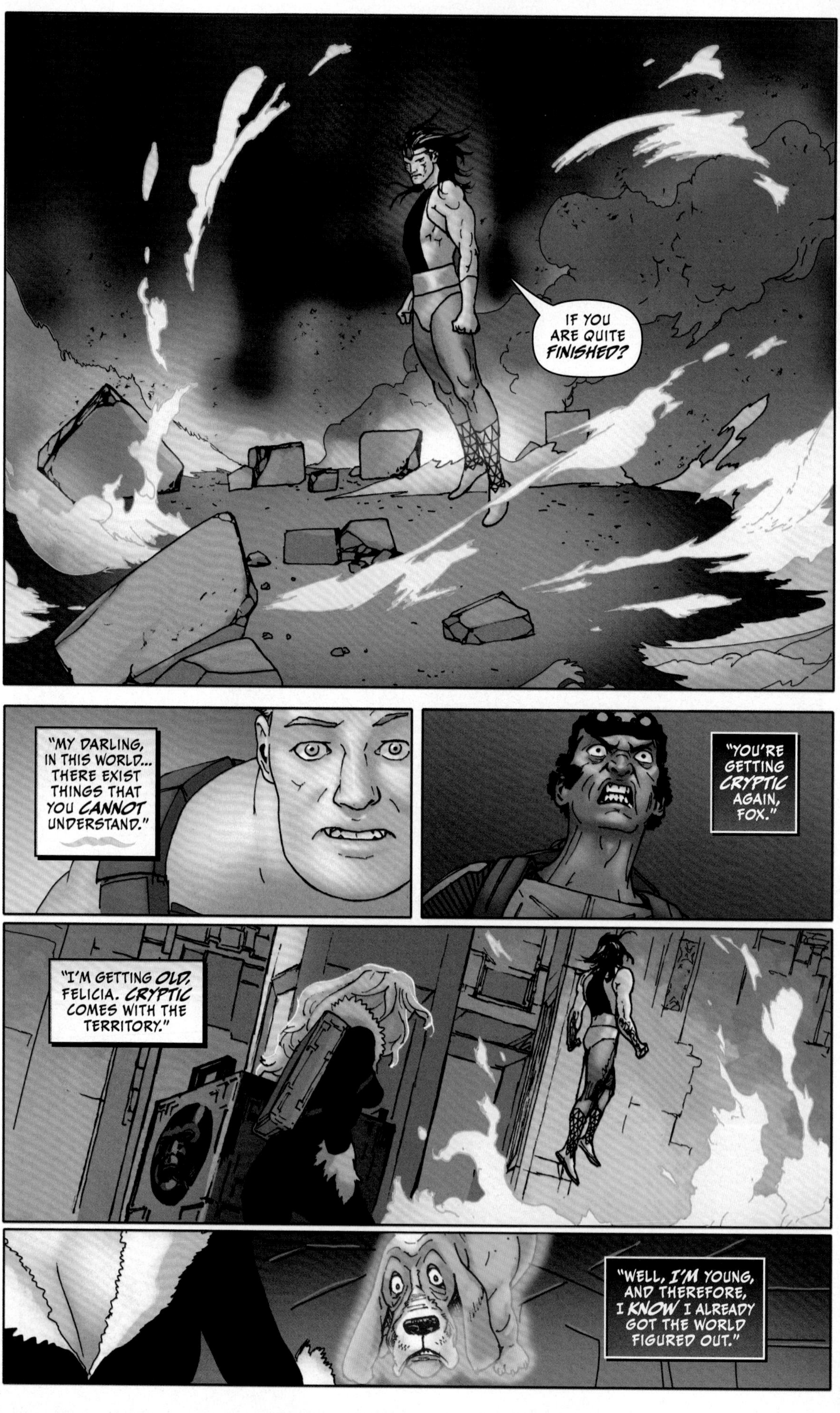
IF YOU ARE QUITE FINISHED?
"MY DARLING, IN THIS WORLD... THERE EXIST THINGS THAT YOU CANNOT UNDERSTAND."
"YOU'RE GETTING CRYPTIC AGAIN, FOX."
"I'M GETTING OLD, FELICIA. CRYPTIC COMES WITH THE TERRITORY."
"WELL, I'M YOUNG, AND THEREFORE, I KNOW I ALREADY GOT THE WORLD FIGURED OUT."

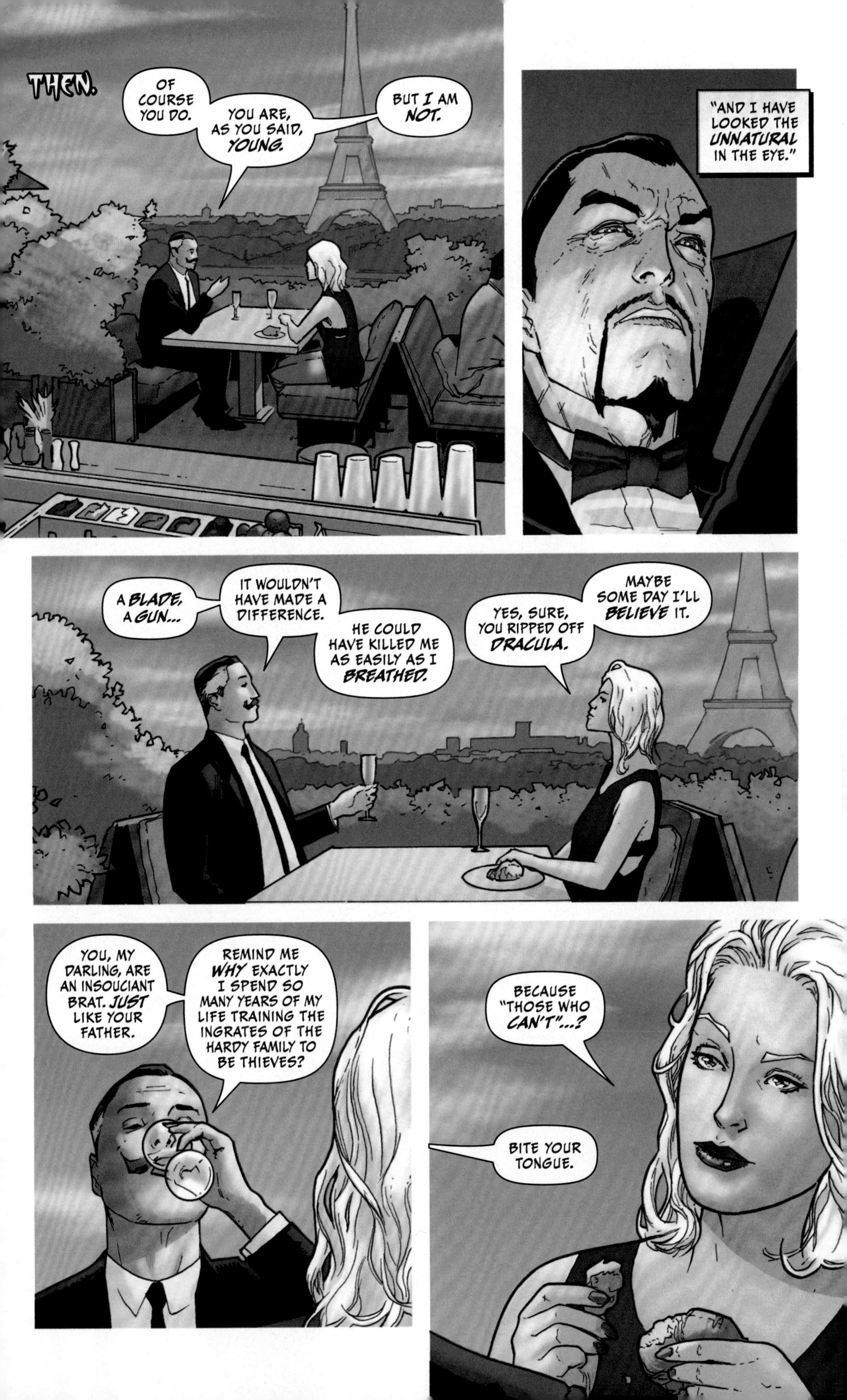
THEN.
OF COURSE YOU DO.
YOU ARE, AS YOU SAID, YOUNG.
BUT I AM NOT.
"AND I HAVE LOOKED THE UNNATURAL IN THE EYE."
A BLADE, A GUN...
IT WOULDN'T HAVE MADE A DIFFERENCE.
HE COULD HAVE KILLED ME AS EASILY AS I BREATHED.
YES, SURE, YOU RIPPED OFF DRACULA.
MAYBE SOME DAY I'LL BELIEVE IT.
YOU, MY DARLING, ARE AN INSOUCIANT BRAT. JUST LIKE YOUR FATHER.
REMIND ME WHY EXACTLY I SPEND SO MANY YEARS OF MY LIFE TRAINING THE INGRATES OF THE HARDY FAMILY TO BE THIEVES?
BECAUSE "THOSE WHO CAN'T"...?
BITE YOUR TONGUE.

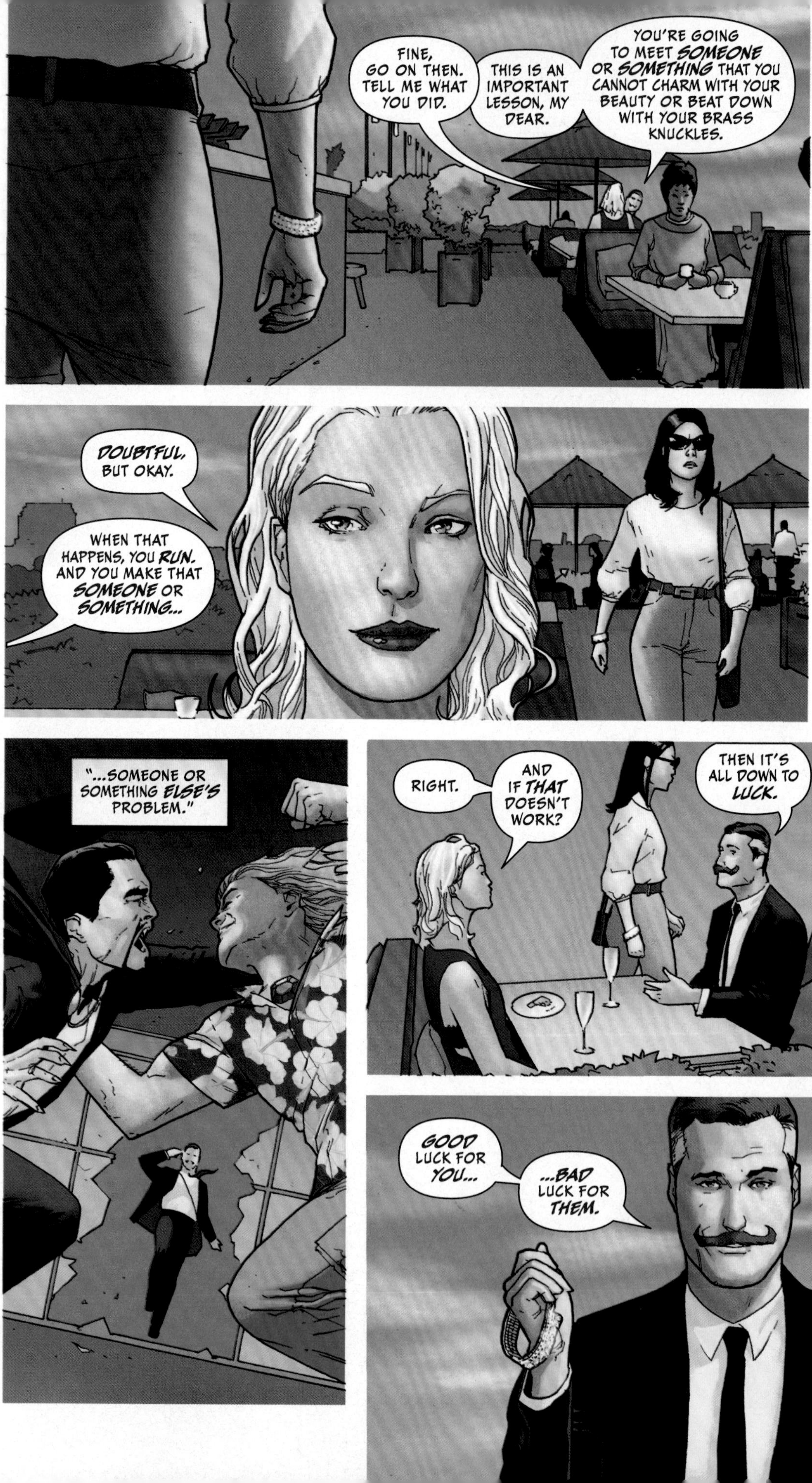
FINE, GO ON THEN. TELL ME WHAT YOU DID.
THIS IS AN IMPORTANT LESSON, MY DEAR.
YOU'RE GOING TO MEET SOMEONE OR SOMETHING THAT YOU CANNOT CHARM WITH YOUR BEAUTY OR BEAT DOWN WITH YOUR BRASS KNUCKLES.
DOUBTFUL, BUT OKAY.
WHEN THAT HAPPENS, YOU RUN. AND YOU MAKE THAT SOMEONE OR SOMETHING...
"...SOMEONE OR SOMETHING ELSE'S PROBLEM."
RIGHT.
AND IF THAT DOESN'T WORK?
THEN IT'S ALL DOWN TO LUCK.
GOOD LUCK FOR YOU...
...BAD LUCK FOR THEM.

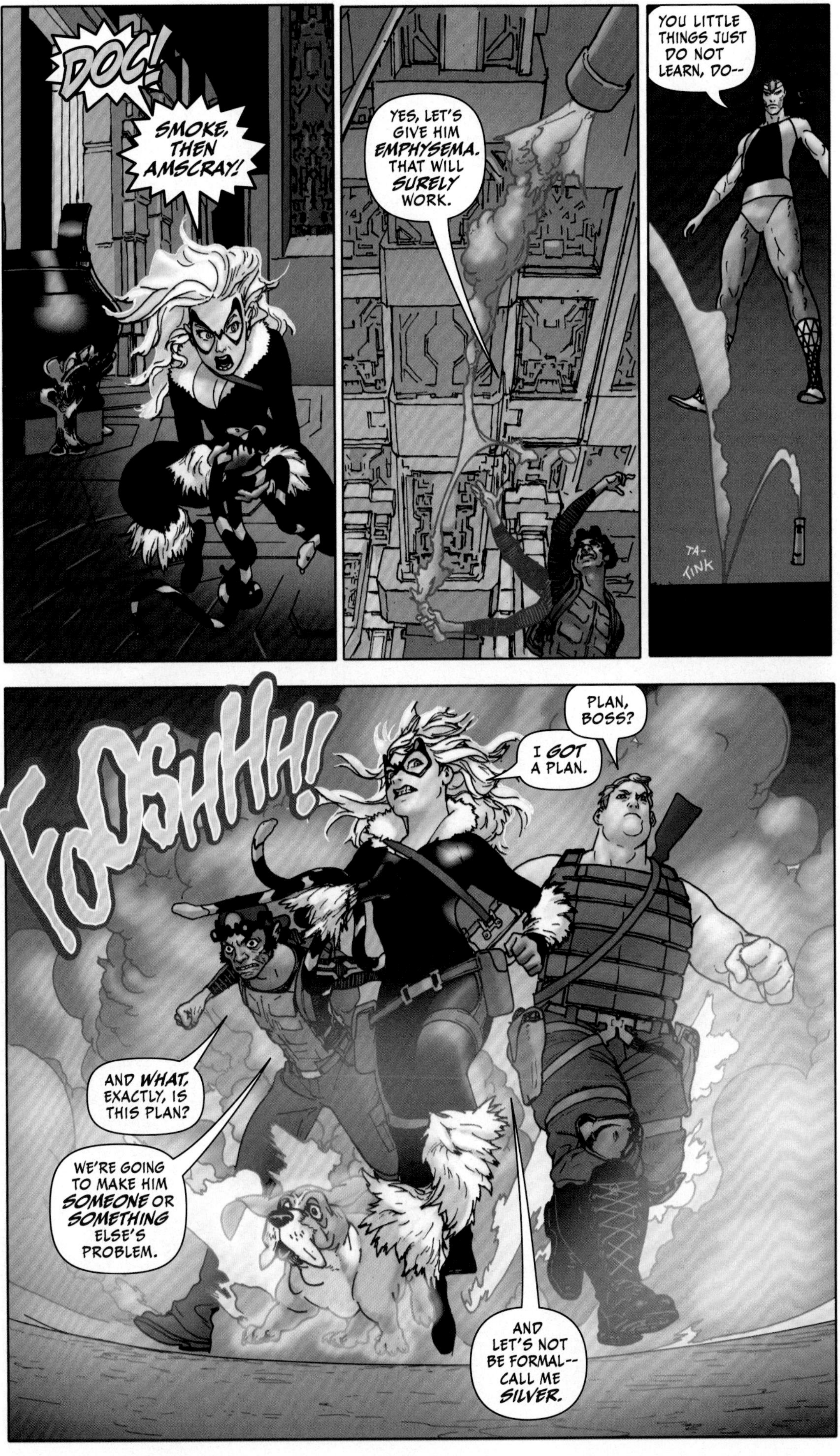
DOC!
SMOKE, THEN AMSCRAY!
YES, LET'S GIVE HIM EMPHYSEMA. THAT WILL SURELY WORK.
YOU LITTLE THINGS JUST DO NOT LEARN, DO--
TA-TINK
FOOSHHH!
PLAN, BOSS?
I GOT A PLAN.
AND WHAT, EXACTLY, IS THIS PLAN?
WE'RE GOING TO MAKE HIM SOMEONE OR SOMETHING ELSE'S PROBLEM.
AND LET'S NOT BE FORMAL-- CALL ME SILVER.

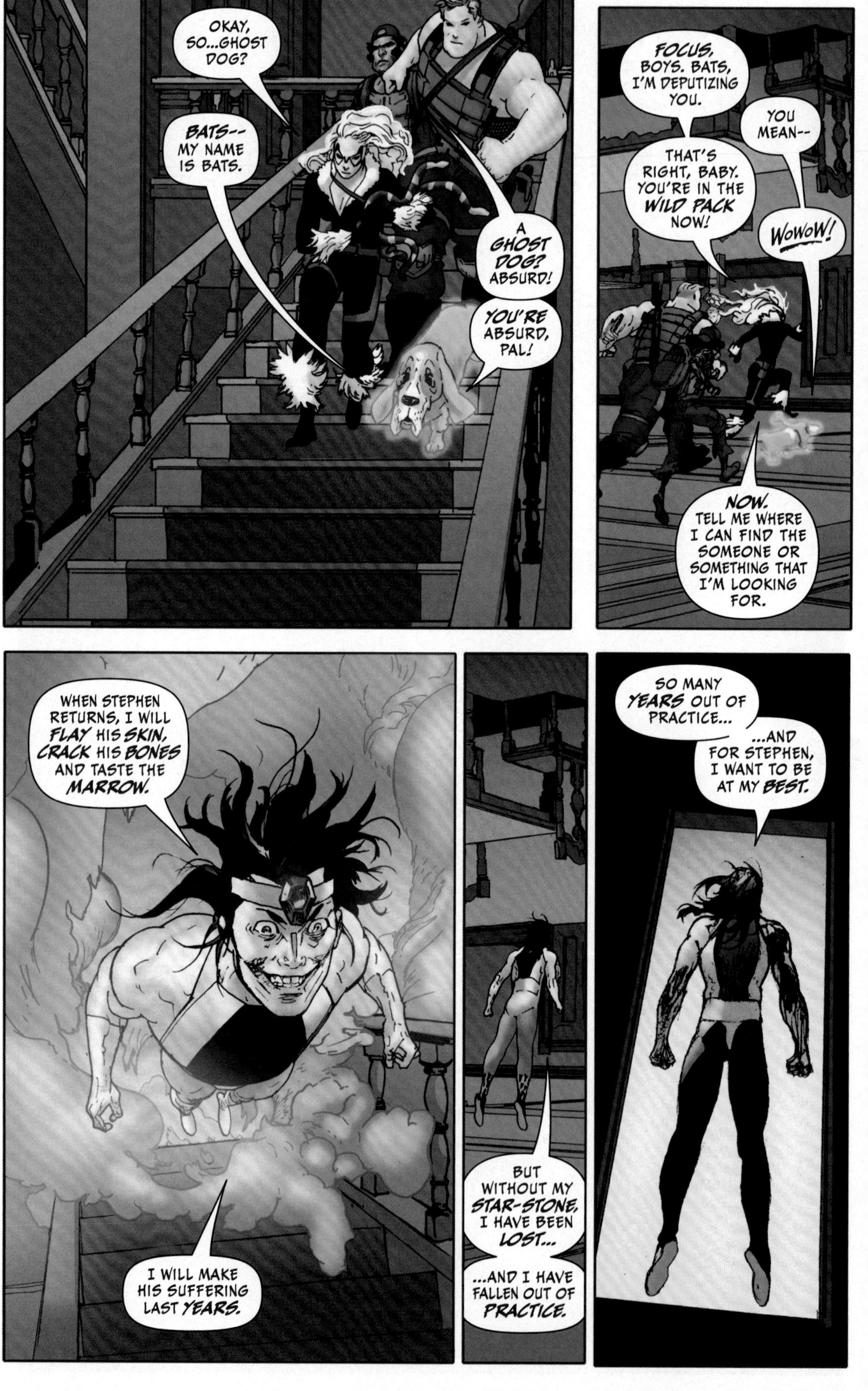
OKAY, SO...GHOST DOG?
BATS-- MY NAME IS BATS.
A GHOST DOG? ABSURD!
YOU'RE ABSURD, PAL!
FOCUS, BOYS. BATS, I'M DEPUTIZING YOU.
YOU MEAN--
THAT'S RIGHT, BABY. YOU'RE IN THE WILD PACK NOW!
WoWoW!
NOW. TELL ME WHERE I CAN FIND THE SOMEONE OR SOMETHING THAT I'M LOOKING FOR.
WHEN STEPHEN RETURNS, I WILL FLAY HIS SKIN, CRACK HIS BONES AND TASTE THE MARROW.
I WILL MAKE HIS SUFFERING LAST YEARS.
BUT WITHOUT MY STAR-STONE, I HAVE BEEN LOST...
...AND I HAVE FALLEN OUT OF PRACTICE.
SO MANY YEARS OUT OF PRACTICE...
...AND FOR STEPHEN, I WANT TO BE AT MY BEST.

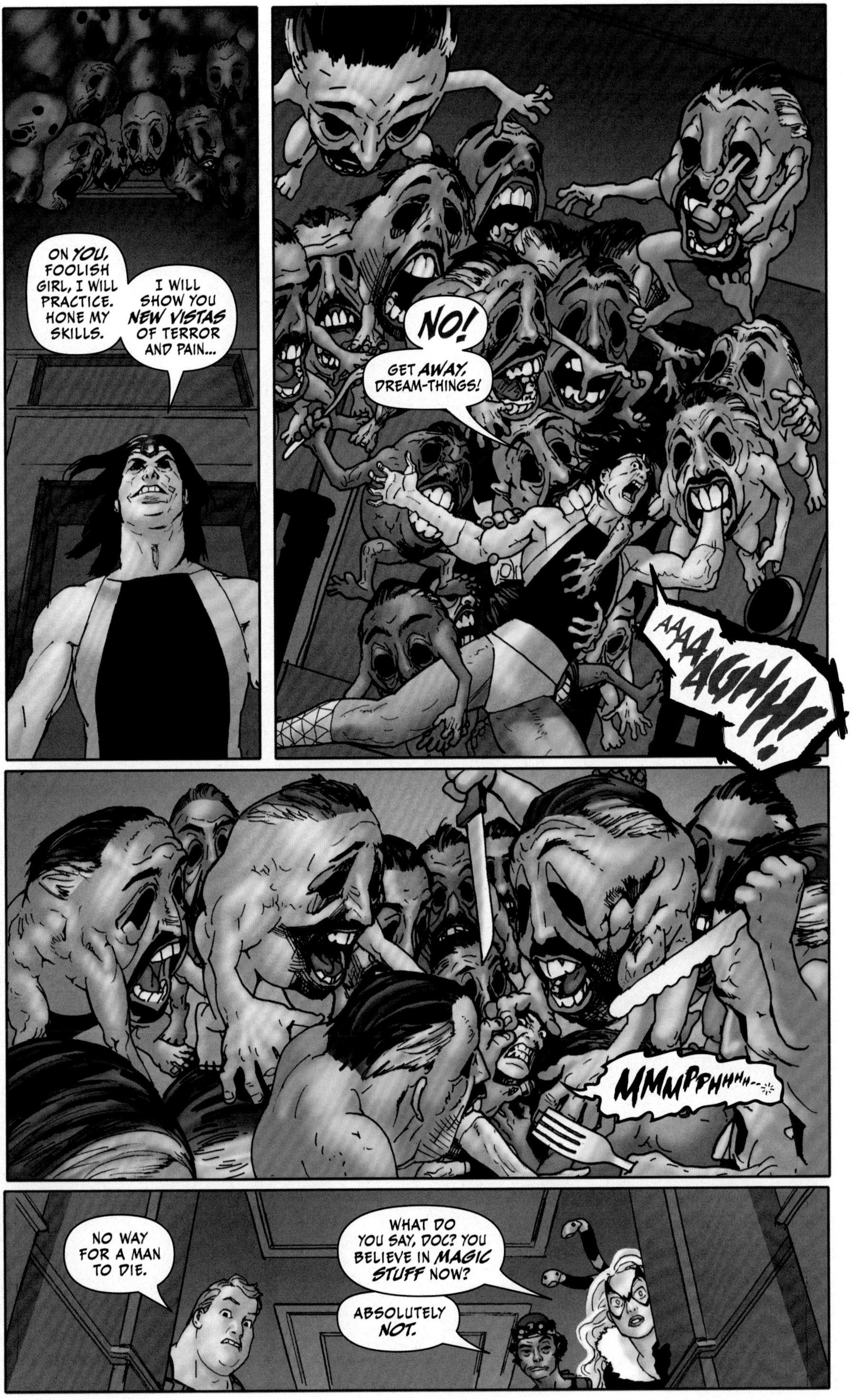
ON YOU, FOOLISH GIRL, I WILL PRACTICE. HONE MY SKILLS.
I WILL SHOW YOU NEW VISTAS OF TERROR AND PAIN...
NO!
GET AWAY, DREAM-THINGS!
AAAAAGHH!
MMMPPHHHH--
NO WAY FOR A MAN TO DIE.
WHAT DO YOU SAY, DOC? YOU BELIEVE IN MAGIC STUFF NOW?
ABSOLUTELY NOT.

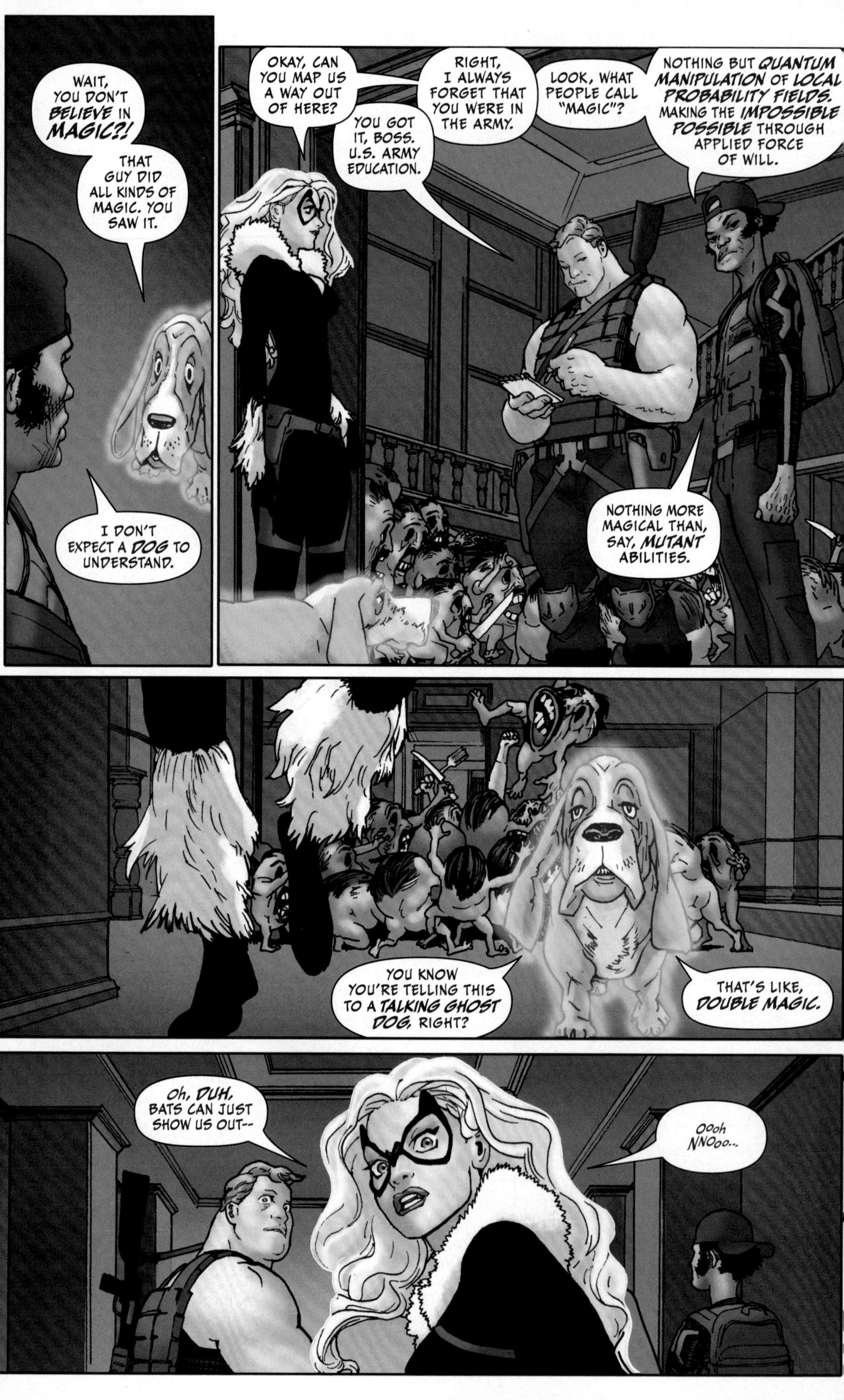
WAIT, YOU DON'T BELIEVE IN MAGIC?!
THAT GUY DID ALL KINDS OF MAGIC. YOU SAW IT.
I DON'T EXPECT A DOG TO UNDERSTAND.
OKAY, CAN YOU MAP US A WAY OUT OF HERE?
YOU GOT IT, BOSS. U.S. ARMY EDUCATION.
RIGHT, I ALWAYS FORGET THAT YOU WERE IN THE ARMY.
LOOK, WHAT PEOPLE CALL "MAGIC"?
NOTHING BUT QUANTUM MANIPULATION OF LOCAL PROBABILITY FIELDS. MAKING THE IMPOSSIBLE POSSIBLE THROUGH APPLIED FORCE OF WILL.
NOTHING MORE MAGICAL THAN, SAY, MUTANT ABILITIES.
YOU KNOW YOU'RE TELLING THIS TO A TALKING GHOST DOG, RIGHT?
THAT'S LIKE, DOUBLE MAGIC.
Oh, DUH, BATS CAN JUST SHOW US OUT--
Oooh NNOoo...

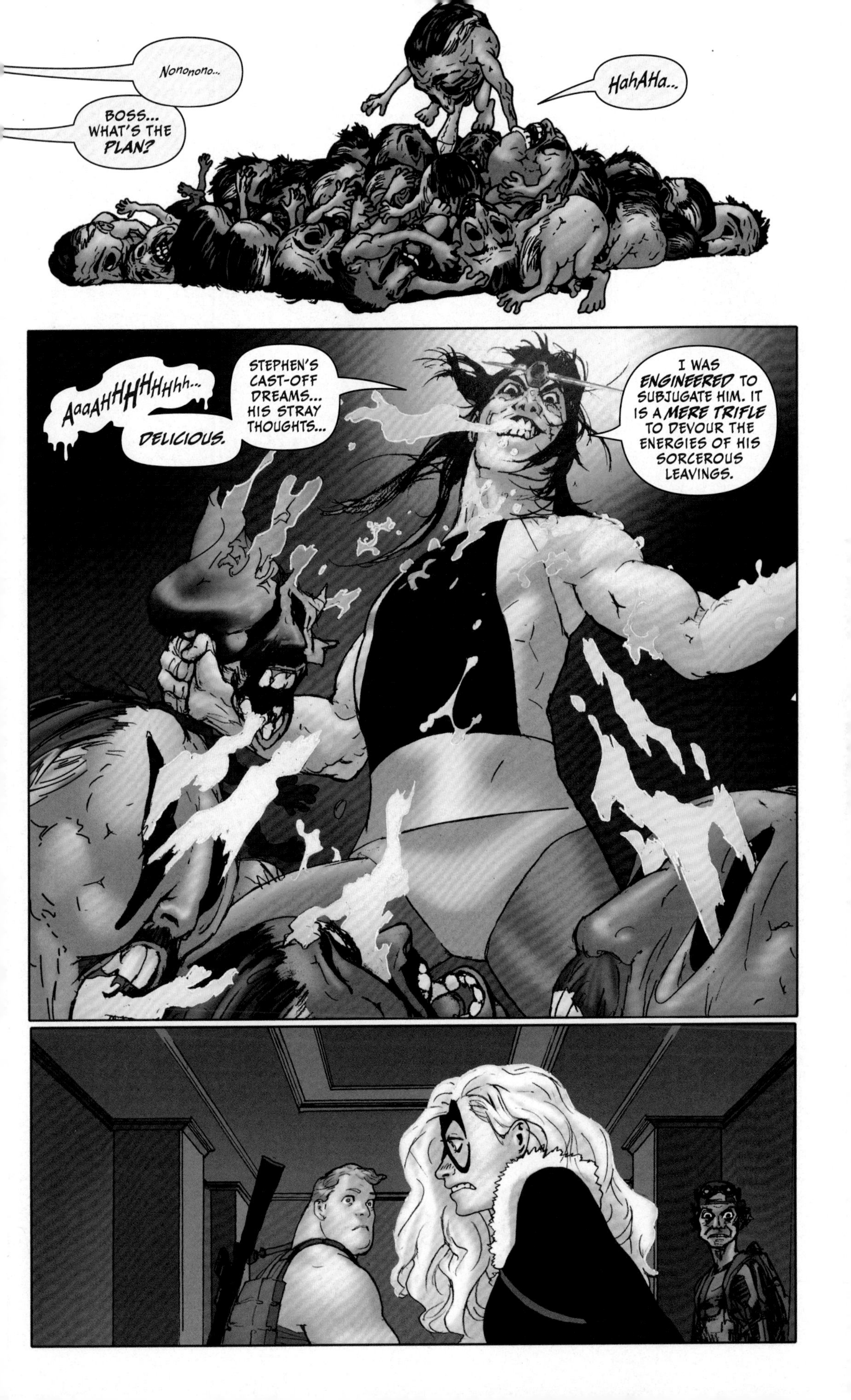
Nononono...
BOSS... WHAT'S THE PLAN?
HahAHa...
AaaAHHHHhhh...
DELICIOUS.
STEPHEN'S CAST-OFF DREAMS... HIS STRAY THOUGHTS...
I WAS ENGINEERED TO SUBJUGATE HIM. IT IS A MERE TRIFLE TO DEVOUR THE ENERGIES OF HIS SORCEROUS LEAVINGS.

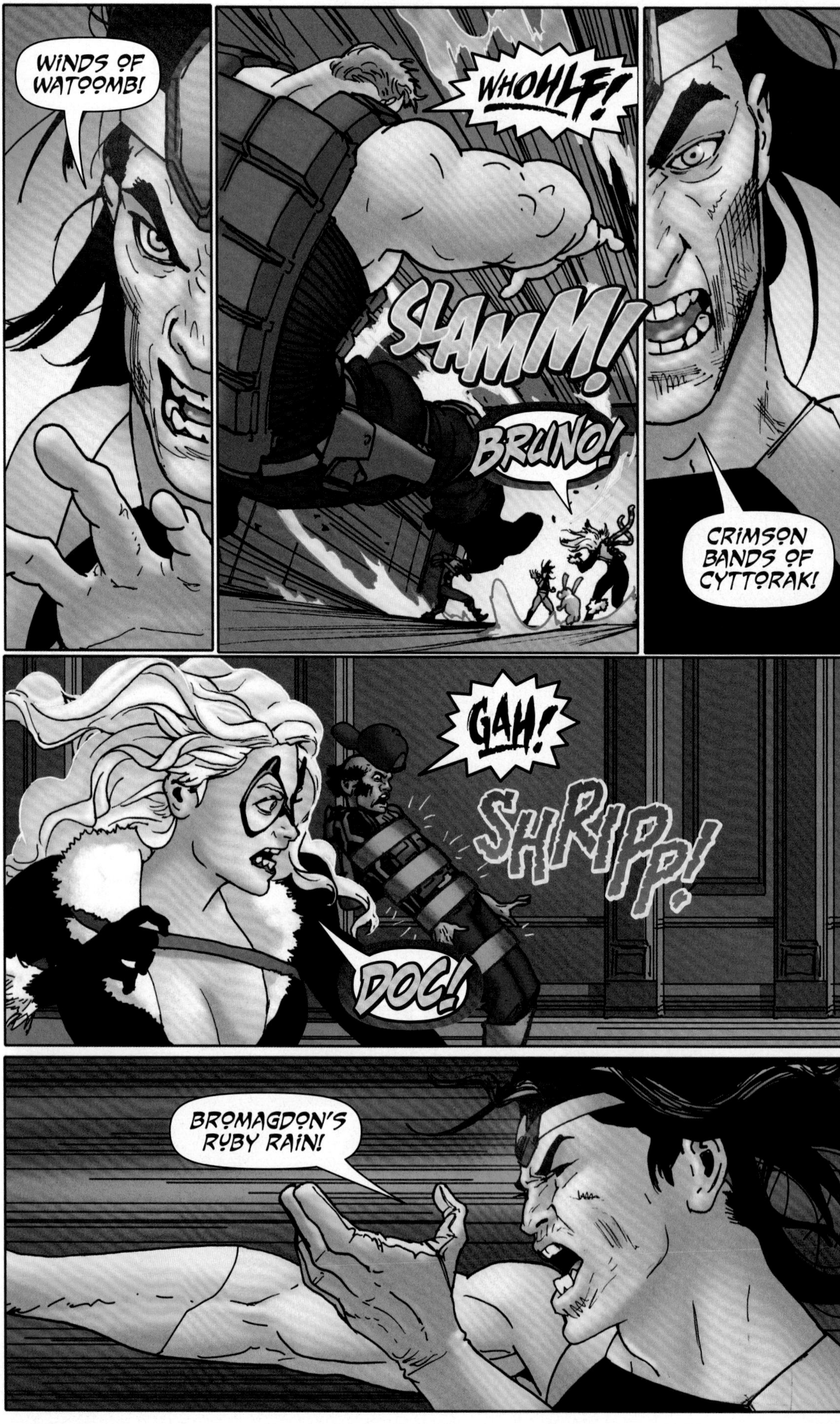
WINDS OF WATOOMB!
WHOHLF!
SLAMM!
BRUNO!
CRIMSON BANDS OF CYTTORAK!
GAH!
SHRIPP!
DOC!
BROMAGDON'S RUBY RAIN!

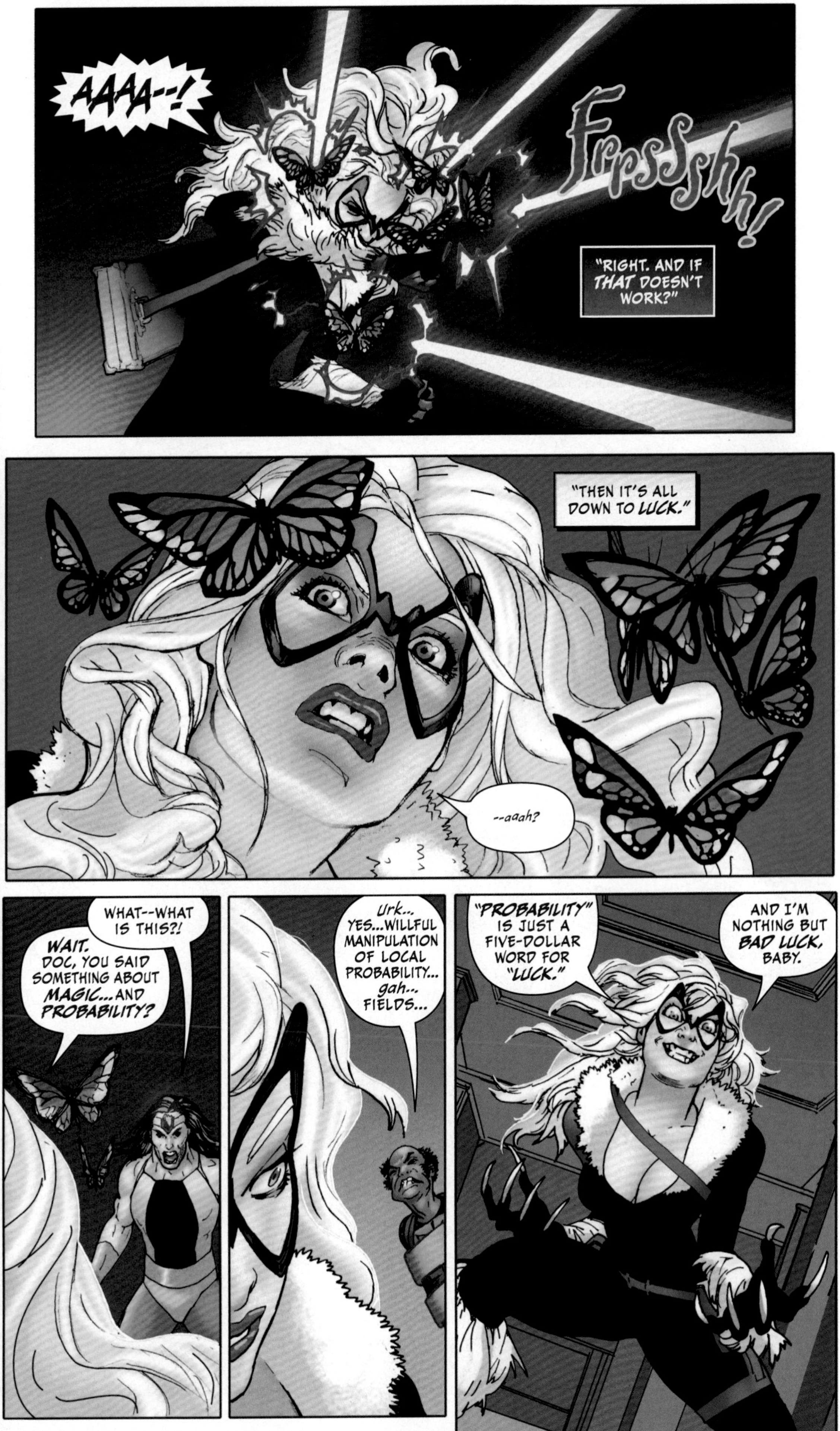
AAAA--!
FRRSSSHH!
"RIGHT. AND IF THAT DOESN'T WORK?"
"THEN IT'S ALL DOWN TO LUCK."
--aaah?
WHAT--WHAT IS THIS?!
WAIT. DOC, YOU SAID SOMETHING ABOUT MAGIC...AND PROBABILITY?
Urk... YES...WILLFUL MANIPULATION OF LOCAL PROBABILITY... gah... FIELDS...
"PROBABILITY" IS JUST A FIVE-DOLLAR WORD FOR "LUCK."
AND I'M NOTHING BUT BAD LUCK, BABY.

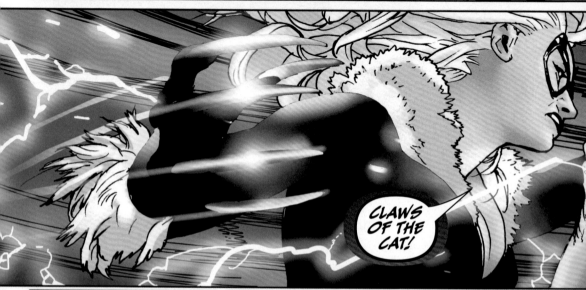

CLAWS OF THE CAT!

Grff...grff... WHAT'S HAPPENING HERE?

SHE... *gah*...HAS AN IMPLANTED *QUANTUM PROBABILITY RIG.*

ENGLISH? OR DOG, THAT WORKS, TOO.

"SHE GENERATES *BAD LUCK*, THE OPPOSITE OF... SO-CALLED '*MAGIC.*'

"WHERE XANDER... *CONSCIOUSLY* ALTERS PROBABILITIES TO MAKE THE *IMPOSSIBLE* HAPPEN...*urk*...

"...*FE--* SILVER SABLE-- UNCONSCIOUSLY *ERODES* THOSE ALTERATIONS, *UNRAVELING* THIS '*MAGIC,*' EMITTING *ENTROPY.*

"*TRANSMUTING* THAT WHICH WOULD HARM HER INTO MERE FANCY."

HARVIN'S HOARY HAMMERS!

FLAME OF TH' FALTIN

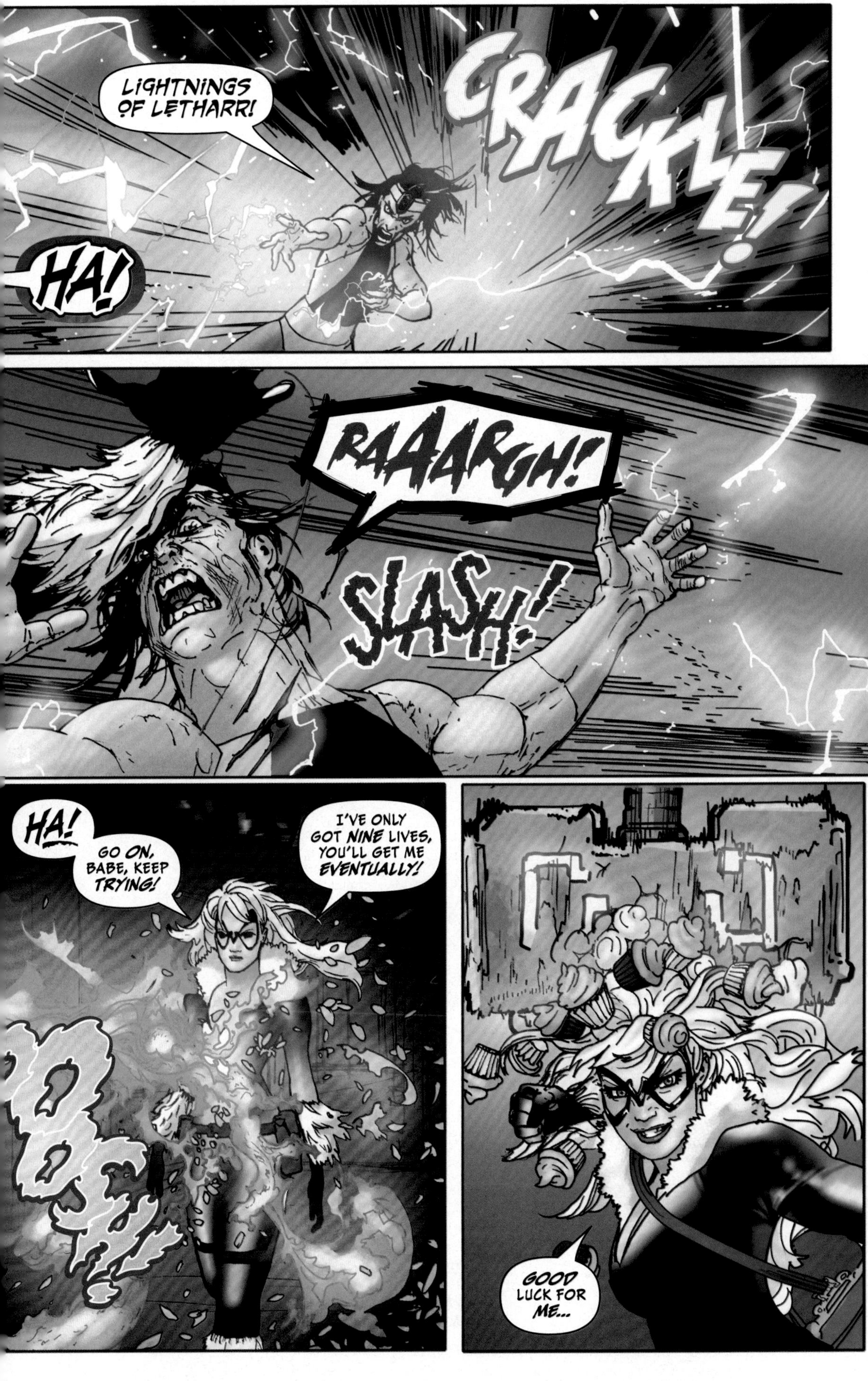
LIGHTNINGS OF LETHARR!
CRACKLE!
HA!
RAAARGH!
SLASH!
HA!
GO ON, BABE, KEEP TRYING!
I'VE ONLY GOT NINE LIVES, YOU'LL GET ME EVENTUALLY!
GOOD LUCK FOR ME...

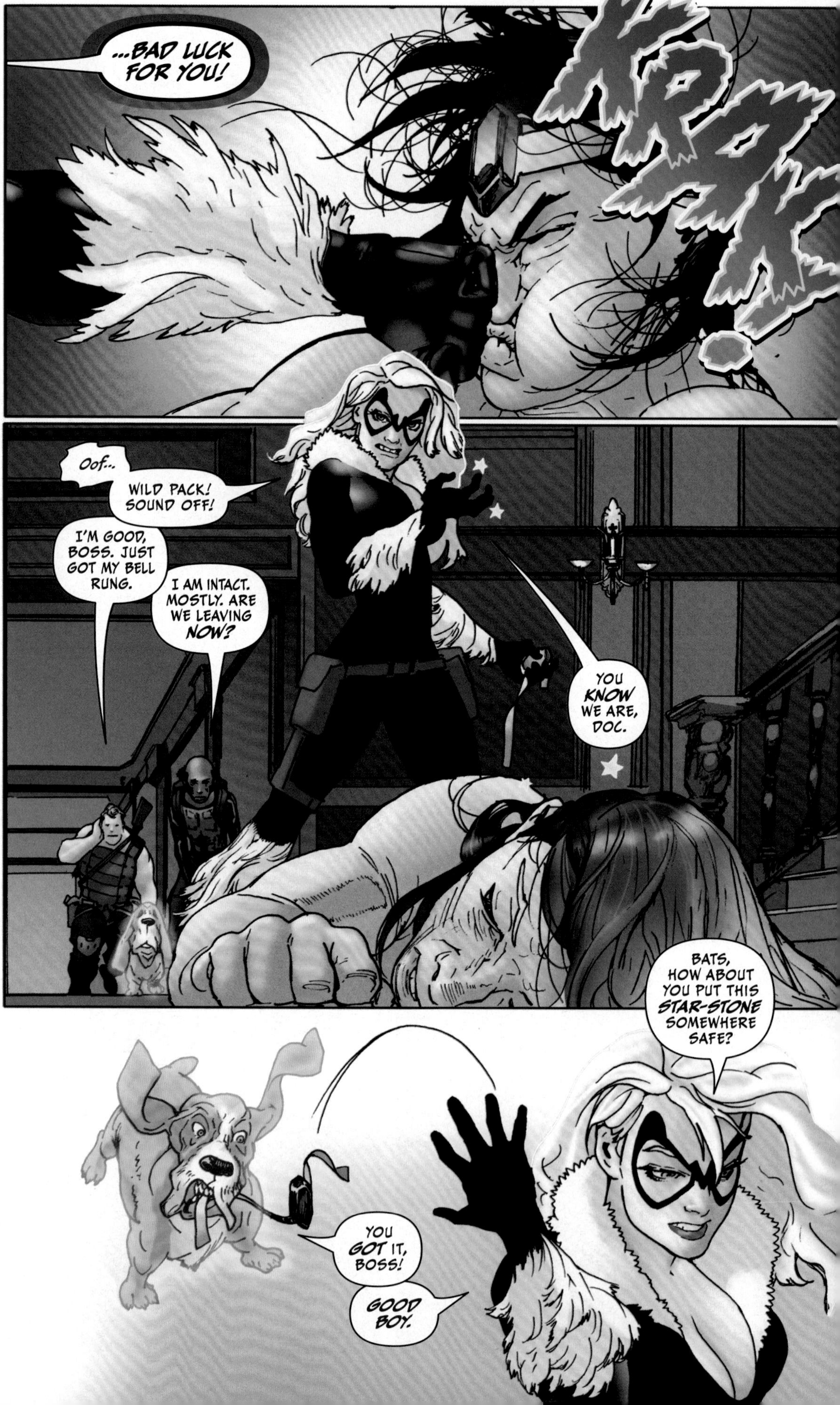
...BAD LUCK FOR YOU!
KRAK!
Oof..
WILD PACK! SOUND OFF!
I'M GOOD, BOSS. JUST GOT MY BELL RUNG.
I AM INTACT. MOSTLY. ARE WE LEAVING NOW?
YOU KNOW WE ARE, DOC.
BATS, HOW ABOUT YOU PUT THIS STAR-STONE SOMEWHERE SAFE?
YOU GOT IT, BOSS!
GOOD BOY.

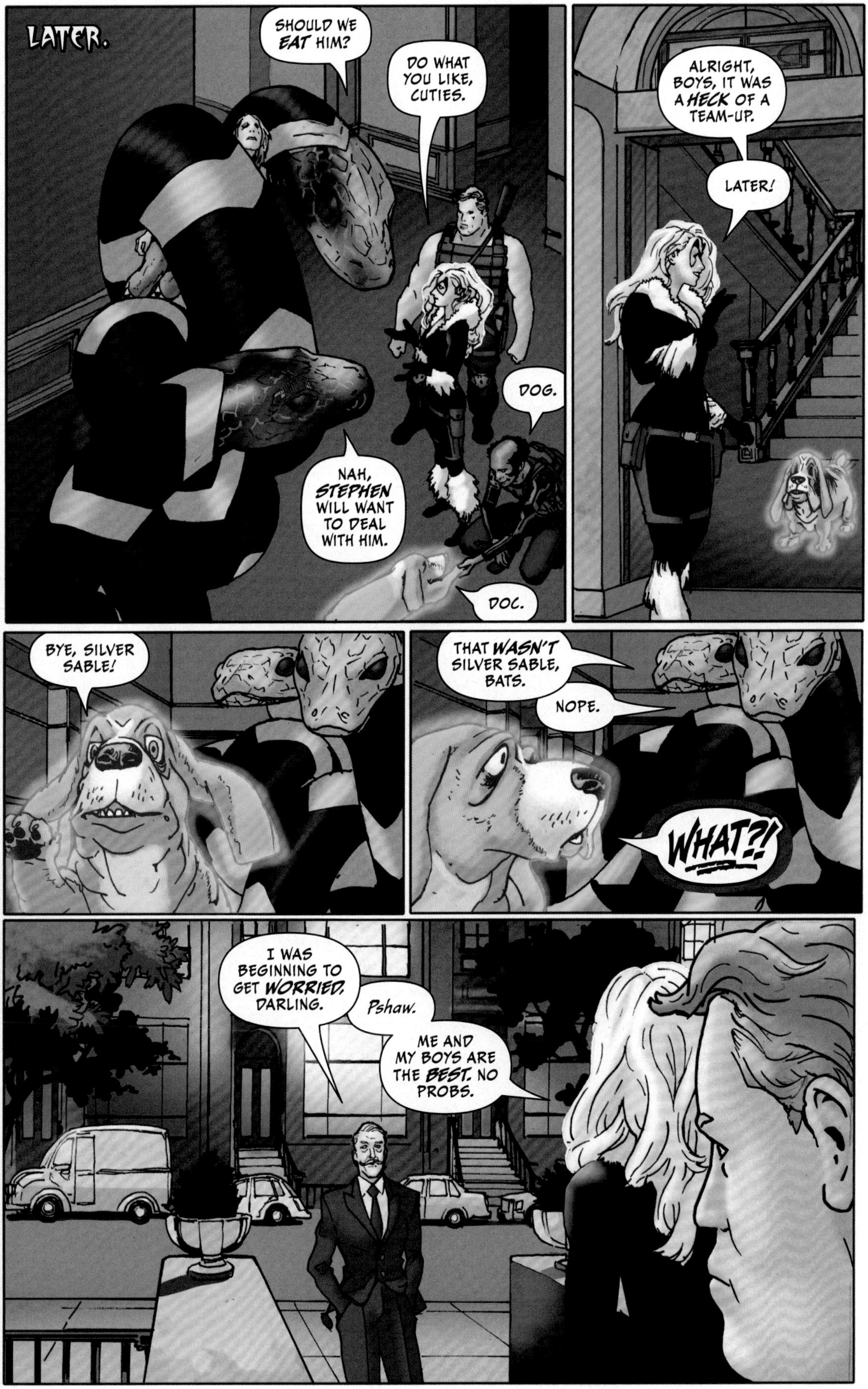
LATER.
SHOULD WE EAT HIM?
DO WHAT YOU LIKE, CUTIES.
NAH, STEPHEN WILL WANT TO DEAL WITH HIM.
DOG.
DOC.
ALRIGHT, BOYS, IT WAS A HECK OF A TEAM-UP.
LATER!
BYE, SILVER SABLE!
THAT WASN'T SILVER SABLE, BATS.
NOPE.
WHAT?!
I WAS BEGINNING TO GET WORRIED, DARLING.
Pshaw.
ME AND MY BOYS ARE THE BEST. NO PROBS.

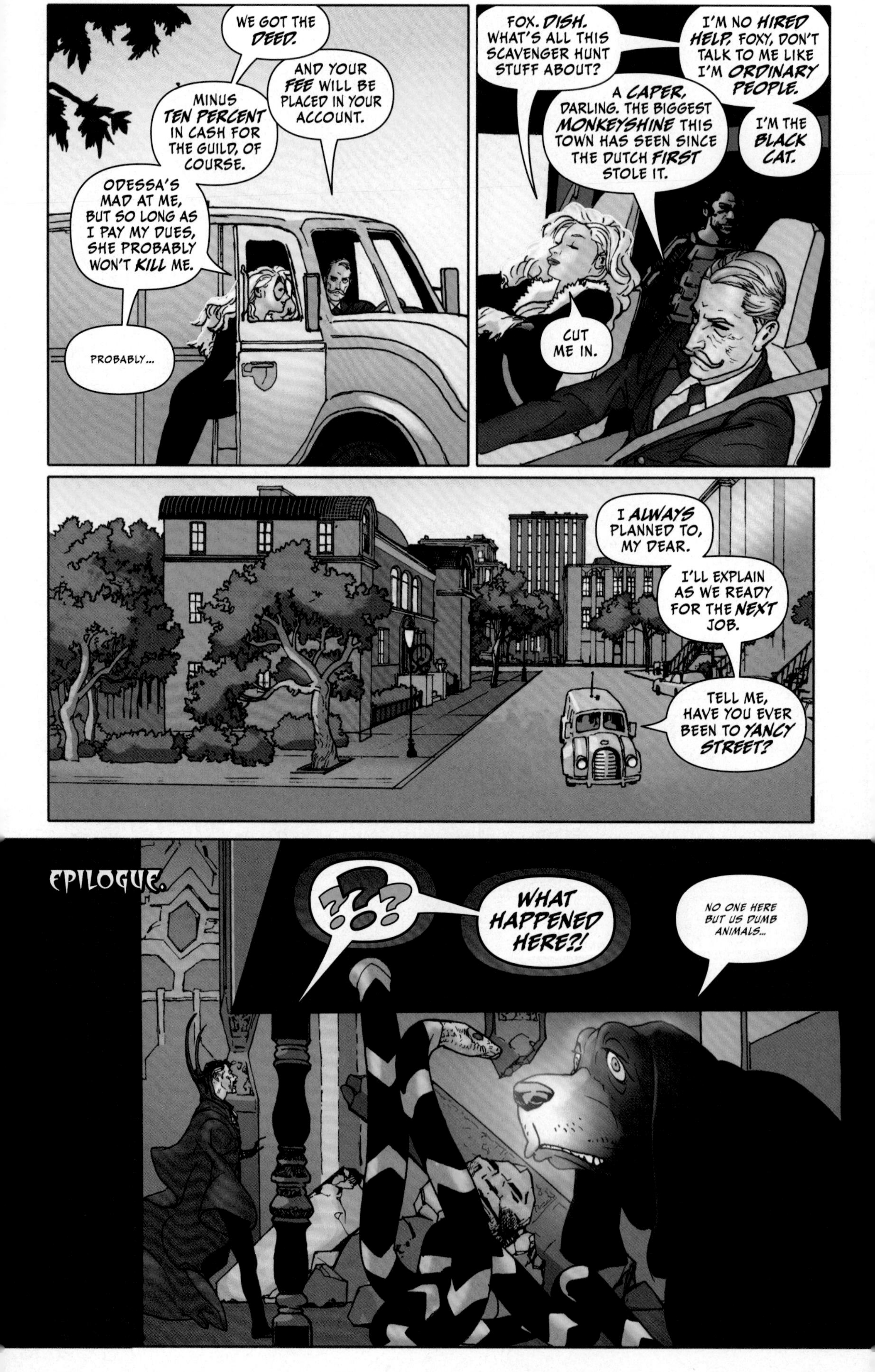
WE GOT THE DEED.
MINUS TEN PERCENT IN CASH FOR THE GUILD, OF COURSE.
AND YOUR FEE WILL BE PLACED IN YOUR ACCOUNT.
ODESSA'S MAD AT ME, BUT SO LONG AS I PAY MY DUES, SHE PROBABLY WON'T KILL ME.
PROBABLY...
FOX. DISH. WHAT'S ALL THIS SCAVENGER HUNT STUFF ABOUT?
I'M NO HIRED HELP, FOXY, DON'T TALK TO ME LIKE I'M ORDINARY PEOPLE.
I'M THE BLACK CAT.
A CAPER, DARLING. THE BIGGEST MONKEYSHINE THIS TOWN HAS SEEN SINCE THE DUTCH FIRST STOLE IT.
CUT ME IN.
I ALWAYS PLANNED TO, MY DEAR.
I'LL EXPLAIN AS WE READY FOR THE NEXT JOB.
TELL ME, HAVE YOU EVER BEEN TO YANCY STREET?
EPILOGUE.
???
WHAT HAPPENED HERE?!
NO ONE HERE BUT US DUMB ANIMALS...

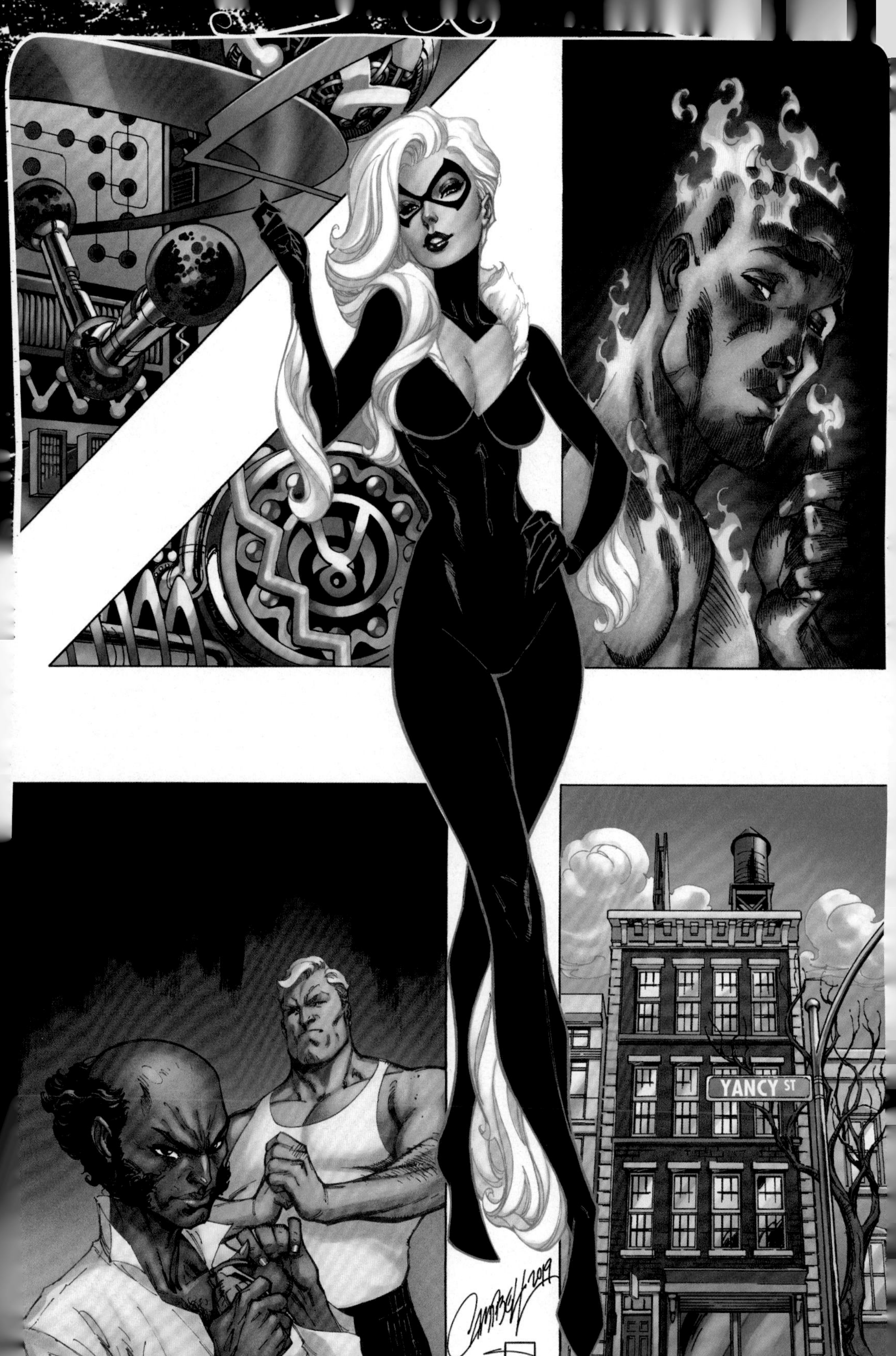
YANCY ST

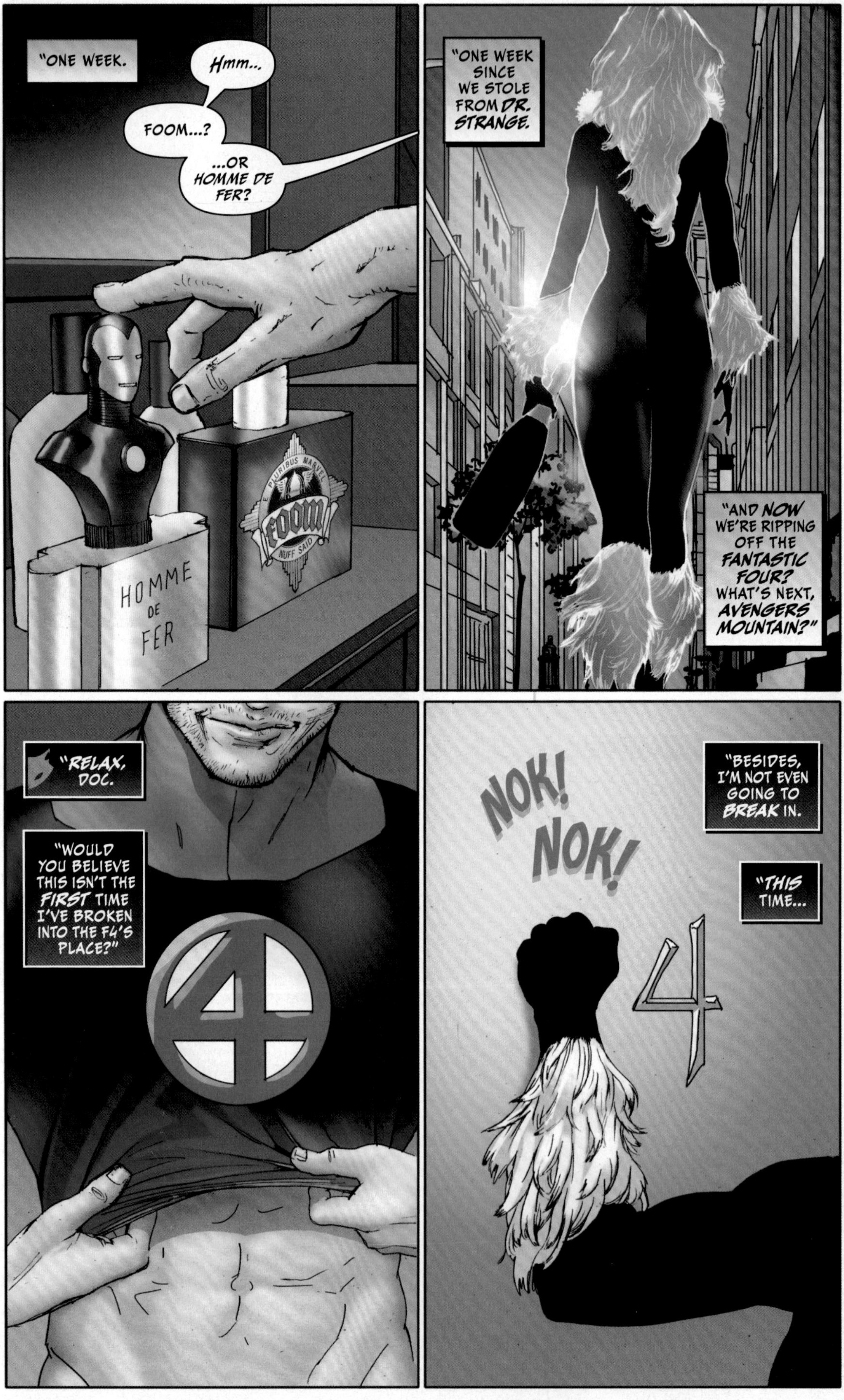
"ONE WEEK.
Hmm...
FOOM...?
...OR HOMME DE FER?
E PLURIBUS MARVEL
FOOM!
NUFF SAID
HOMME DE FER
"ONE WEEK SINCE WE STOLE FROM DR. STRANGE.
"AND NOW WE'RE RIPPING OFF THE FANTASTIC FOUR? WHAT'S NEXT, AVENGERS MOUNTAIN?"
"RELAX, DOC.
"WOULD YOU BELIEVE THIS ISN'T THE FIRST TIME I'VE BROKEN INTO THE F4'S PLACE?"
NOK!
NOK!
"BESIDES, I'M NOT EVEN GOING TO BREAK IN.
"THIS TIME...

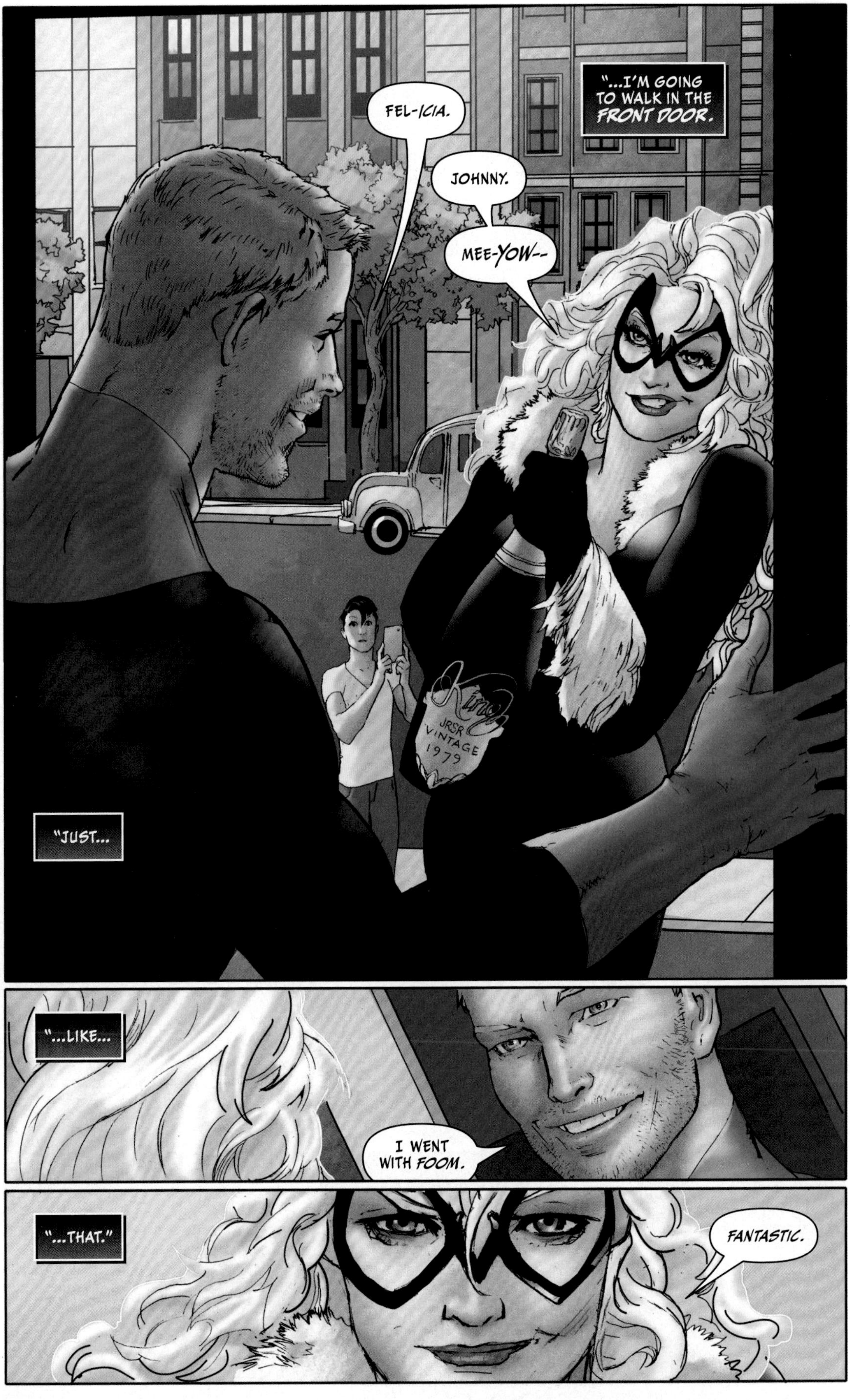
"...I'M GOING TO WALK IN THE FRONT DOOR.
FEL-ICIA.
JOHNNY.
MEE-YOW--
King JRSR VINTAGE 1979
"JUST...
"...LIKE...
I WENT WITH FOOM.
"...THAT."
FANTASTIC.

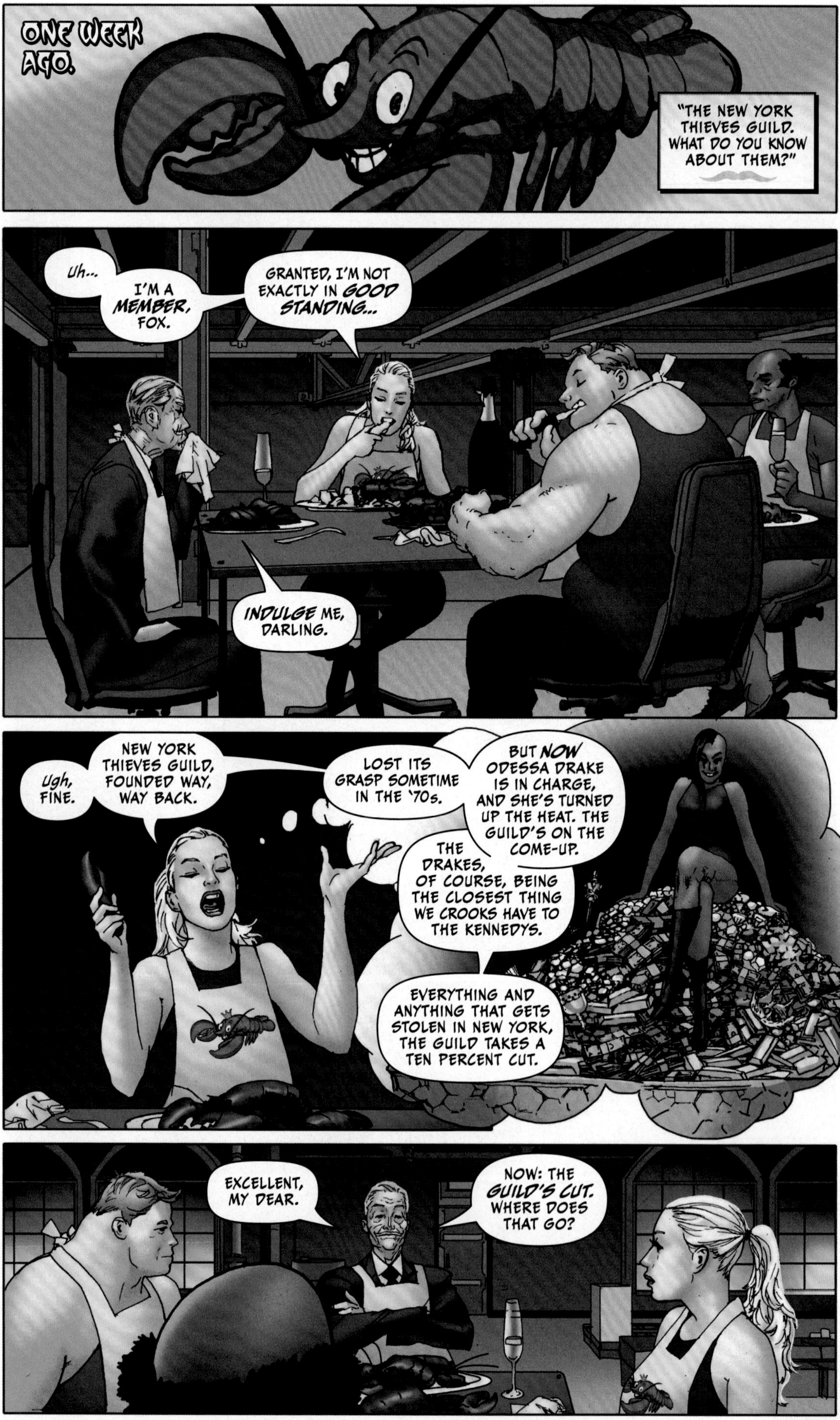
ONE WEEK AGO.
"THE NEW YORK THIEVES GUILD. WHAT DO YOU KNOW ABOUT THEM?"
Uh...
I'M A MEMBER, FOX.
GRANTED, I'M NOT EXACTLY IN GOOD STANDING...
INDULGE ME, DARLING.
Ugh, FINE.
NEW YORK THIEVES GUILD, FOUNDED WAY, WAY BACK.
LOST ITS GRASP SOMETIME IN THE '70s.
BUT NOW ODESSA DRAKE IS IN CHARGE, AND SHE'S TURNED UP THE HEAT. THE GUILD'S ON THE COME-UP.
THE DRAKES, OF COURSE, BEING THE CLOSEST THING WE CROOKS HAVE TO THE KENNEDYS.
EVERYTHING AND ANYTHING THAT GETS STOLEN IN NEW YORK, THE GUILD TAKES A TEN PERCENT CUT.
EXCELLENT, MY DEAR.
NOW: THE GUILD'S CUT. WHERE DOES THAT GO?

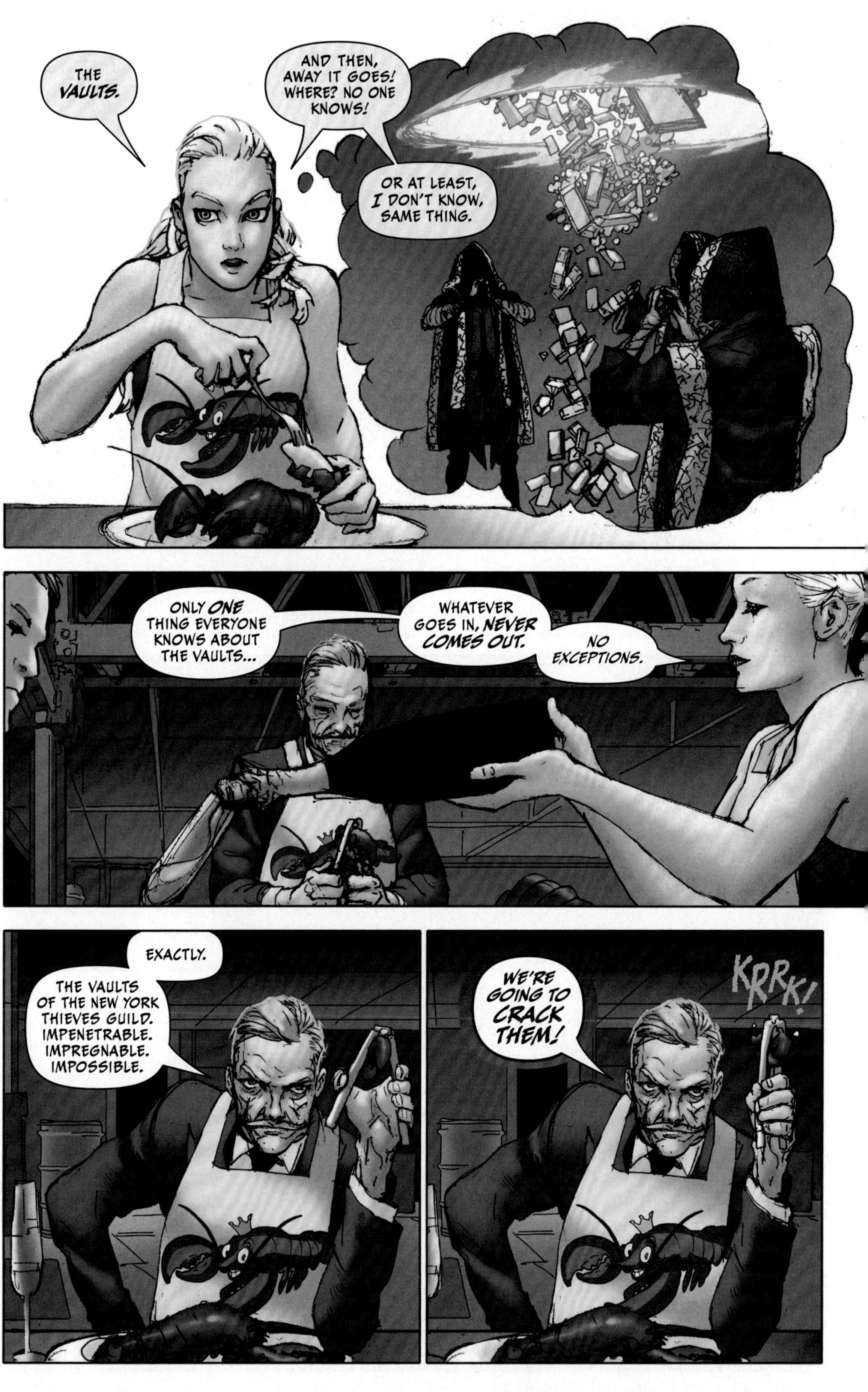
THE VAULTS.
AND THEN, AWAY IT GOES! WHERE? NO ONE KNOWS!
OR AT LEAST, I DON'T KNOW, SAME THING.
ONLY ONE THING EVERYONE KNOWS ABOUT THE VAULTS...
WHATEVER GOES IN, NEVER COMES OUT.
NO EXCEPTIONS.
EXACTLY.
THE VAULTS OF THE NEW YORK THIEVES GUILD. IMPENETRABLE. IMPREGNABLE. IMPOSSIBLE.
KRRK!
WE'RE GOING TO CRACK THEM!

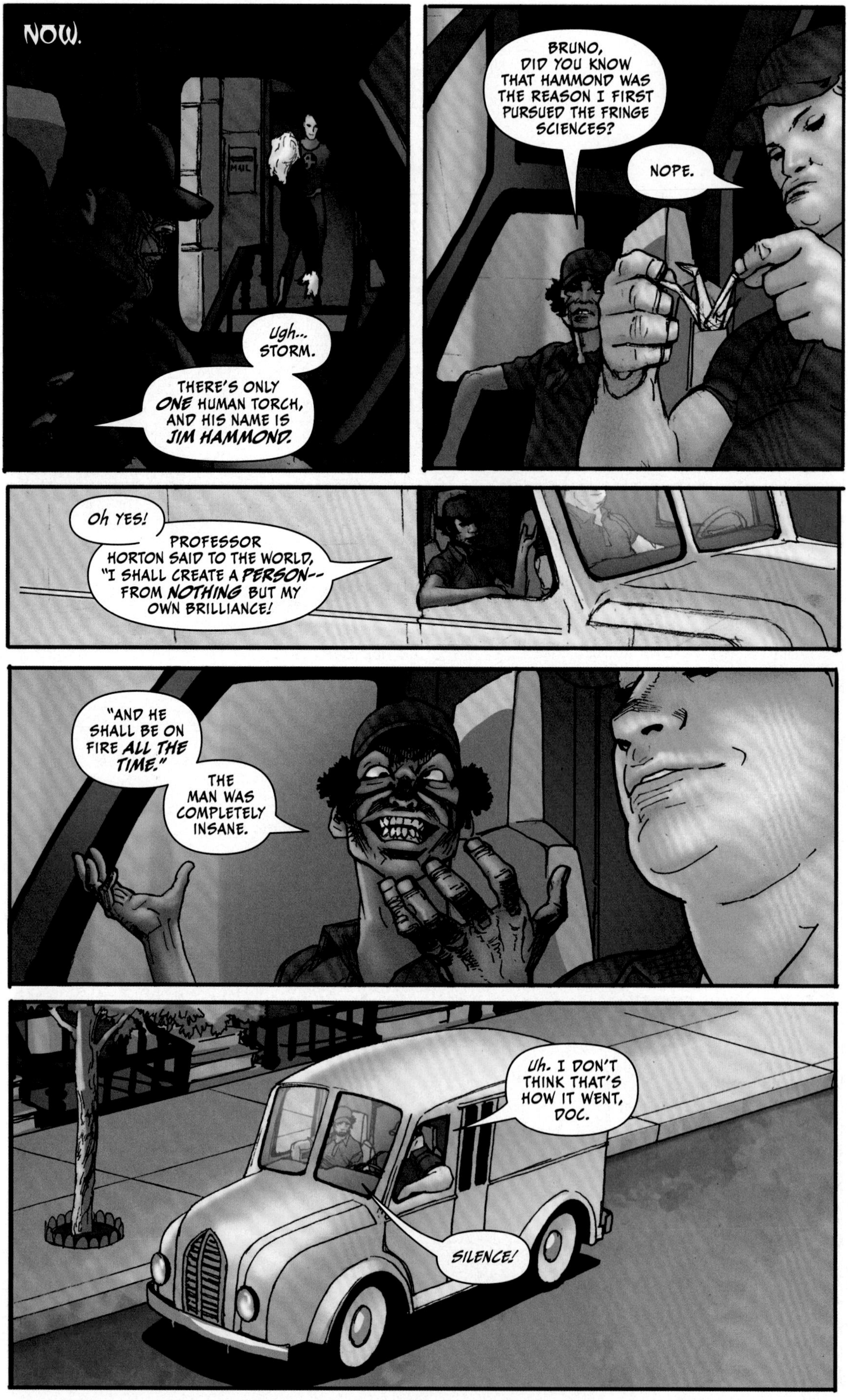
NOW.
Ugh... STORM.
THERE'S ONLY ONE HUMAN TORCH, AND HIS NAME IS JIM HAMMOND.
BRUNO, DID YOU KNOW THAT HAMMOND WAS THE REASON I FIRST PURSUED THE FRINGE SCIENCES?
NOPE.
Oh YES!
PROFESSOR HORTON SAID TO THE WORLD, "I SHALL CREATE A PERSON-- FROM NOTHING BUT MY OWN BRILLIANCE!
"AND HE SHALL BE ON FIRE ALL THE TIME."
THE MAN WAS COMPLETELY INSANE.
Uh. I DON'T THINK THAT'S HOW IT WENT, DOC.
SILENCE!

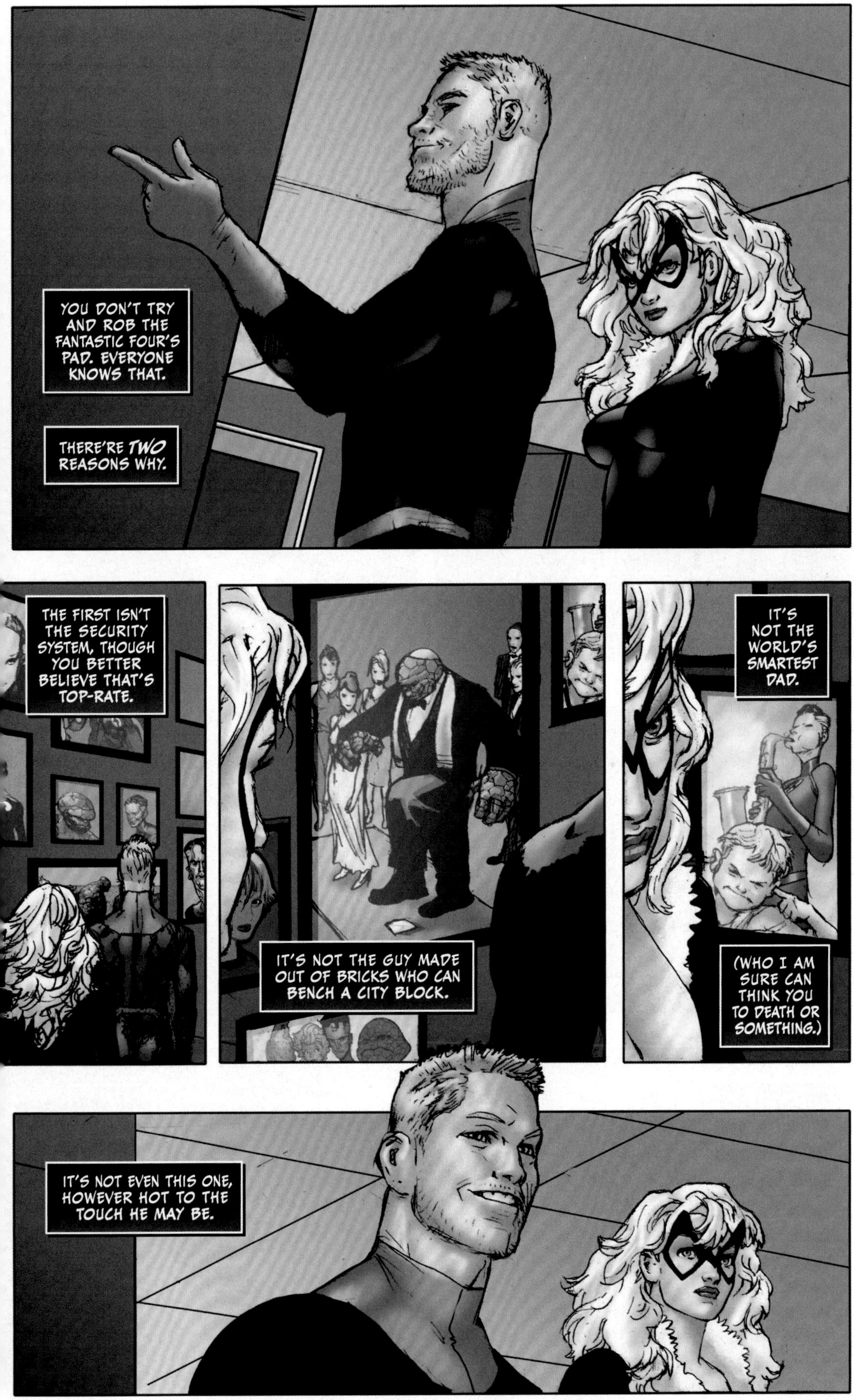
YOU DON'T TRY AND ROB THE FANTASTIC FOUR'S PAD. EVERYONE KNOWS THAT.
THERE'RE TWO REASONS WHY.
THE FIRST ISN'T THE SECURITY SYSTEM, THOUGH YOU BETTER BELIEVE THAT'S TOP-RATE.
IT'S NOT THE GUY MADE OUT OF BRICKS WHO CAN BENCH A CITY BLOCK.
IT'S NOT THE WORLD'S SMARTEST DAD.
(WHO I AM SURE CAN THINK YOU TO DEATH OR SOMETHING.)
IT'S NOT EVEN THIS ONE, HOWEVER HOT TO THE TOUCH HE MAY BE.

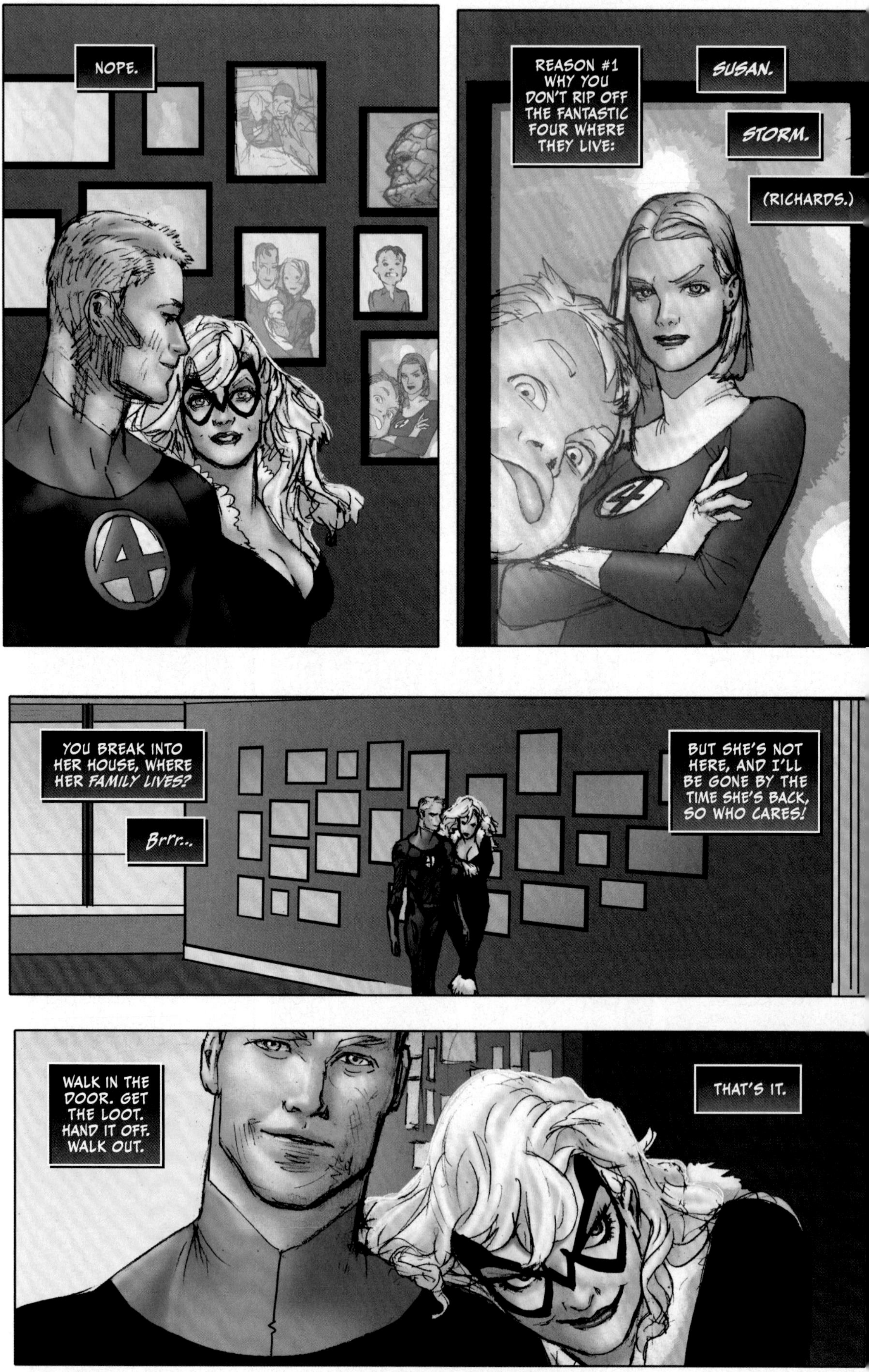
NOPE.
REASON #1 WHY YOU DON'T RIP OFF THE FANTASTIC FOUR WHERE THEY LIVE:
SUSAN.
STORM.
(RICHARDS.)
YOU BREAK INTO HER HOUSE, WHERE HER FAMILY LIVES?
Brrr...
BUT SHE'S NOT HERE, AND I'LL BE GONE BY THE TIME SHE'S BACK, SO WHO CARES!
WALK IN THE DOOR. GET THE LOOT. HAND IT OFF. WALK OUT.
THAT'S IT.

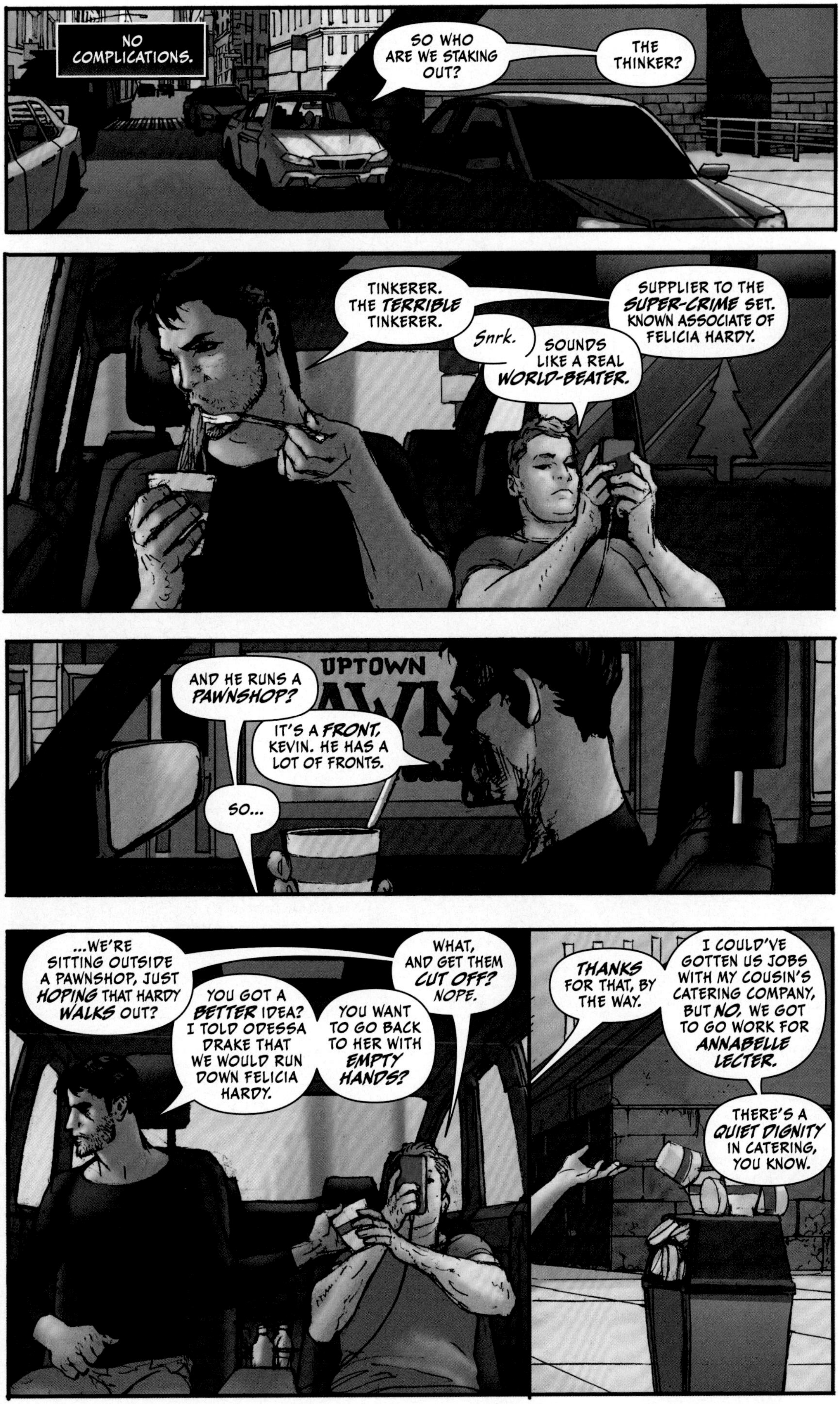
NO COMPLICATIONS.
SO WHO ARE WE STAKING OUT?
THE THINKER?
TINKERER. THE TERRIBLE TINKERER.
SUPPLIER TO THE SUPER-CRIME SET. KNOWN ASSOCIATE OF FELICIA HARDY.
Snrk.
SOUNDS LIKE A REAL WORLD-BEATER.
UPTOWN
AND HE RUNS A PAWNSHOP?
IT'S A FRONT, KEVIN. HE HAS A LOT OF FRONTS.
SO...
...WE'RE SITTING OUTSIDE A PAWNSHOP, JUST HOPING THAT HARDY WALKS OUT?
YOU GOT A BETTER IDEA? I TOLD ODESSA DRAKE THAT WE WOULD RUN DOWN FELICIA HARDY.
YOU WANT TO GO BACK TO HER WITH EMPTY HANDS?
WHAT, AND GET THEM CUT OFF? NOPE.
THANKS FOR THAT, BY THE WAY.
I COULD'VE GOTTEN US JOBS WITH MY COUSIN'S CATERING COMPANY, BUT NO, WE GOT TO GO WORK FOR ANNABELLE LECTER.
THERE'S A QUIET DIGNITY IN CATERING, YOU KNOW.

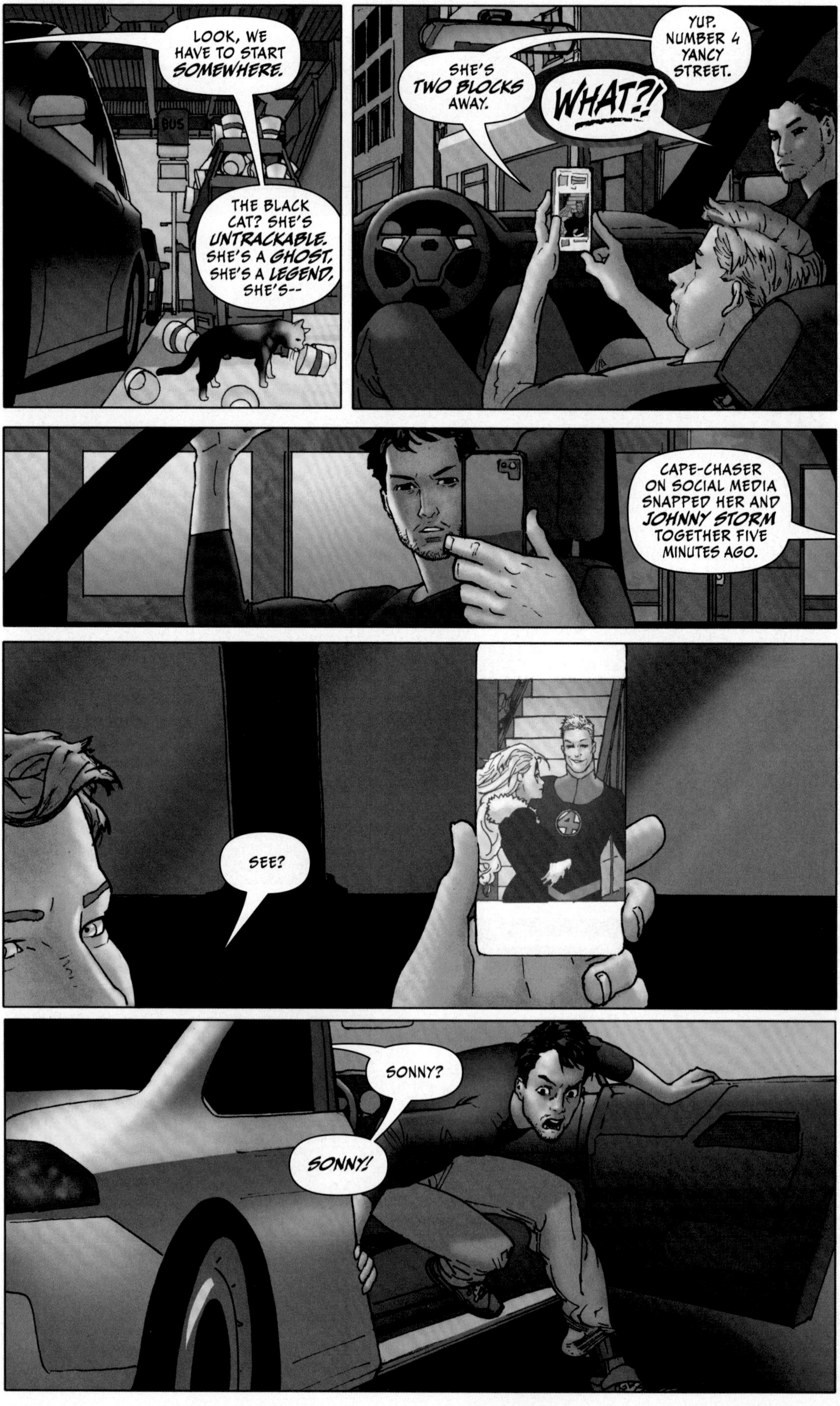
LOOK, WE HAVE TO START SOMEWHERE.
THE BLACK CAT? SHE'S UNTRACKABLE. SHE'S A GHOST, SHE'S A LEGEND, SHE'S--
SHE'S TWO BLOCKS AWAY.
WHAT?!
YUP. NUMBER 4 YANCY STREET.
CAPE-CHASER ON SOCIAL MEDIA SNAPPED HER AND JOHNNY STORM TOGETHER FIVE MINUTES AGO.
SEE?
SONNY?
SONNY!

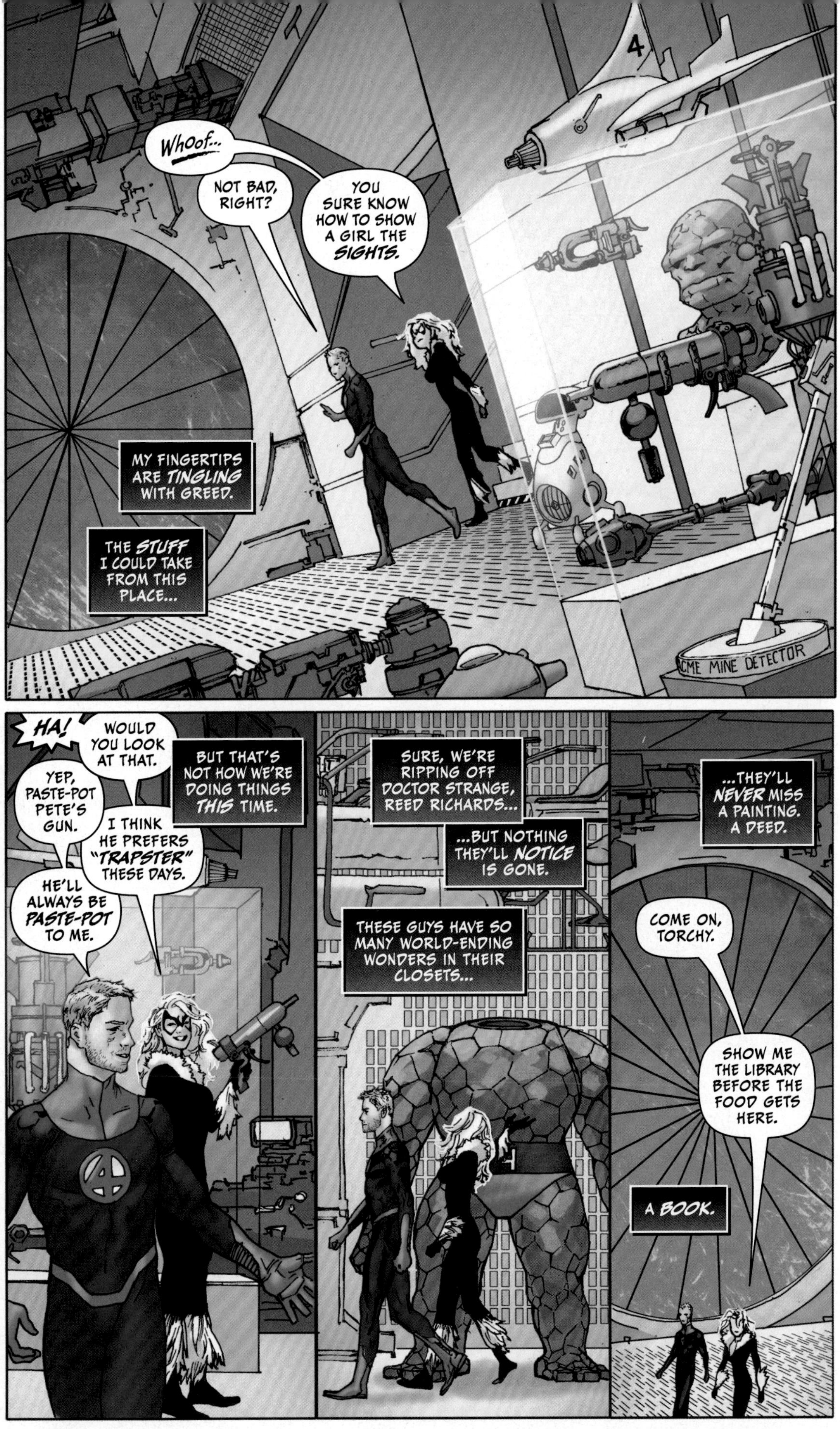

Whoof...
NOT BAD, RIGHT?
YOU SURE KNOW HOW TO SHOW A GIRL THE SIGHTS.
MY FINGERTIPS ARE TINGLING WITH GREED.
THE STUFF I COULD TAKE FROM THIS PLACE...
ACME MINE DETECTOR
HA!
WOULD YOU LOOK AT THAT.
YEP, PASTE-POT PETE'S GUN.
I THINK HE PREFERS "TRAPSTER" THESE DAYS.
HE'LL ALWAYS BE PASTE-POT TO ME.
BUT THAT'S NOT HOW WE'RE DOING THINGS THIS TIME.
SURE, WE'RE RIPPING OFF DOCTOR STRANGE, REED RICHARDS...
...BUT NOTHING THEY'LL NOTICE IS GONE.
THESE GUYS HAVE SO MANY WORLD-ENDING WONDERS IN THEIR CLOSETS...
...THEY'LL NEVER MISS A PAINTING. A DEED.
COME ON, TORCHY.
SHOW ME THE LIBRARY BEFORE THE FOOD GETS HERE.
A BOOK.

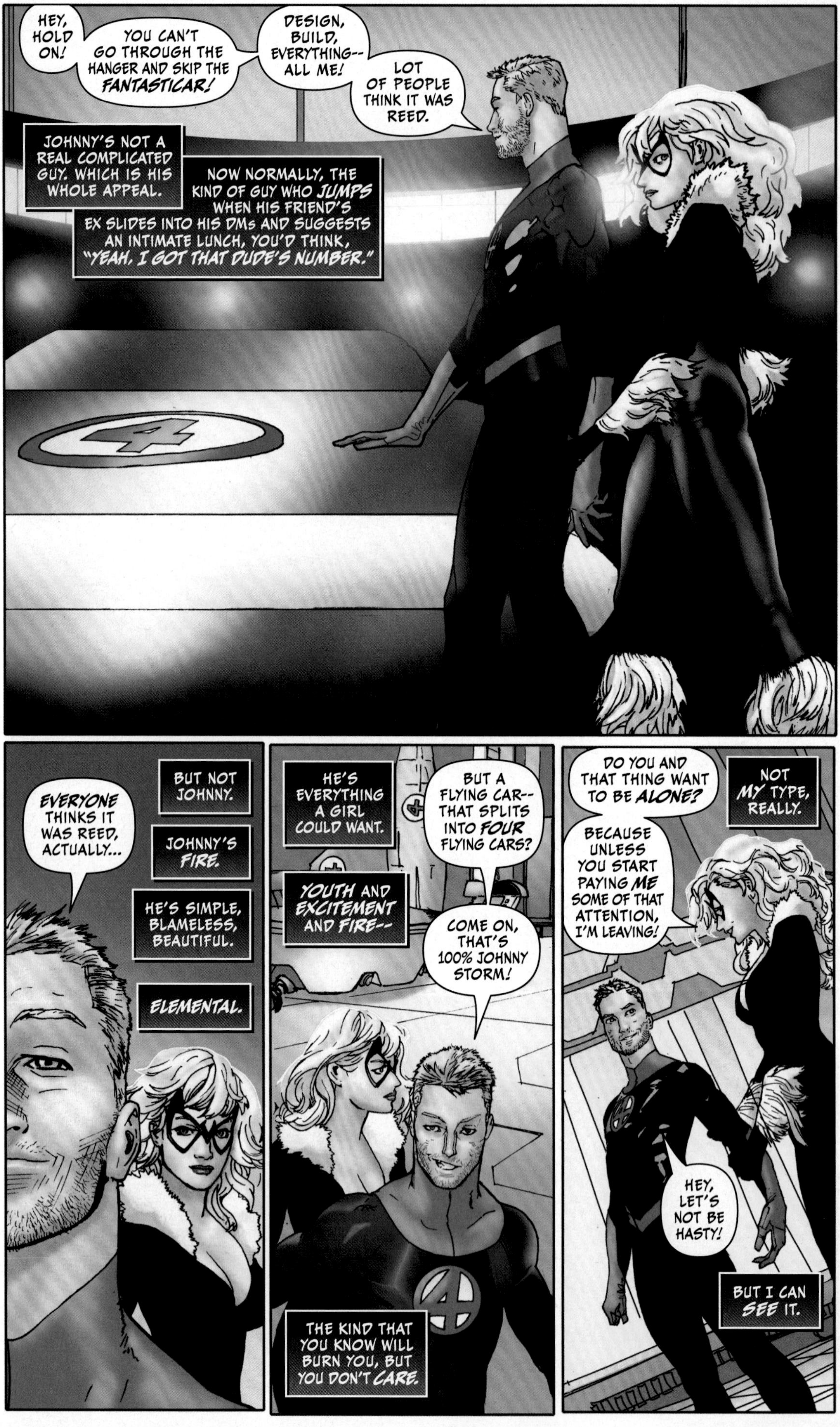
HEY, HOLD ON!
YOU CAN'T GO THROUGH THE HANGER AND SKIP THE FANTASTICAR!
DESIGN, BUILD, EVERYTHING-- ALL ME!
LOT OF PEOPLE THINK IT WAS REED.
JOHNNY'S NOT A REAL COMPLICATED GUY. WHICH IS HIS WHOLE APPEAL.
NOW NORMALLY, THE KIND OF GUY WHO JUMPS WHEN HIS FRIEND'S EX SLIDES INTO HIS DMs AND SUGGESTS AN INTIMATE LUNCH, YOU'D THINK, "YEAH, I GOT THAT DUDE'S NUMBER."
EVERYONE THINKS IT WAS REED, ACTUALLY...
BUT NOT JOHNNY.
JOHNNY'S FIRE.
HE'S SIMPLE, BLAMELESS, BEAUTIFUL.
ELEMENTAL.
HE'S EVERYTHING A GIRL COULD WANT.
BUT A FLYING CAR-- THAT SPLITS INTO FOUR FLYING CARS?
YOUTH AND EXCITEMENT AND FIRE--
COME ON, THAT'S 100% JOHNNY STORM!
THE KIND THAT YOU KNOW WILL BURN YOU, BUT YOU DON'T CARE.
DO YOU AND THAT THING WANT TO BE ALONE?
NOT MY TYPE, REALLY.
BECAUSE UNLESS YOU START PAYING ME SOME OF THAT ATTENTION, I'M LEAVING!
HEY, LET'S NOT BE HASTY!
BUT I CAN SEE IT.

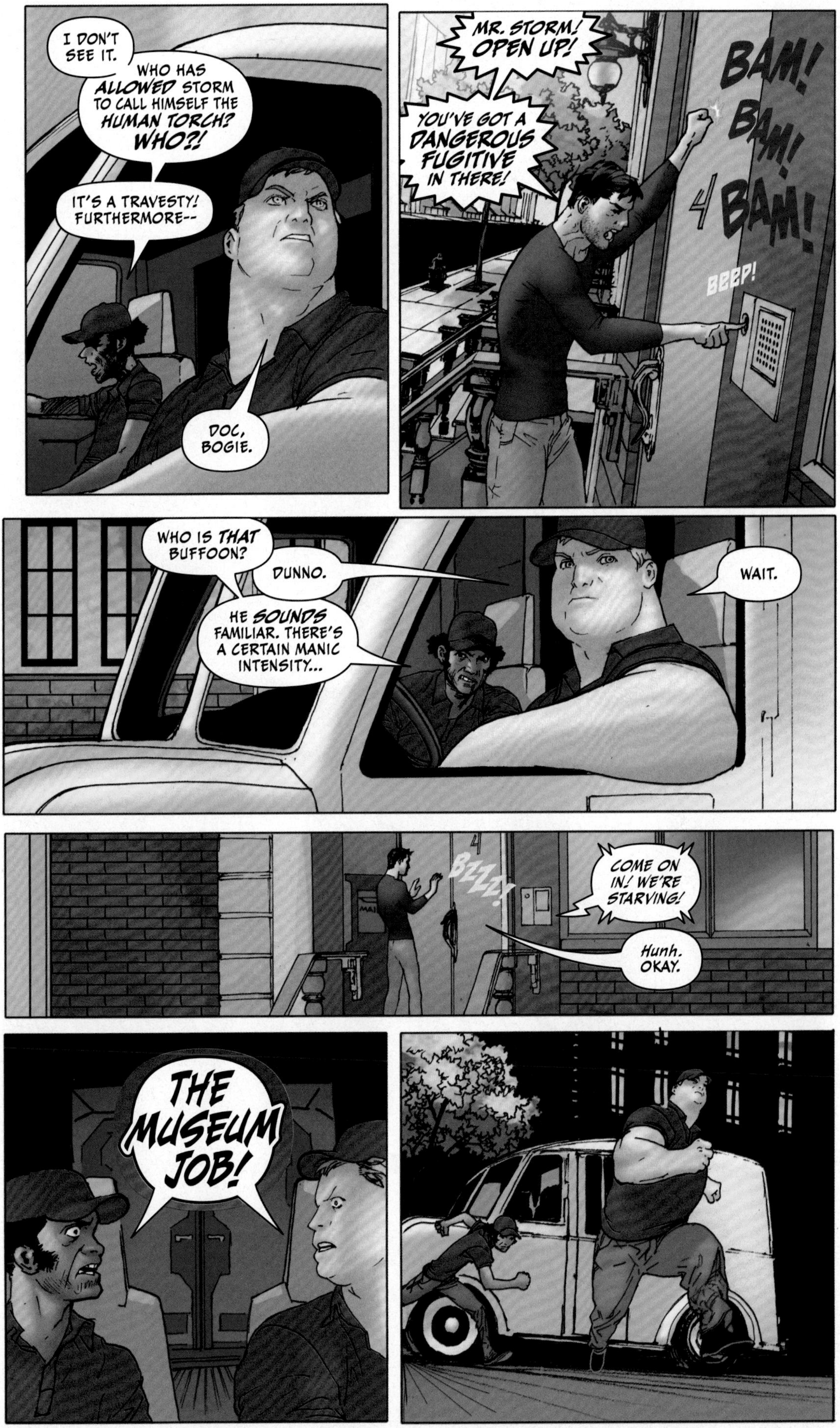
I DON'T SEE IT.
WHO HAS ALLOWED STORM TO CALL HIMSELF THE HUMAN TORCH? WHO?!
IT'S A TRAVESTY! FURTHERMORE--
DOC, BOGIE.
MR. STORM! OPEN UP!
YOU'VE GOT A DANGEROUS FUGITIVE IN THERE!
BAM! BAM! BAM!
BEEP!
WHO IS THAT BUFFOON?
DUNNO.
HE SOUNDS FAMILIAR. THERE'S A CERTAIN MANIC INTENSITY...
WAIT.
BZZZ!
COME ON IN! WE'RE STARVING!
Hunh. OKAY.
THE MUSEUM JOB!

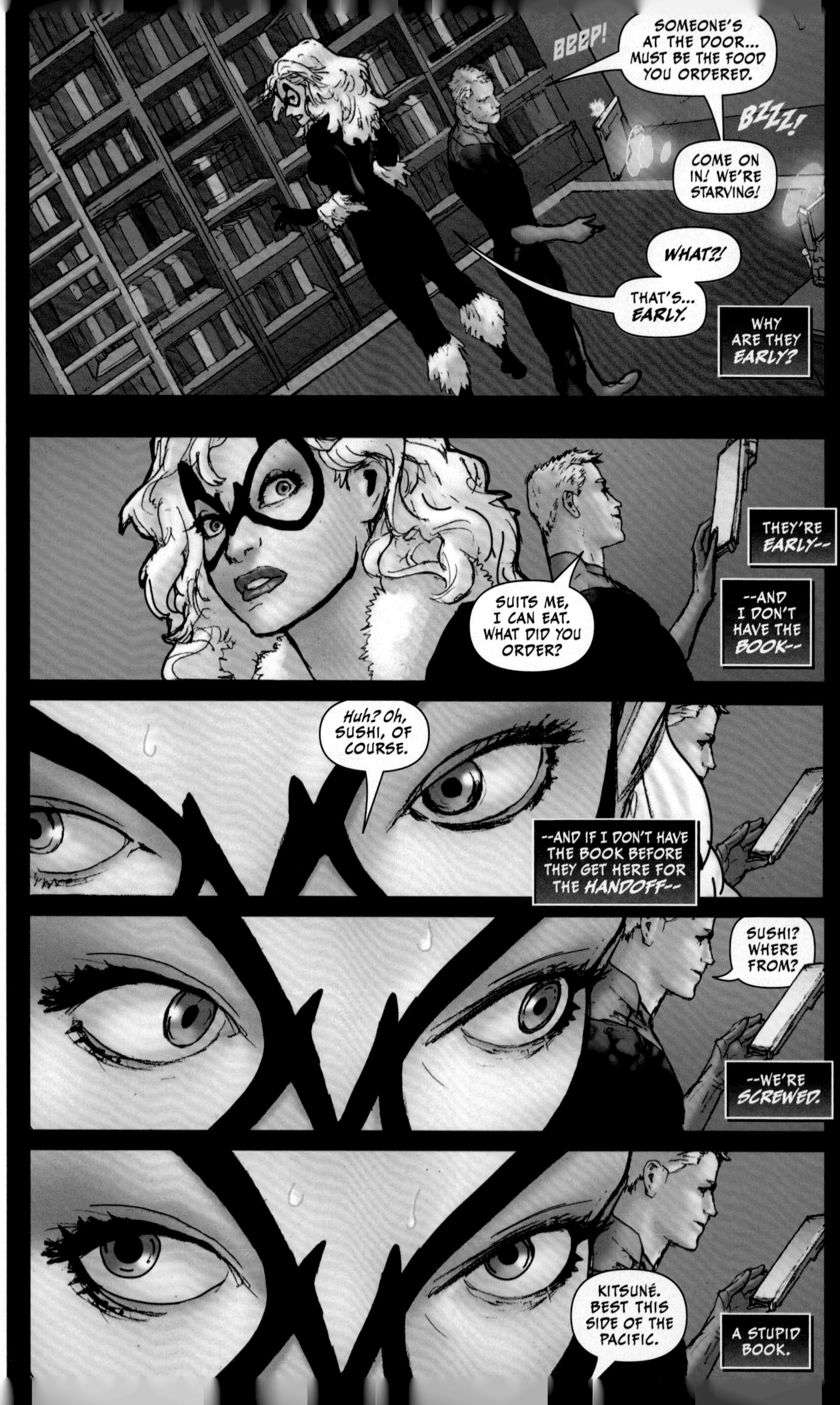
BEEP!
SOMEONE'S AT THE DOOR... MUST BE THE FOOD YOU ORDERED.
BZZZ!
COME ON IN! WE'RE STARVING!
WHAT?!
THAT'S... EARLY.
WHY ARE THEY EARLY?
THEY'RE EARLY--
--AND I DON'T HAVE THE BOOK--
SUITS ME, I CAN EAT. WHAT DID YOU ORDER?
Huh? Oh, SUSHI, OF COURSE.
--AND IF I DON'T HAVE THE BOOK BEFORE THEY GET HERE FOR THE HANDOFF--
SUSHI? WHERE FROM?
--WE'RE SCREWED.
KITSUNÉ. BEST THIS SIDE OF THE PACIFIC.
A STUPID BOOK.

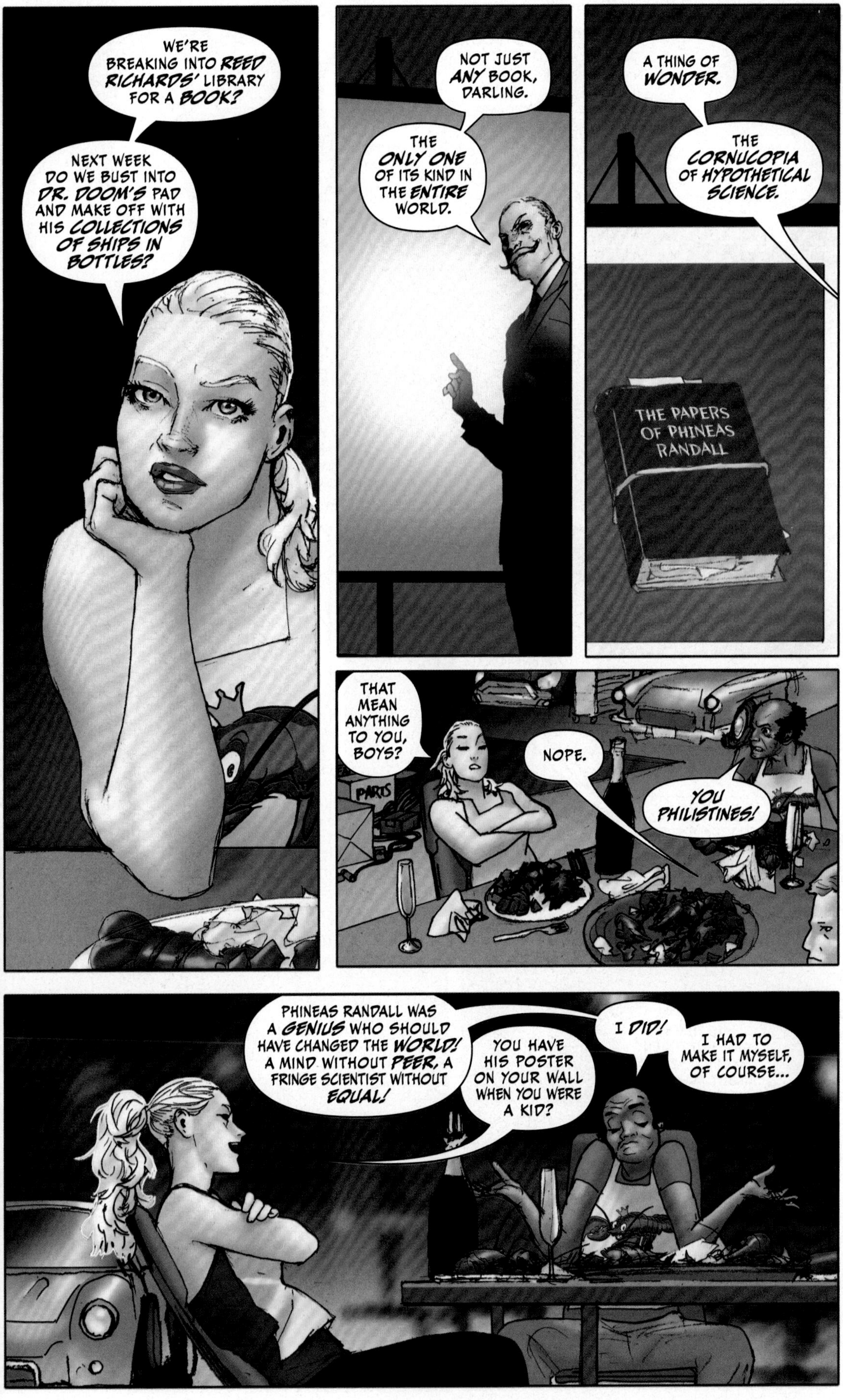

WE'RE BREAKING INTO REED RICHARDS' LIBRARY FOR A BOOK?
NEXT WEEK DO WE BUST INTO DR. DOOM'S PAD AND MAKE OFF WITH HIS COLLECTIONS OF SHIPS IN BOTTLES?
NOT JUST ANY BOOK, DARLING.
THE ONLY ONE OF ITS KIND IN THE ENTIRE WORLD.
A THING OF WONDER.
THE CORNUCOPIA OF HYPOTHETICAL SCIENCE.
THE PAPERS OF PHINEAS RANDALL
THAT MEAN ANYTHING TO YOU, BOYS?
NOPE.
YOU PHILISTINES!
PARTS
PHINEAS RANDALL WAS A GENIUS WHO SHOULD HAVE CHANGED THE WORLD! A MIND WITHOUT PEER, A FRINGE SCIENTIST WITHOUT EQUAL!
YOU HAVE HIS POSTER ON YOUR WALL WHEN YOU WERE A KID?
I DID!
I HAD TO MAKE IT MYSELF, OF COURSE...

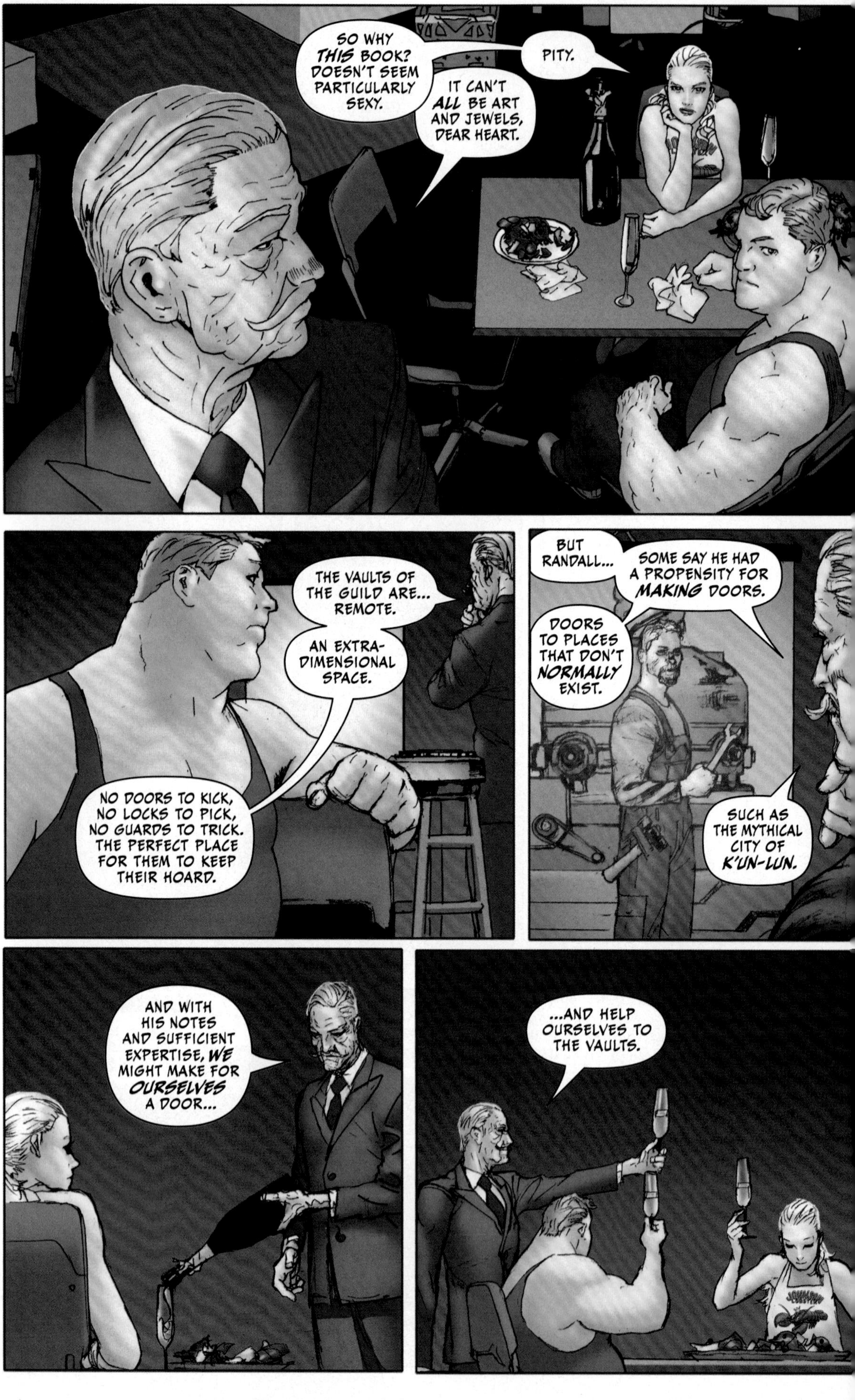
SO WHY *THIS* BOOK? DOESN'T SEEM PARTICULARLY SEXY.
PITY.
IT CAN'T *ALL* BE ART AND JEWELS, DEAR HEART.
THE VAULTS OF THE GUILD ARE... REMOTE.
AN EXTRA-DIMENSIONAL SPACE.
NO DOORS TO KICK, NO LOCKS TO PICK, NO GUARDS TO TRICK. THE PERFECT PLACE FOR THEM TO KEEP THEIR HOARD.
BUT RANDALL...
SOME SAY HE HAD A PROPENSITY FOR *MAKING* DOORS.
DOORS TO PLACES THAT DON'T *NORMALLY* EXIST.
SUCH AS THE MYTHICAL CITY OF *K'UN-LUN.*
AND WITH HIS NOTES AND SUFFICIENT EXPERTISE, *WE* MIGHT MAKE FOR *OURSELVES* A DOOR...
...AND HELP OURSELVES TO THE VAULTS.

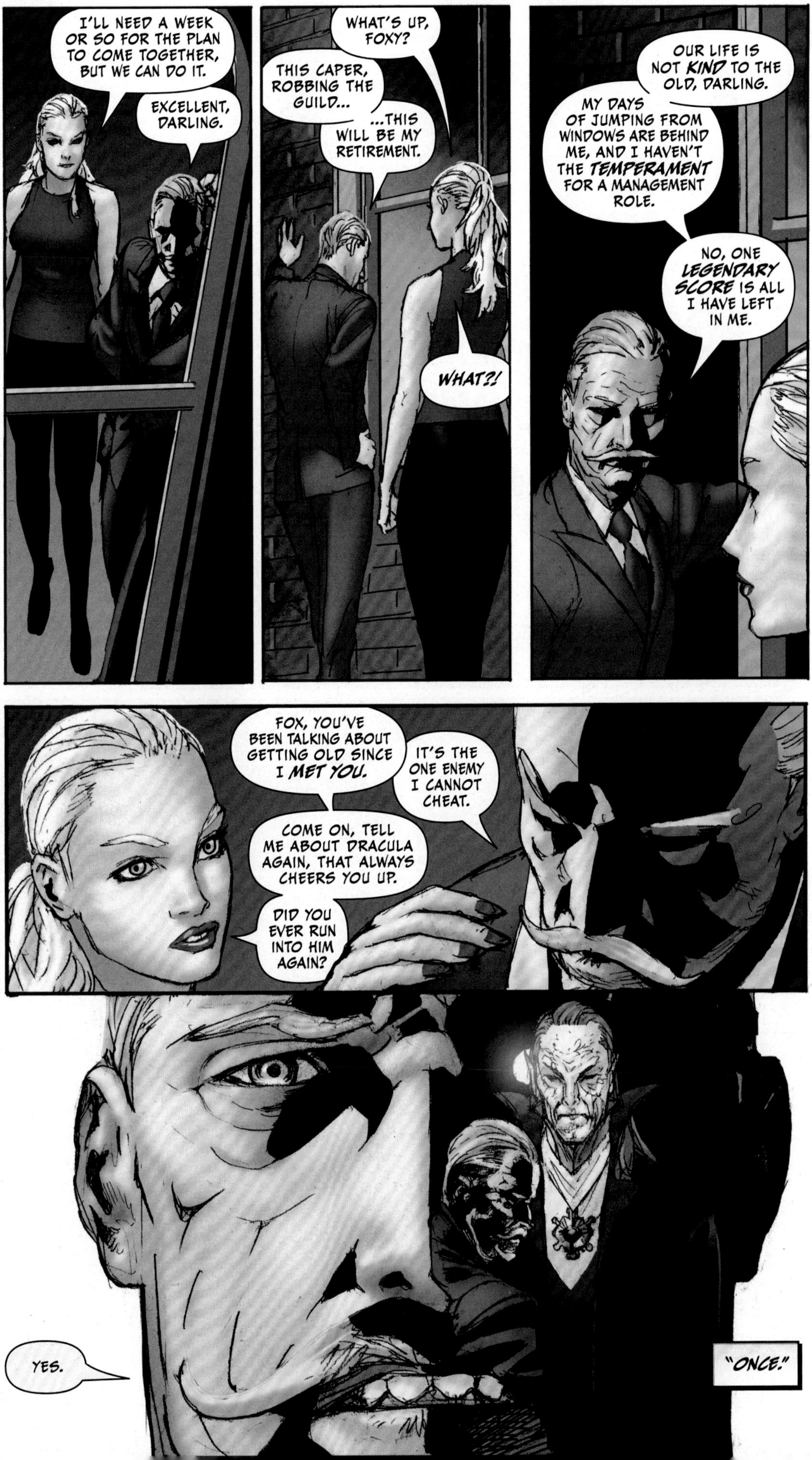
I'LL NEED A WEEK OR SO FOR THE PLAN TO COME TOGETHER, BUT WE CAN DO IT.
EXCELLENT, DARLING.
WHAT'S UP, FOXY?
THIS CAPER, ROBBING THE GUILD...
...THIS WILL BE MY RETIREMENT.
WHAT?!
OUR LIFE IS NOT KIND TO THE OLD, DARLING.
MY DAYS OF JUMPING FROM WINDOWS ARE BEHIND ME, AND I HAVEN'T THE TEMPERAMENT FOR A MANAGEMENT ROLE.
NO, ONE LEGENDARY SCORE IS ALL I HAVE LEFT IN ME.
FOX, YOU'VE BEEN TALKING ABOUT GETTING OLD SINCE I MET YOU.
IT'S THE ONE ENEMY I CANNOT CHEAT.
COME ON, TELL ME ABOUT DRACULA AGAIN, THAT ALWAYS CHEERS YOU UP.
DID YOU EVER RUN INTO HIM AGAIN?
YES.
"ONCE."

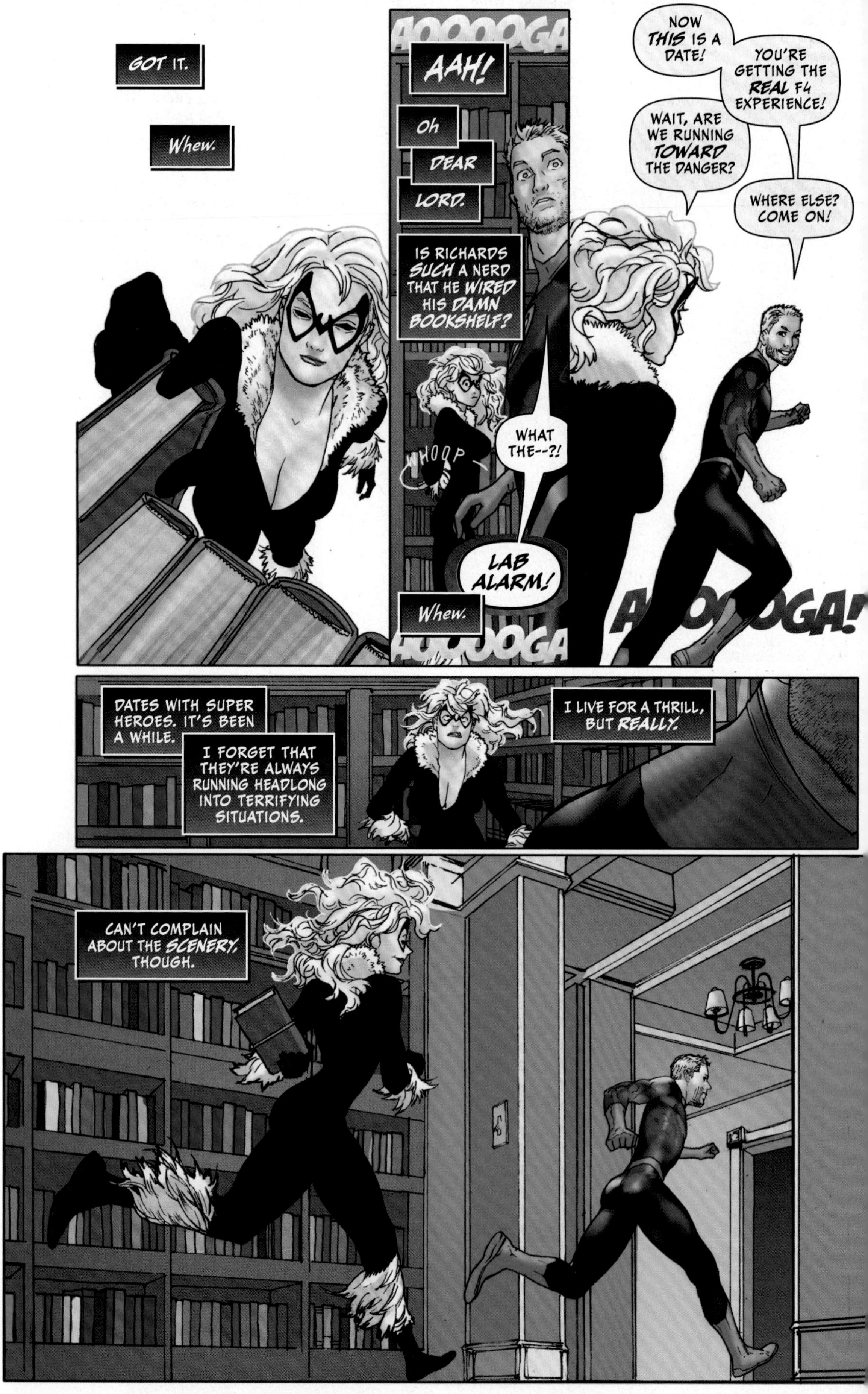
GOT IT.
Whew.
AOOOOGA
AAH!
Oh
DEAR
LORD.
IS RICHARDS SUCH A NERD THAT HE WIRED HIS DAMN BOOKSHELF?
WHOOP
WHAT THE--?!
LAB ALARM!
Whew.
AOOOOGA
NOW THIS IS A DATE!
YOU'RE GETTING THE REAL F4 EXPERIENCE!
WAIT, ARE WE RUNNING TOWARD THE DANGER?
WHERE ELSE? COME ON!
AOOOOGA!
DATES WITH SUPER HEROES. IT'S BEEN A WHILE.
I FORGET THAT THEY'RE ALWAYS RUNNING HEADLONG INTO TERRIFYING SITUATIONS.
I LIVE FOR A THRILL, BUT REALLY.
CAN'T COMPLAIN ABOUT THE SCENERY, THOUGH.

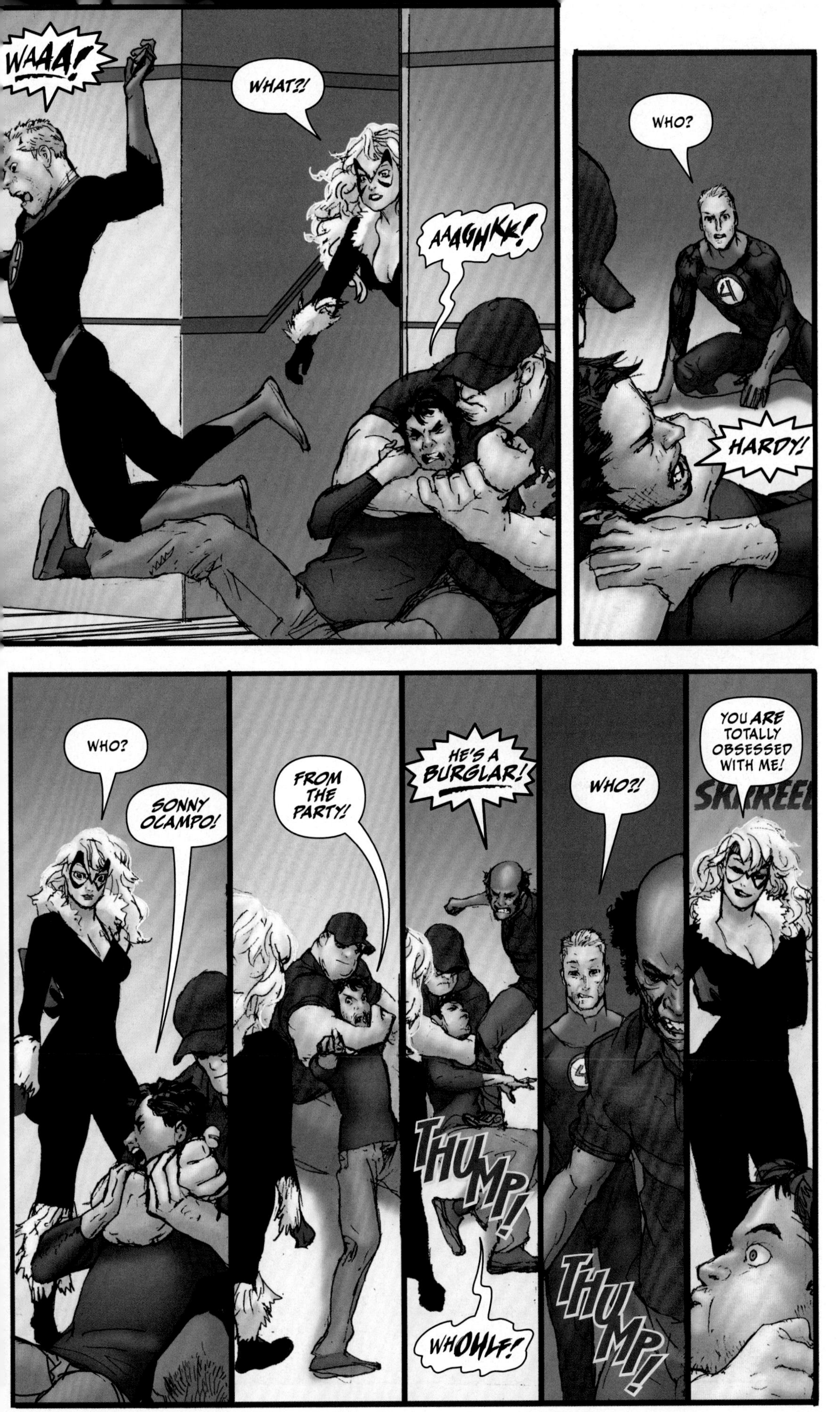
WAAA!
WHAT?!
AAAGHKK!
WHO?
HARDY!
WHO?
SONNY OCAMPO!
FROM THE PARTY!
HE'S A BURGLAR!
THUMP!
WHOULF!
WHO?!
THUMP!
SKREEE
YOU ARE TOTALLY OBSESSED WITH ME!

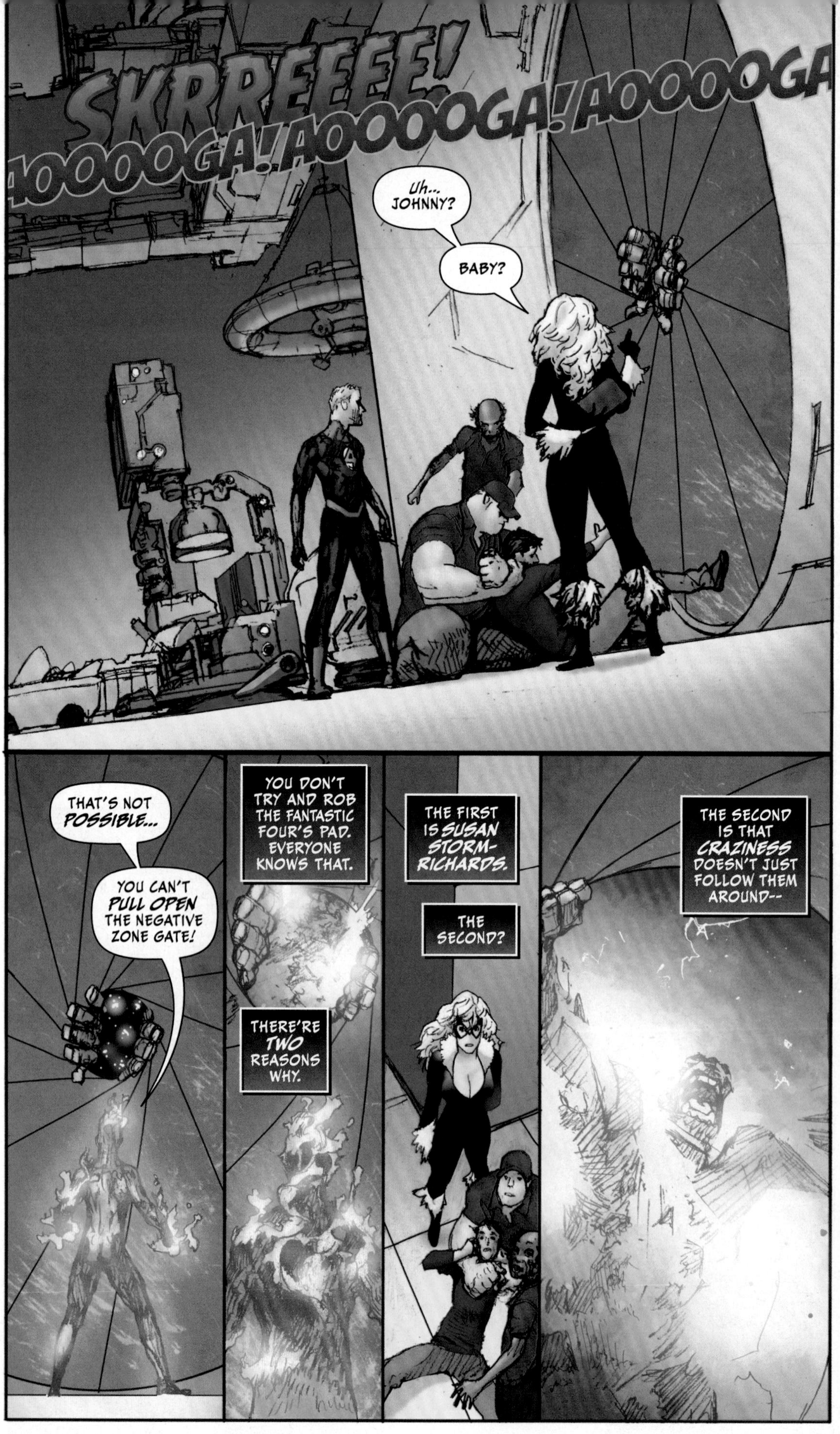
SKRREEEE!
AOOOOOGA! AOOOOOGA! AOOOOOGA
Uh... JOHNNY?
BABY?
THAT'S NOT POSSIBLE...
YOU CAN'T PULL OPEN THE NEGATIVE ZONE GATE!
YOU DON'T TRY AND ROB THE FANTASTIC FOUR'S PAD. EVERYONE KNOWS THAT.
THERE'RE TWO REASONS WHY.
THE FIRST IS SUSAN STORM-RICHARDS.
THE SECOND?
THE SECOND IS THAT CRAZINESS DOESN'T JUST FOLLOW THEM AROUND--

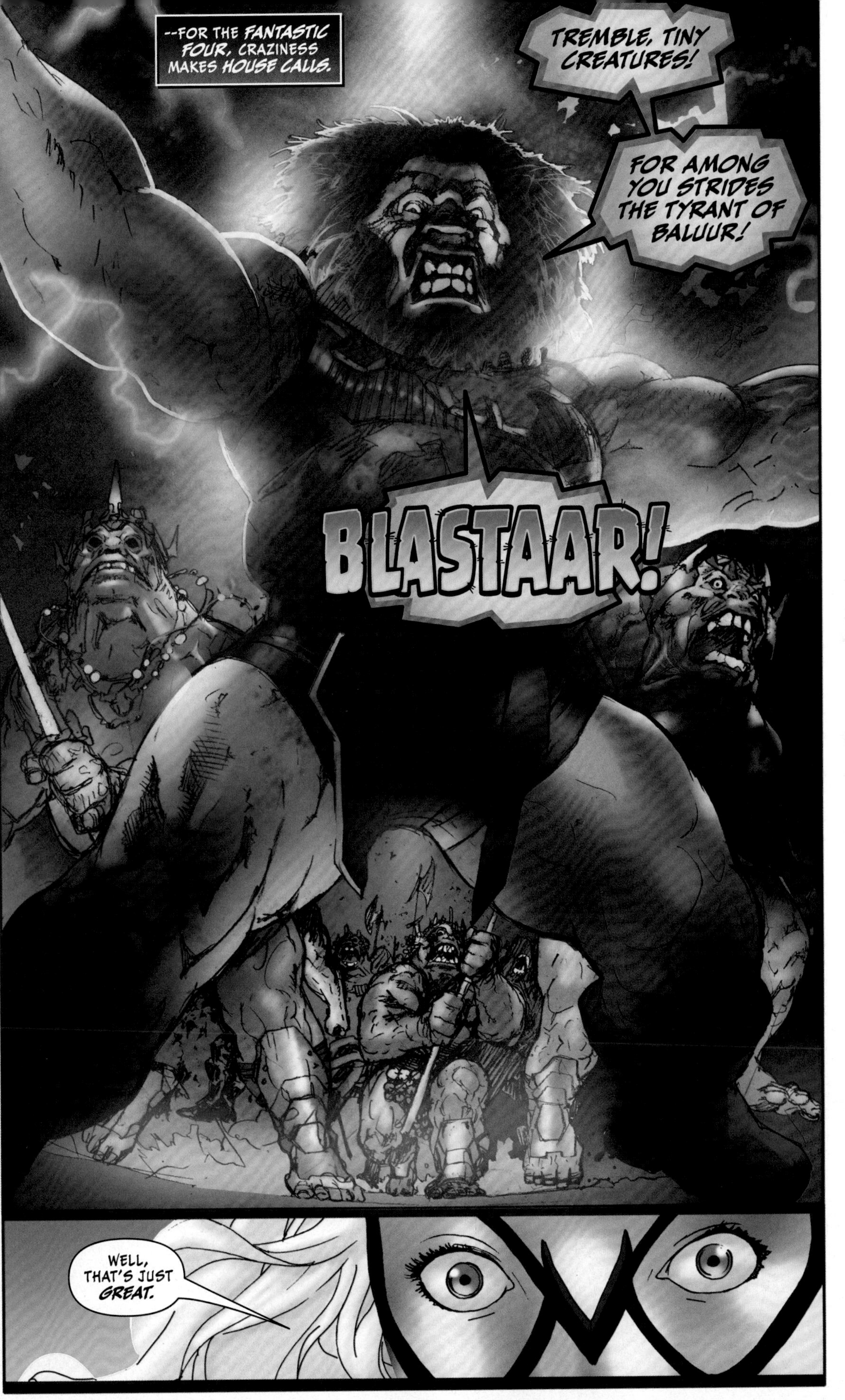
--FOR THE FANTASTIC FOUR, CRAZINESS MAKES HOUSE CALLS.
TREMBLE, TINY CREATURES!
FOR AMONG YOU STRIDES THE TYRANT OF BALUUR!
BLASTAAR!
WELL, THAT'S JUST GREAT.

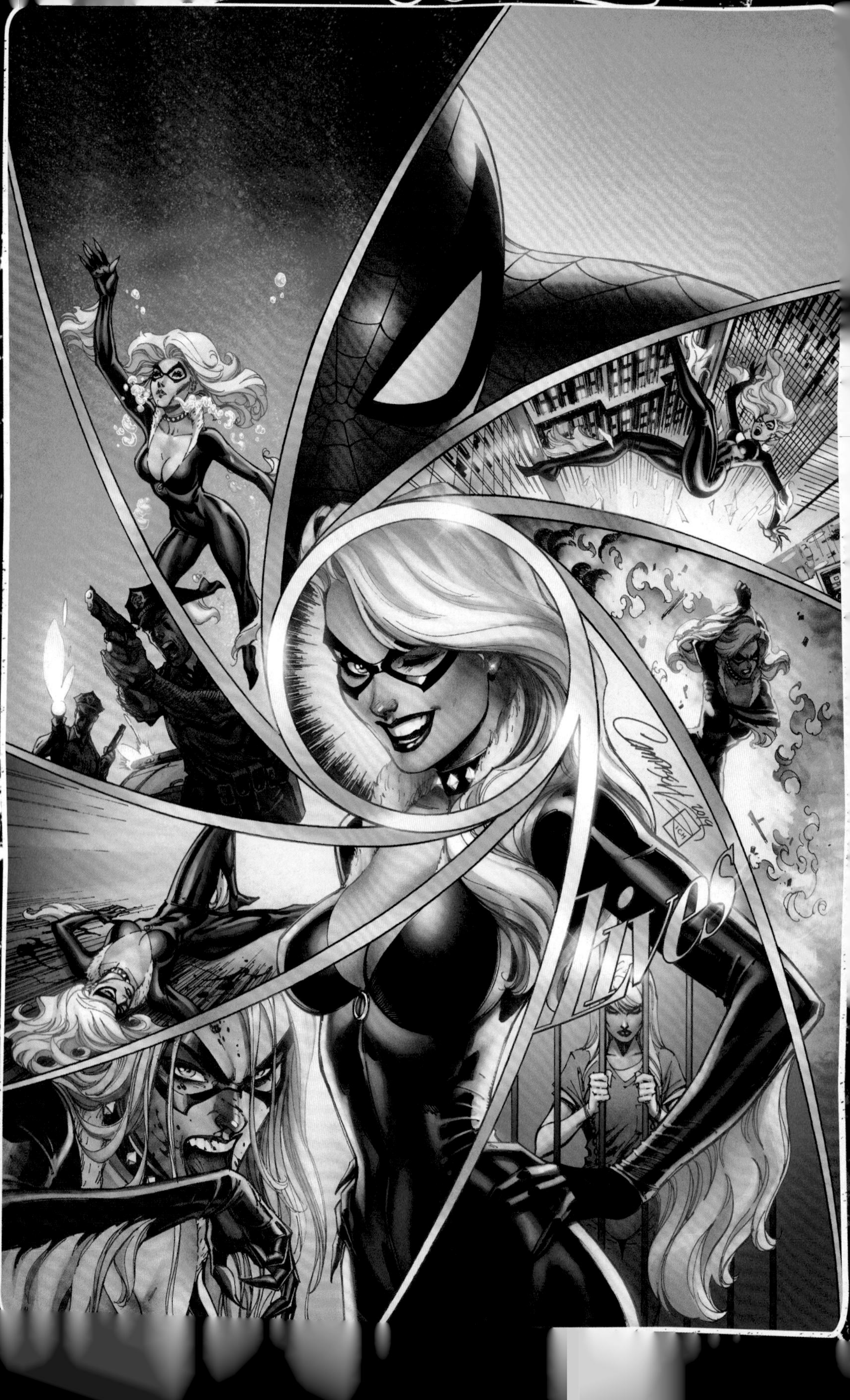
Lives

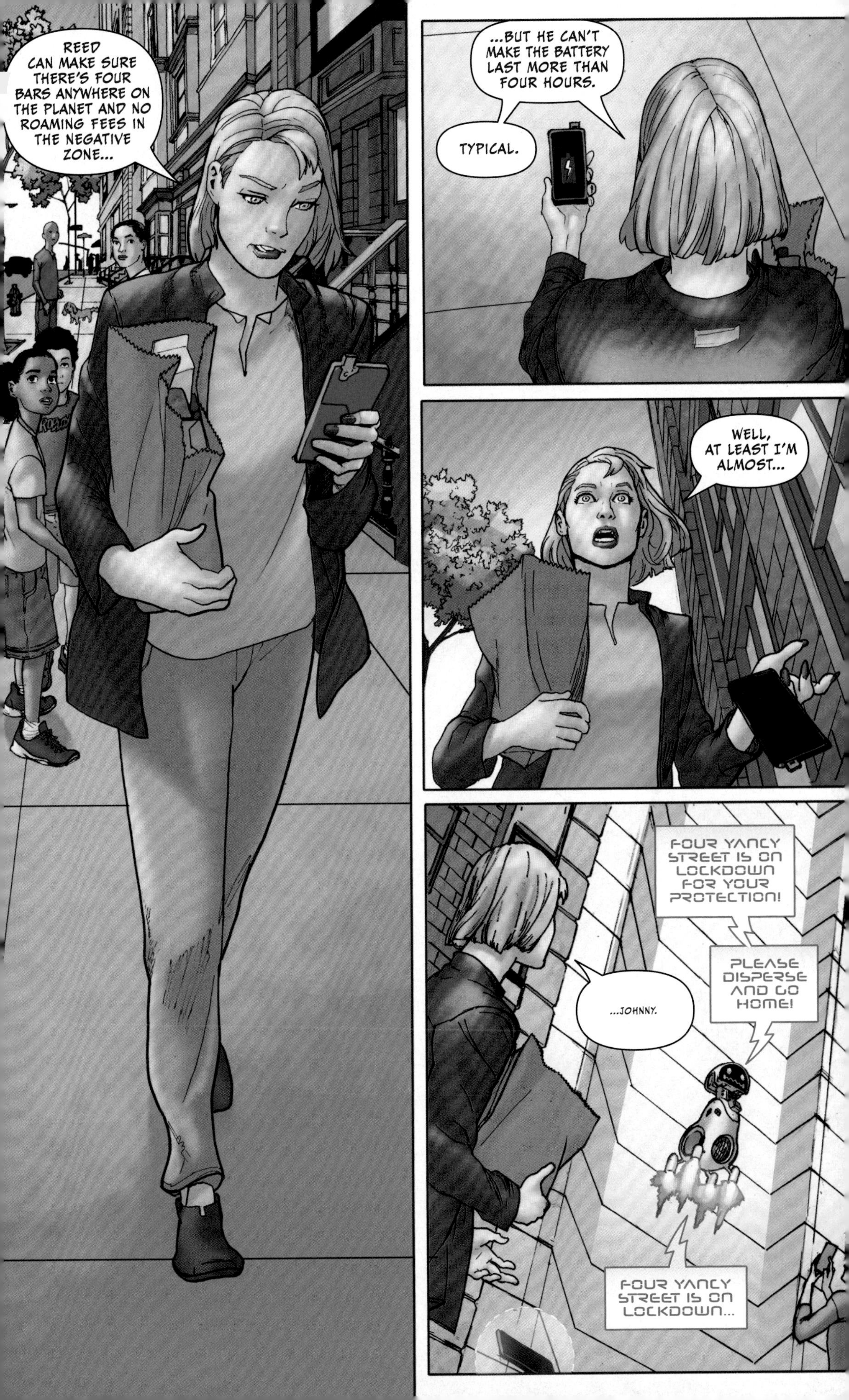
REED CAN MAKE SURE THERE'S FOUR BARS ANYWHERE ON THE PLANET AND NO ROAMING FEES IN THE NEGATIVE ZONE...
...BUT HE CAN'T MAKE THE BATTERY LAST MORE THAN FOUR HOURS.
TYPICAL.
WELL, AT LEAST I'M ALMOST...
FOUR YANCY STREET IS ON LOCKDOWN FOR YOUR PROTECTION!
PLEASE DISPERSE AND GO HOME!
...JOHNNY.
FOUR YANCY STREET IS ON LOCKDOWN...

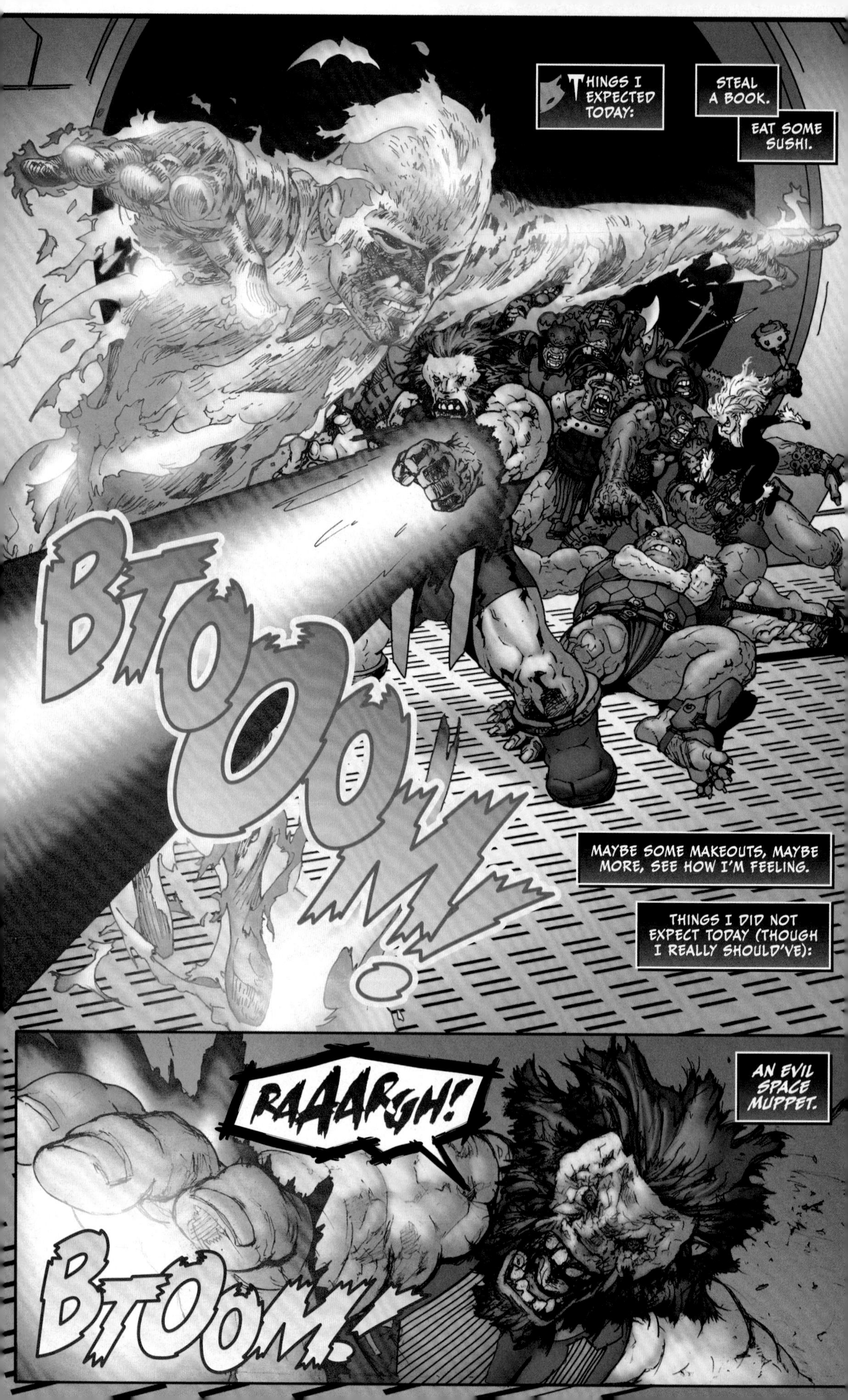

THINGS I EXPECTED TODAY:
STEAL A BOOK.
EAT SOME SUSHI.
BTOOOM!
MAYBE SOME MAKEOUTS, MAYBE MORE, SEE HOW I'M FEELING.
THINGS I DID NOT EXPECT TODAY (THOUGH I REALLY SHOULD'VE):
AN EVIL SPACE MUPPET.
RAAARGH!
BTOOM!

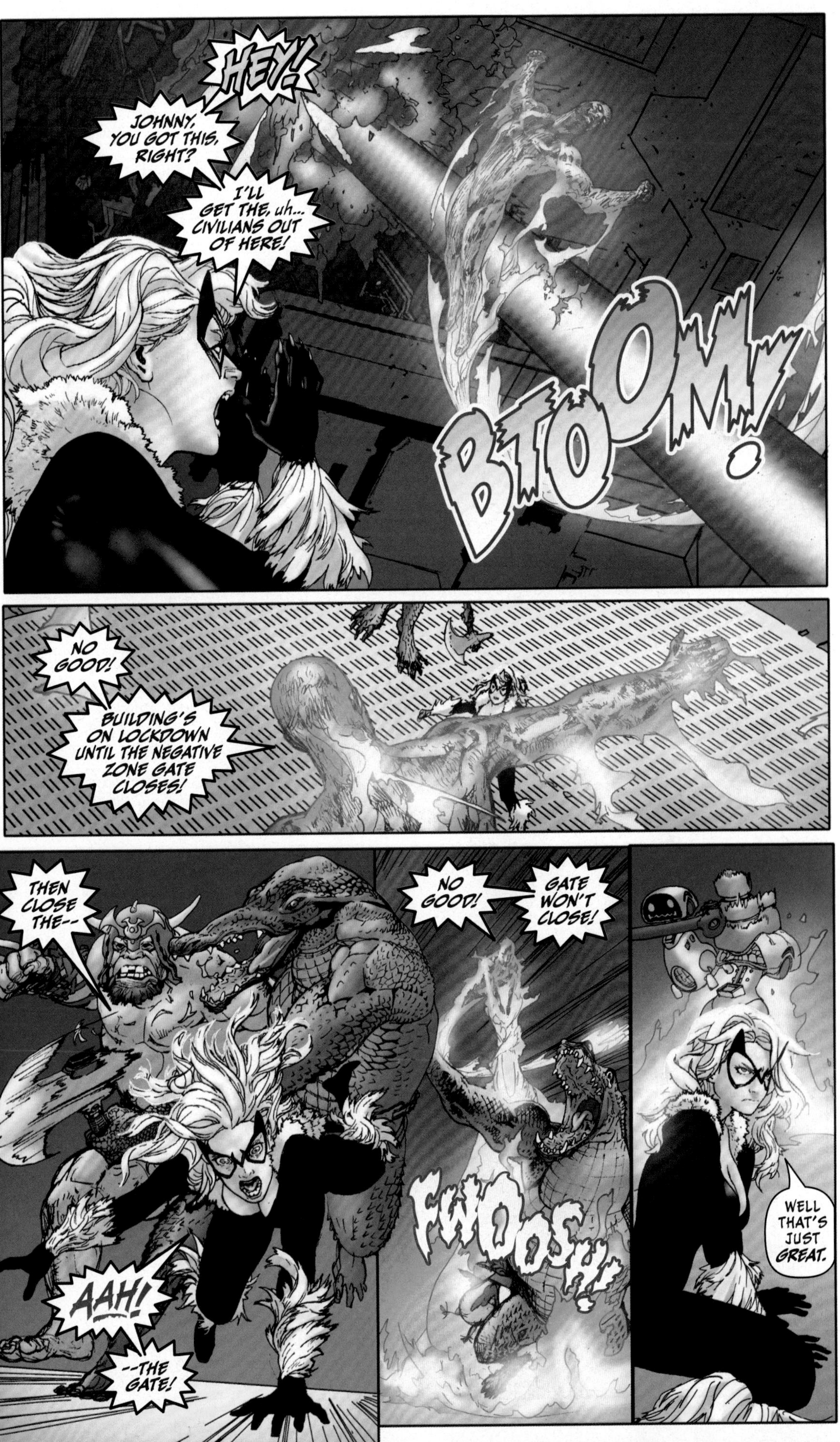
HEY!
JOHNNY, YOU GOT THIS, RIGHT?
I'LL GET THE, uh... CIVILIANS OUT OF HERE!
BTOOM!
NO GOOD!
BUILDING'S ON LOCKDOWN UNTIL THE NEGATIVE ZONE GATE CLOSES!
THEN CLOSE THE--
AAH!
--THE GATE!
NO GOOD!
GATE WON'T CLOSE!
FWOOSH!!
WELL THAT'S JUST GREAT.

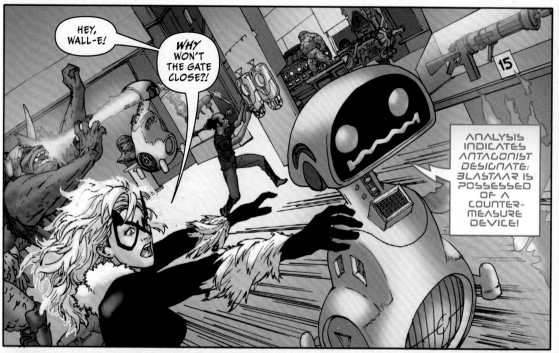

HEY, WALL-E!

WHY WON'T THE GATE CLOSE?!

ANALYSIS INDICATES ANTAGONIST DESIGNATE: BLASTAAR IS POSSESSED OF A COUNTER-MEASURE DEVICE!

NEGATIVE ZONE GATE COMPROMISED!

SUGGESTION: TAKE POSSESSION--

AAAH!

SQUARKK! ☀

BTOOM!

YOU. PRETTY ONE.

YOU PLEASE ME.

DON'T.

SERIOUSLY, MAN, DON'T.

YOU WILL BE MY EARTH-WIFE.

WELL, THAT'S--

--JUST--

--GREAT.

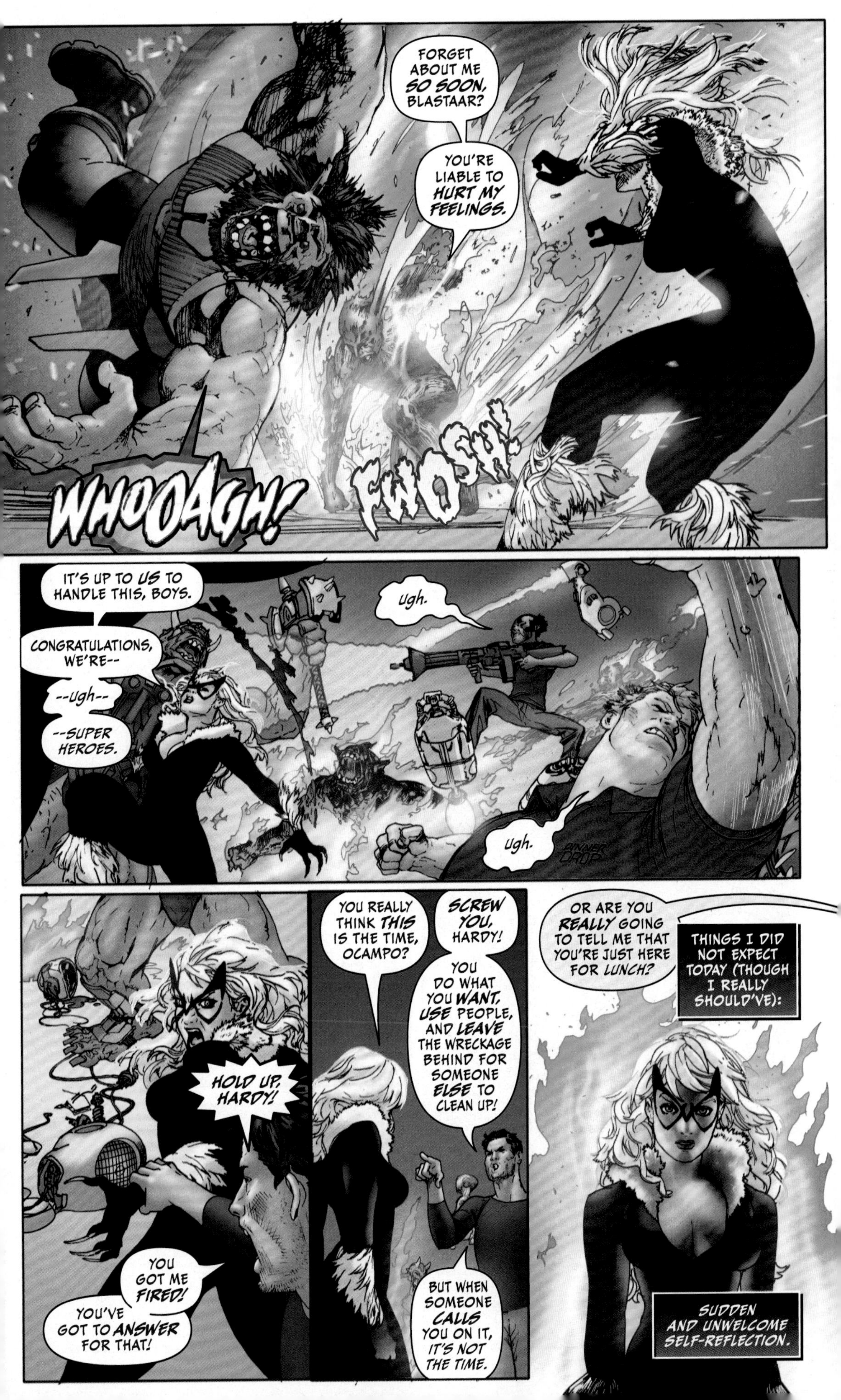
FORGET ABOUT ME SO SOON, BLASTAAR?
YOU'RE LIABLE TO HURT MY FEELINGS.
WHOOAGH!
FWOSH!
IT'S UP TO US TO HANDLE THIS, BOYS.
CONGRATULATIONS, WE'RE--
--UGH--
--SUPER HEROES.
UGH.
UGH.
HOLD UP, HARDY!
YOU GOT ME FIRED!
YOU'VE GOT TO ANSWER FOR THAT!
YOU REALLY THINK THIS IS THE TIME, OCAMPO?
SCREW YOU, HARDY!
YOU DO WHAT YOU WANT, USE PEOPLE, AND LEAVE THE WRECKAGE BEHIND FOR SOMEONE ELSE TO CLEAN UP!
BUT WHEN SOMEONE CALLS YOU ON IT, IT'S NOT THE TIME.
OR ARE YOU REALLY GOING TO TELL ME THAT YOU'RE JUST HERE FOR LUNCH?
THINGS I DID NOT EXPECT TODAY (THOUGH I REALLY SHOULD'VE):
SUDDEN AND UNWELCOME SELF-REFLECTION.

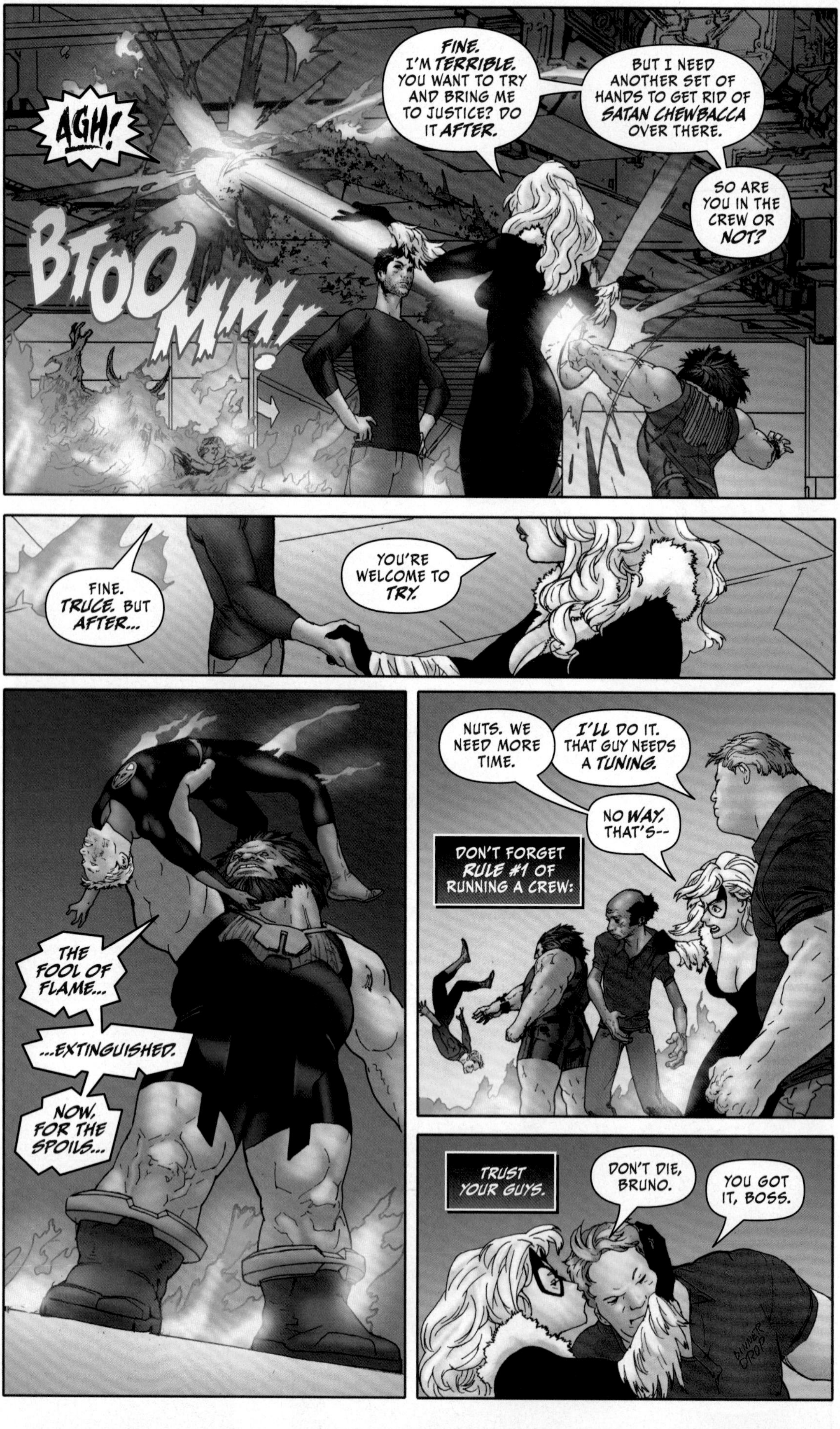
AGH!
BTOOMM!
FINE. I'M TERRIBLE. YOU WANT TO TRY AND BRING ME TO JUSTICE? DO IT AFTER.
BUT I NEED ANOTHER SET OF HANDS TO GET RID OF SATAN CHEWBACCA OVER THERE.
SO ARE YOU IN THE CREW OR NOT?
FINE. TRUCE. BUT AFTER...
YOU'RE WELCOME TO TRY.
THE FOOL OF FLAME...
...EXTINGUISHED.
NOW, FOR THE SPOILS...
NUTS. WE NEED MORE TIME.
I'LL DO IT. THAT GUY NEEDS A TUNING.
NO WAY. THAT'S--
DON'T FORGET RULE #1 OF RUNNING A CREW:
TRUST YOUR GUYS.
DON'T DIE, BRUNO.
YOU GOT IT, BOSS.

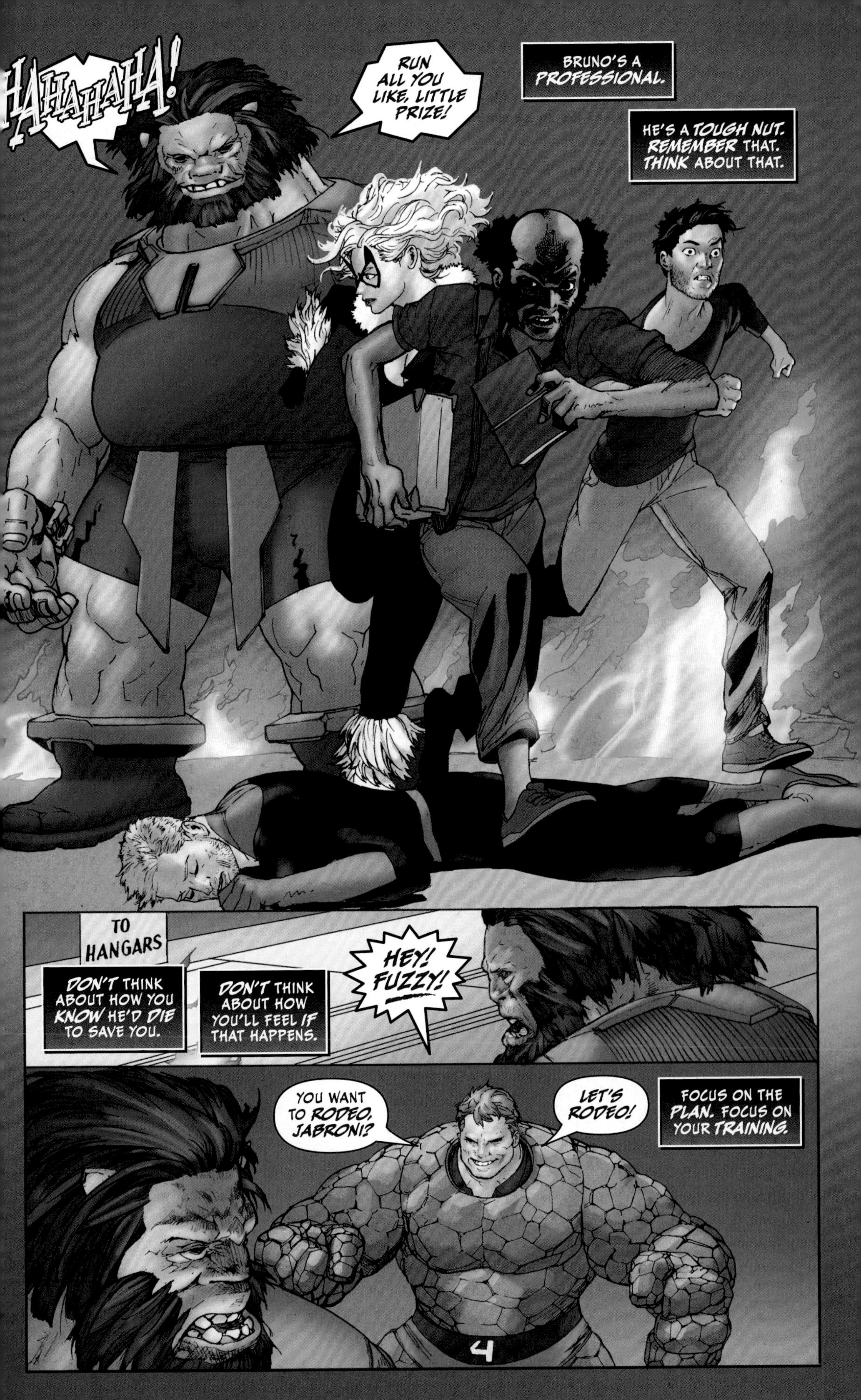

HAHAHAHA!
RUN ALL YOU LIKE, LITTLE PRIZE!
BRUNO'S A PROFESSIONAL.
HE'S A TOUGH NUT. REMEMBER THAT. THINK ABOUT THAT.
TO HANGARS
DON'T THINK ABOUT HOW YOU KNOW HE'D DIE TO SAVE YOU.
DON'T THINK ABOUT HOW YOU'LL FEEL IF THAT HAPPENS.
HEY! FUZZY!
YOU WANT TO RODEO, JABRONI?
LET'S RODEO!
FOCUS ON THE PLAN. FOCUS ON YOUR TRAINING.
4

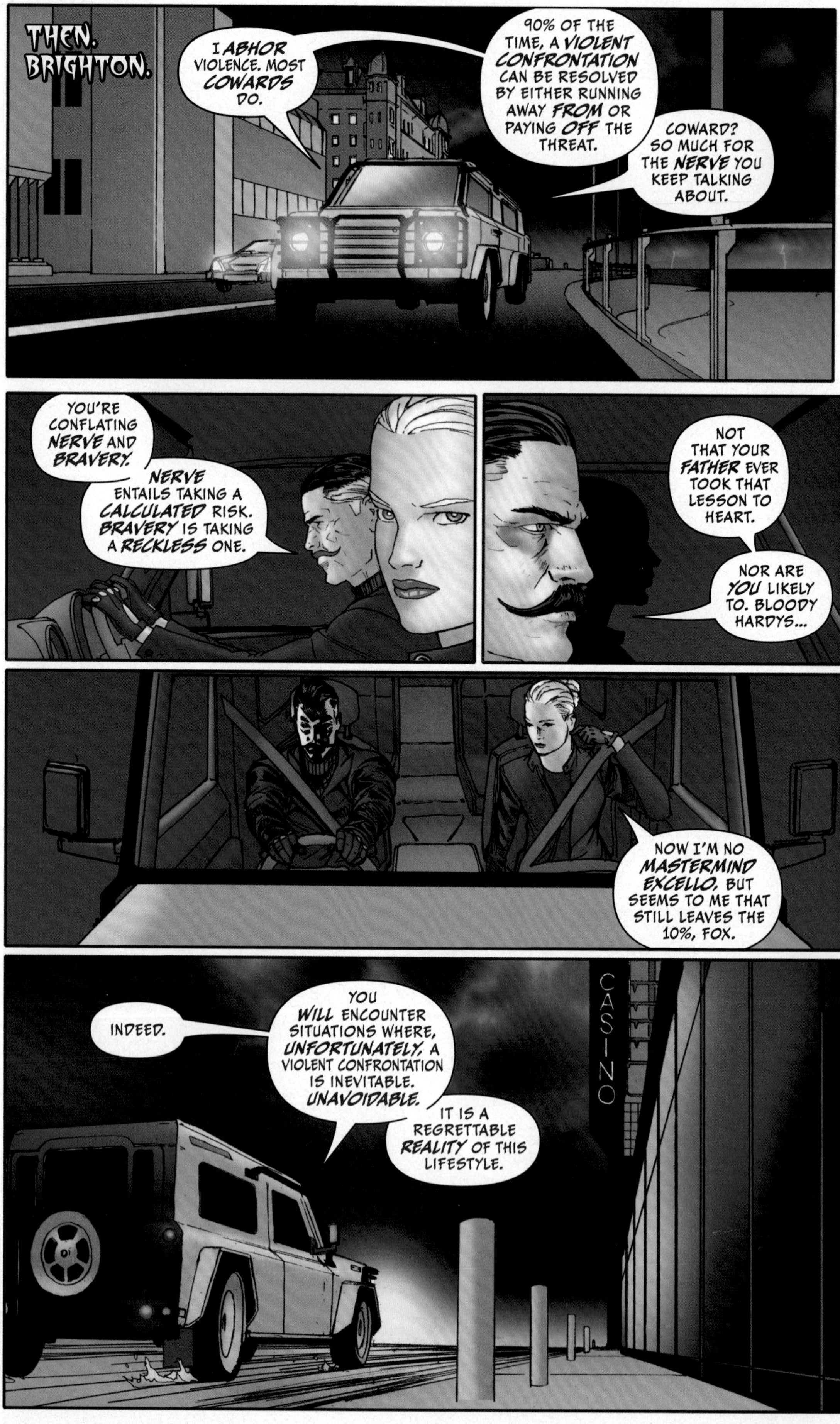
THEN. BRIGHTON.
I ABHOR VIOLENCE. MOST COWARDS DO.
90% OF THE TIME, A VIOLENT CONFRONTATION CAN BE RESOLVED BY EITHER RUNNING AWAY FROM OR PAYING OFF THE THREAT.
COWARD? SO MUCH FOR THE NERVE YOU KEEP TALKING ABOUT.
YOU'RE CONFLATING NERVE AND BRAVERY.
NERVE ENTAILS TAKING A CALCULATED RISK. BRAVERY IS TAKING A RECKLESS ONE.
NOT THAT YOUR FATHER EVER TOOK THAT LESSON TO HEART.
NOR ARE YOU LIKELY TO. BLOODY HARDYS...
NOW I'M NO MASTERMIND EXCELLO, BUT SEEMS TO ME THAT STILL LEAVES THE 10%, FOX.
INDEED.
YOU WILL ENCOUNTER SITUATIONS WHERE, UNFORTUNATELY, A VIOLENT CONFRONTATION IS INEVITABLE. UNAVOIDABLE.
IT IS A REGRETTABLE REALITY OF THIS LIFESTYLE.
CASINO

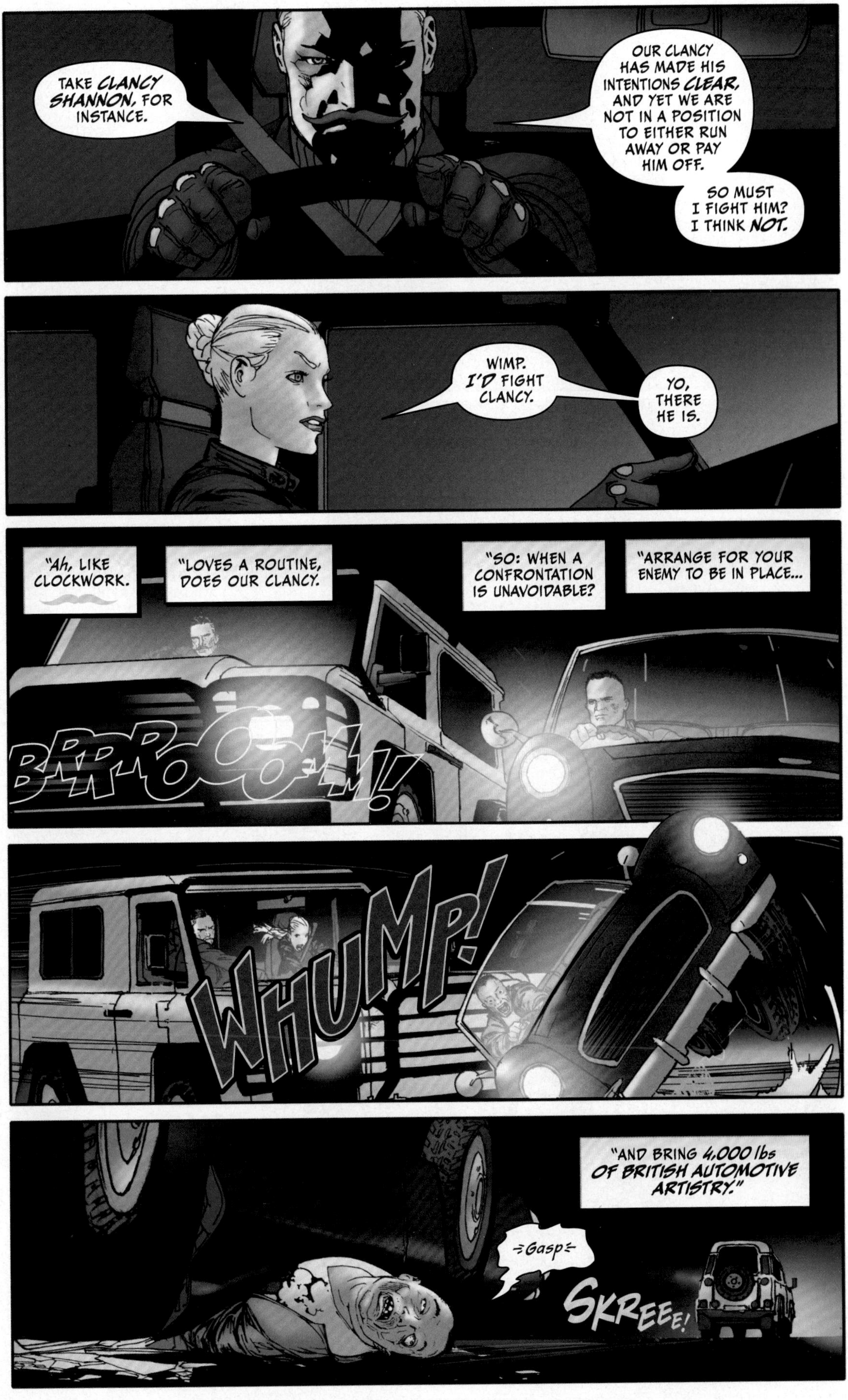
TAKE CLANCY SHANNON, FOR INSTANCE.
OUR CLANCY HAS MADE HIS INTENTIONS CLEAR, AND YET WE ARE NOT IN A POSITION TO EITHER RUN AWAY OR PAY HIM OFF.
SO MUST I FIGHT HIM? I THINK NOT.
WIMP. I'D FIGHT CLANCY.
YO, THERE HE IS.
"Ah, LIKE CLOCKWORK.
"LOVES A ROUTINE, DOES OUR CLANCY.
"SO: WHEN A CONFRONTATION IS UNAVOIDABLE?
"ARRANGE FOR YOUR ENEMY TO BE IN PLACE...
BRRROOOM!!
WHUMP!
"AND BRING 4,000 lbs OF BRITISH AUTOMOTIVE ARTISTRY."
Gasp
SKREEEE!

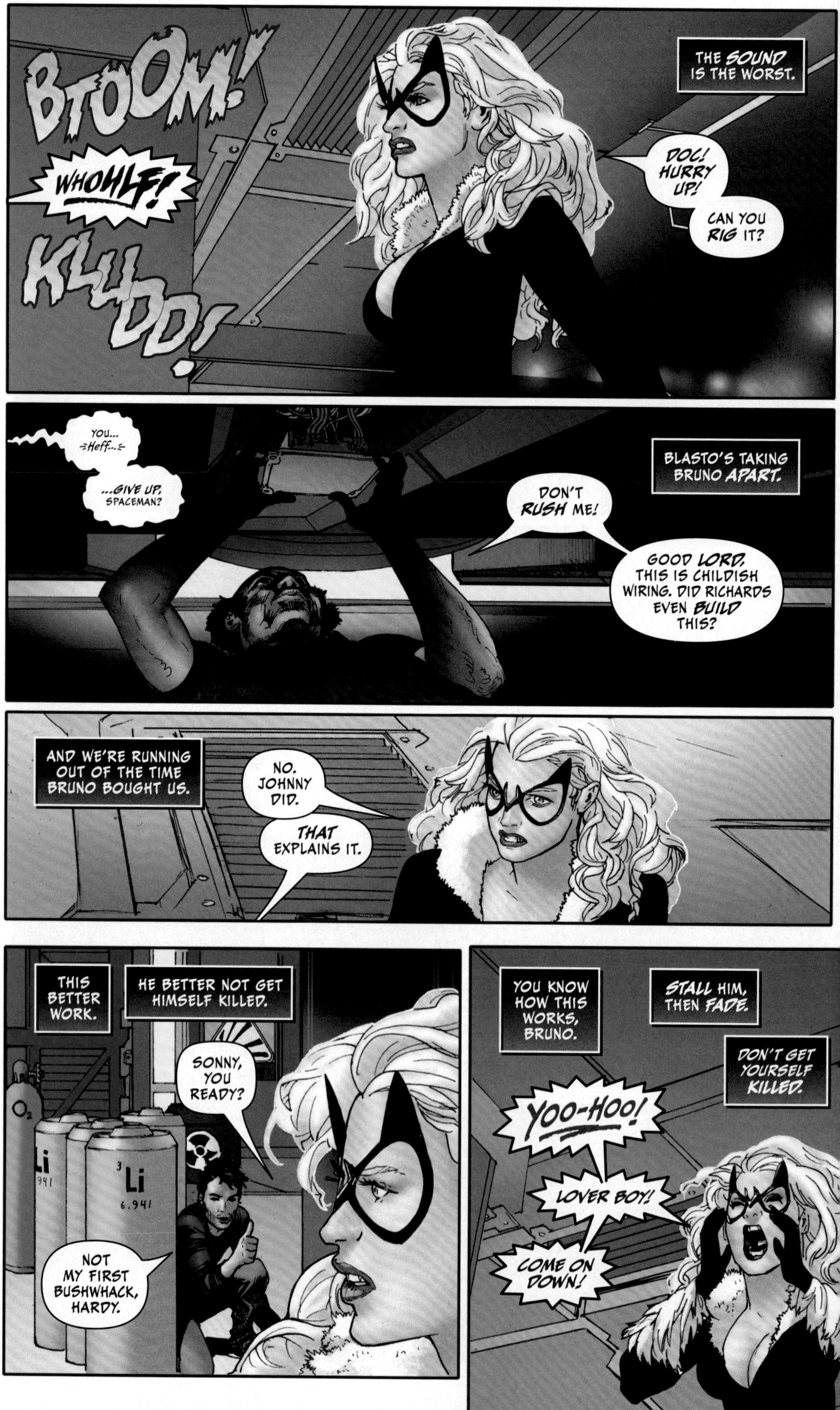
BTOOM!
WHOHLF!
KLUDD!
THE SOUND IS THE WORST.
DOC! HURRY UP!
CAN YOU RIG IT?
YOU... Heff...
...GIVE UP, SPACEMAN?
BLASTO'S TAKING BRUNO APART.
DON'T RUSH ME!
GOOD LORD, THIS IS CHILDISH WIRING. DID RICHARDS EVEN BUILD THIS?
AND WE'RE RUNNING OUT OF THE TIME BRUNO BOUGHT US.
NO. JOHNNY DID.
THAT EXPLAINS IT.
THIS BETTER WORK.
HE BETTER NOT GET HIMSELF KILLED.
SONNY, YOU READY?
NOT MY FIRST BUSHWHACK, HARDY.
YOU KNOW HOW THIS WORKS, BRUNO.
STALL HIM, THEN FADE.
DON'T GET YOURSELF KILLED.
YOO-HOO!
LOVER BOY!
COME ON DOWN!

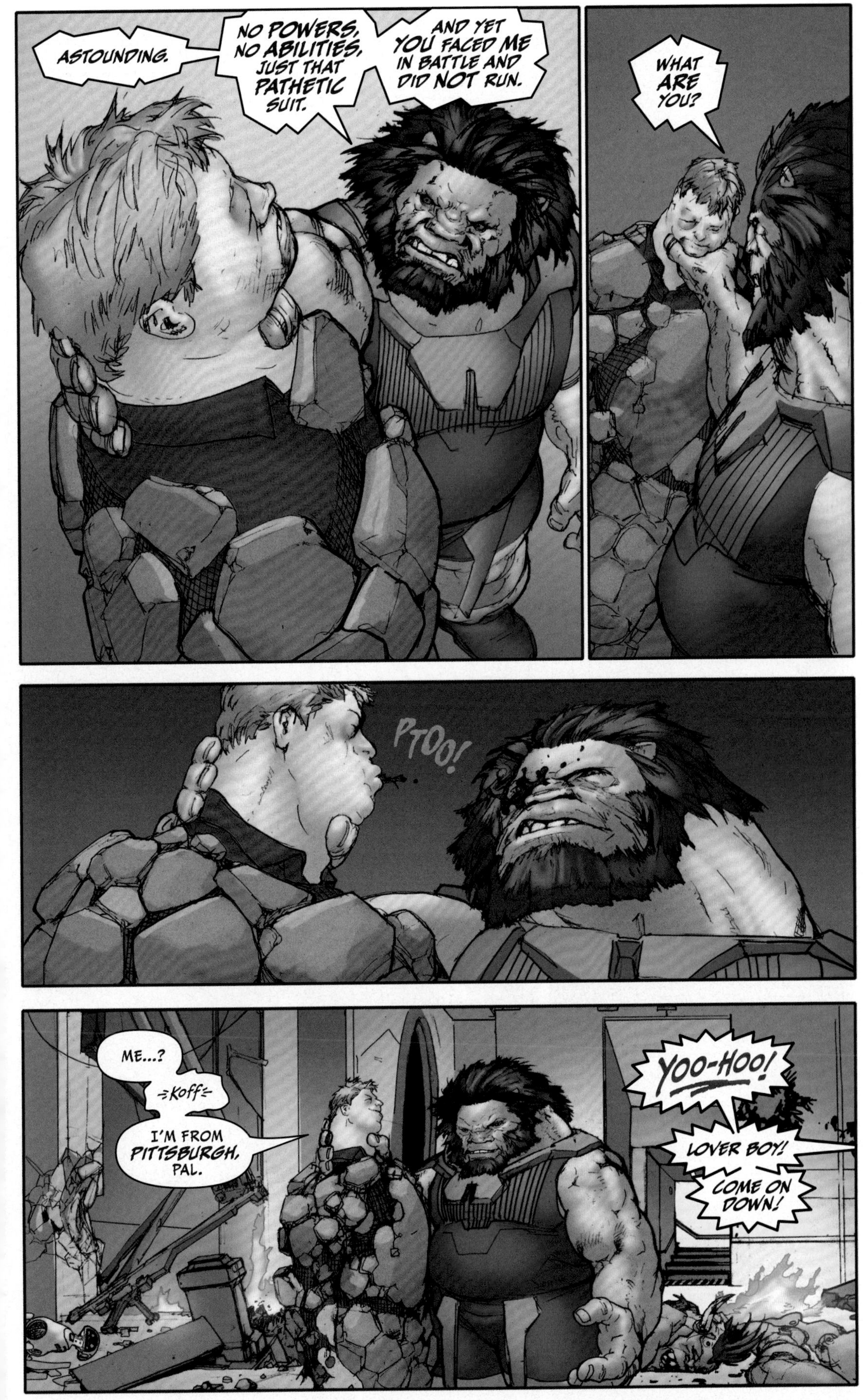
ASTOUNDING.
NO POWERS, NO ABILITIES, JUST THAT PATHETIC SUIT.
AND YET YOU FACED ME IN BATTLE AND DID NOT RUN.
WHAT ARE YOU?
PTOO!
ME...?
KOFF
I'M FROM PITTSBURGH, PAL.
YOO-HOO!
LOVER BOY!
COME ON DOWN!

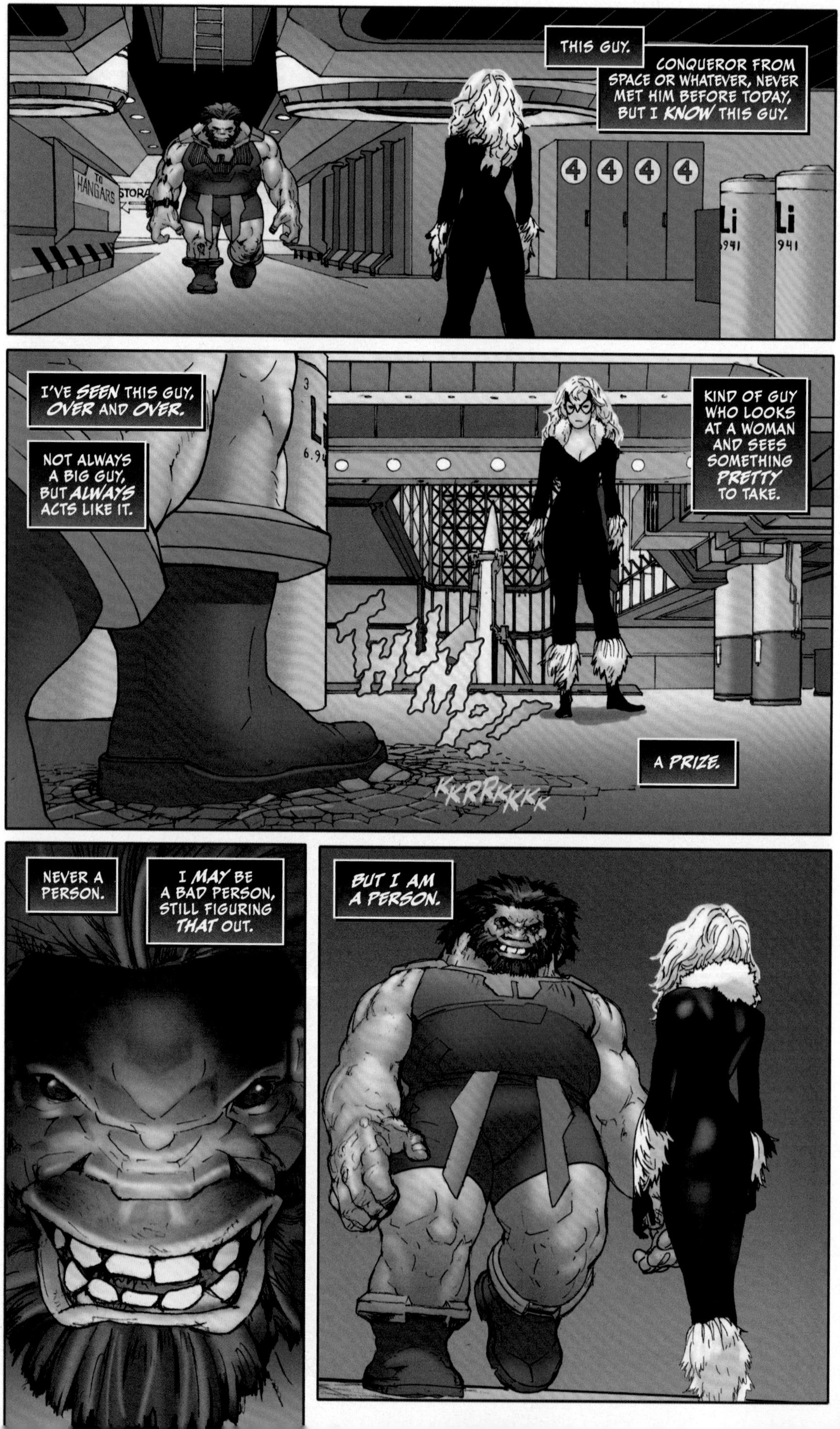
THIS GUY.
CONQUEROR FROM SPACE OR WHATEVER, NEVER MET HIM BEFORE TODAY, BUT I KNOW THIS GUY.
TO HANGARS
STORA
4 4 4 4
Li 6.941
Li 6.941
I'VE SEEN THIS GUY, OVER AND OVER.
NOT ALWAYS A BIG GUY, BUT ALWAYS ACTS LIKE IT.
KIND OF GUY WHO LOOKS AT A WOMAN AND SEES SOMETHING PRETTY TO TAKE.
THUMP!!
KKRRKKKK
A PRIZE.
NEVER A PERSON.
I MAY BE A BAD PERSON, STILL FIGURING THAT OUT.
BUT I AM A PERSON.

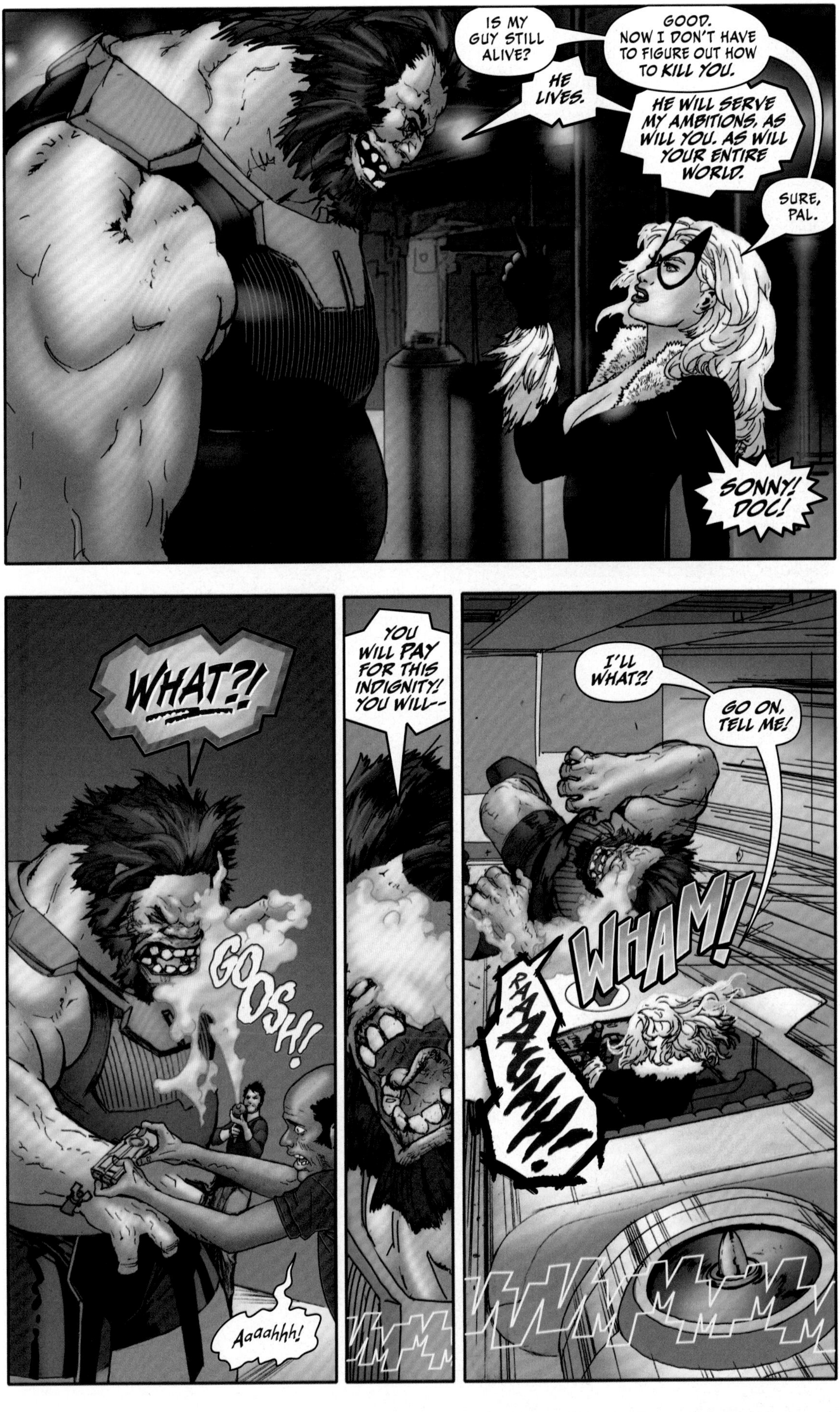
IS MY GUY STILL ALIVE?
HE LIVES.
GOOD. NOW I DON'T HAVE TO FIGURE OUT HOW TO KILL YOU.
HE WILL SERVE MY AMBITIONS, AS WILL YOU. AS WILL YOUR ENTIRE WORLD.
SURE, PAL.
SONNY! DOC!
WHAT?!
GOOSH!
Aaaahhh!
YOU WILL PAY FOR THIS INDIGNITY! YOU WILL--
I'LL WHAT?!
GO ON, TELL ME!
WHAM!
RAAAUGHH!
WHMMMM

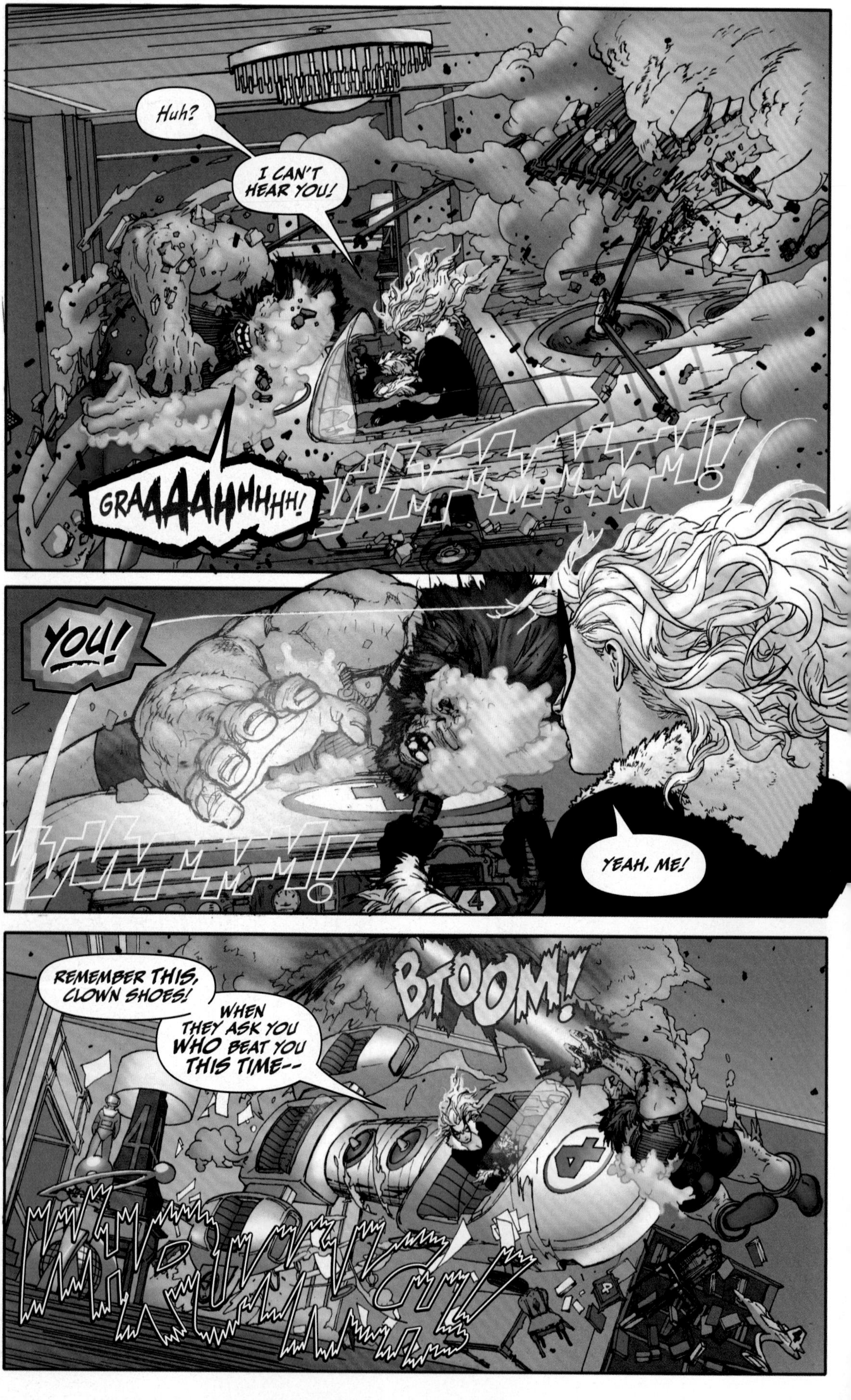
Huh?
I CAN'T HEAR YOU!
GRAAAAHHHHH!
YOU!
YEAH, ME!
REMEMBER THIS, CLOWN SHOES!
WHEN THEY ASK YOU WHO BEAT YOU THIS TIME--
BTOOM!

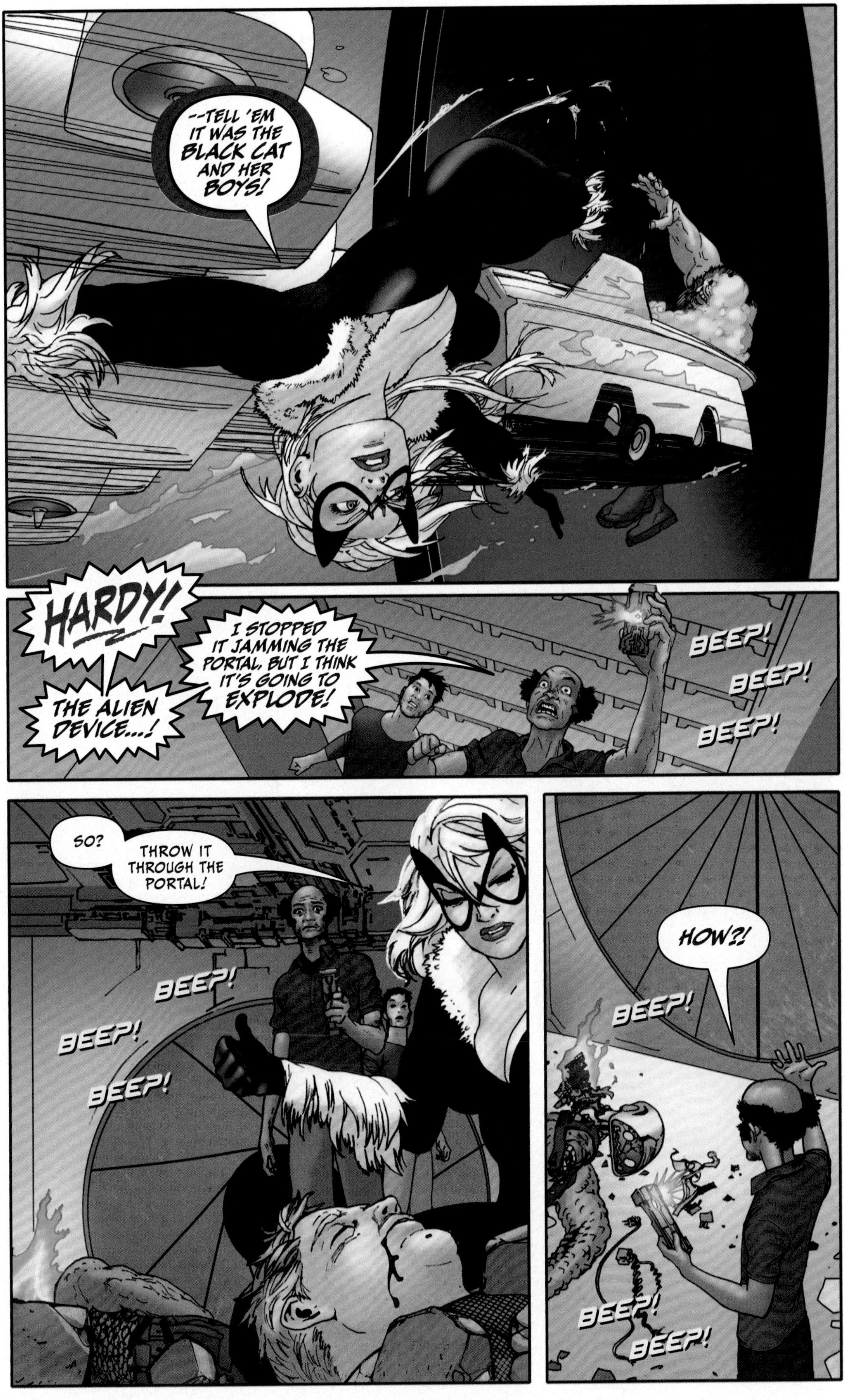
--TELL 'EM IT WAS THE BLACK CAT AND HER BOYS!
HARDY!
THE ALIEN DEVICE...!
I STOPPED IT JAMMING THE PORTAL, BUT I THINK IT'S GOING TO EXPLODE!
BEEP!
BEEP!
BEEP!
SO?
THROW IT THROUGH THE PORTAL!
BEEP!
BEEP!
BEEP!
HOW?!
BEEP!
BEEP!
BEEP!

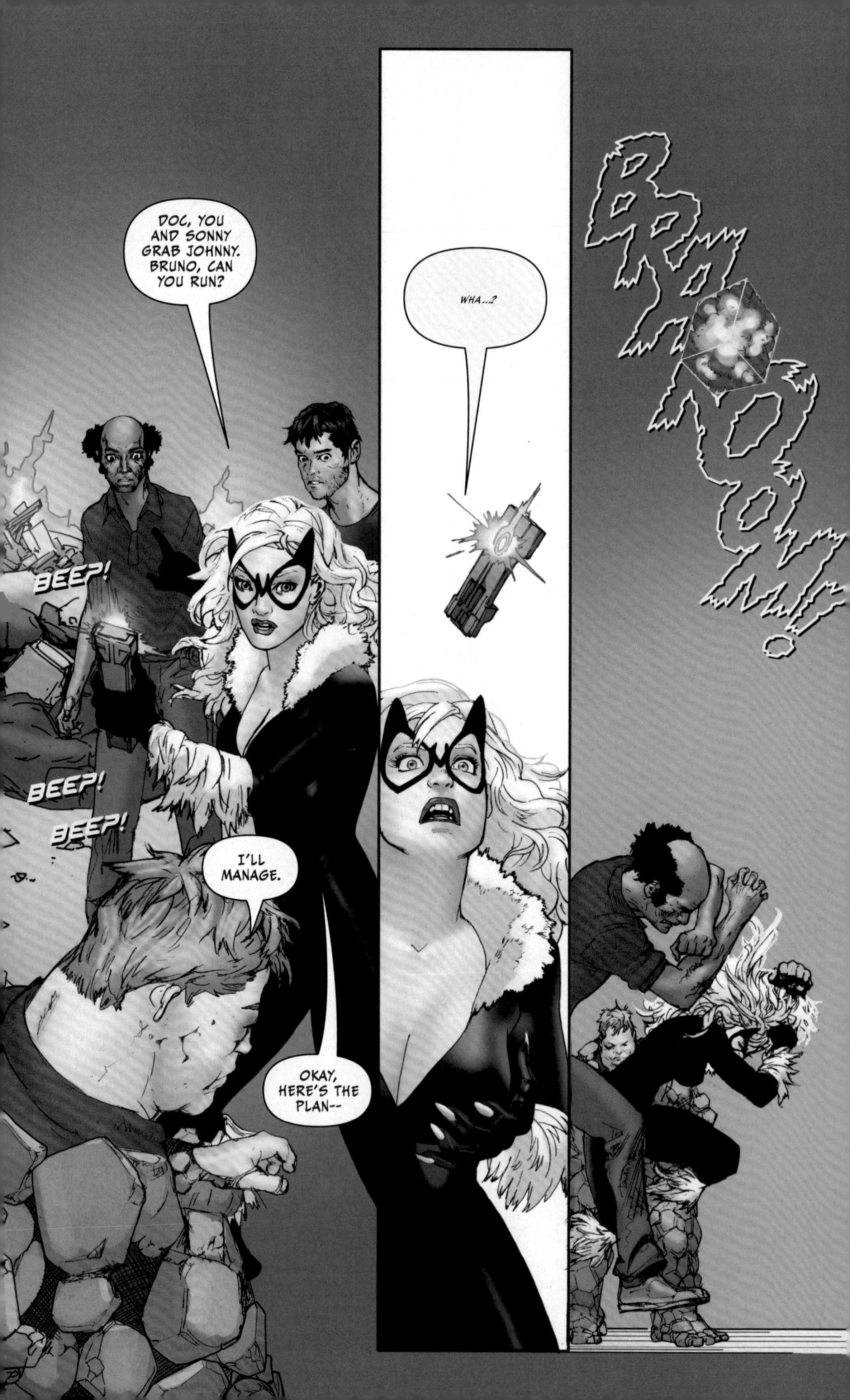
DOC, YOU AND SONNY GRAB JOHNNY. BRUNO, CAN YOU RUN?
BEEP!
BEEP!
BEEP!
I'LL MANAGE.
OKAY, HERE'S THE PLAN--
WHA...?
BRA-KOOM!!

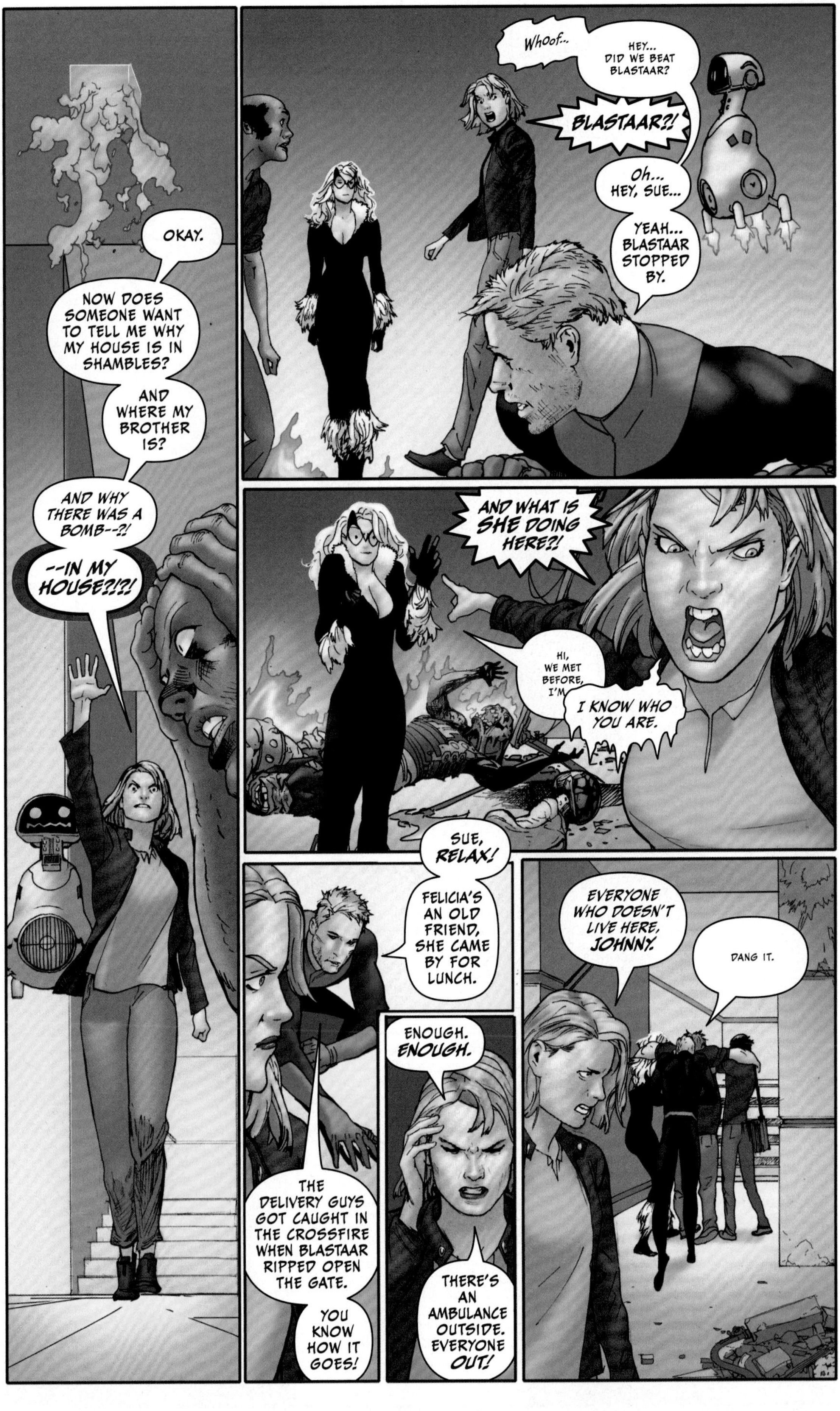
OKAY.
NOW DOES SOMEONE WANT TO TELL ME WHY MY HOUSE IS IN SHAMBLES?
AND WHERE MY BROTHER IS?
AND WHY THERE WAS A BOMB--?!
--IN MY HOUSE?!?!
Whoof...
HEY... DID WE BEAT BLASTAAR?
BLASTAAR?!
Oh... HEY, SUE...
YEAH... BLASTAAR STOPPED BY.
AND WHAT IS SHE DOING HERE?!
HI, WE MET BEFORE, I'M
I KNOW WHO YOU ARE.
SUE, RELAX!
FELICIA'S AN OLD FRIEND, SHE CAME BY FOR LUNCH.
THE DELIVERY GUYS GOT CAUGHT IN THE CROSSFIRE WHEN BLASTAAR RIPPED OPEN THE GATE.
YOU KNOW HOW IT GOES!
ENOUGH. ENOUGH.
THERE'S AN AMBULANCE OUTSIDE. EVERYONE OUT!
EVERYONE WHO DOESN'T LIVE HERE, JOHNNY.
DANG IT.

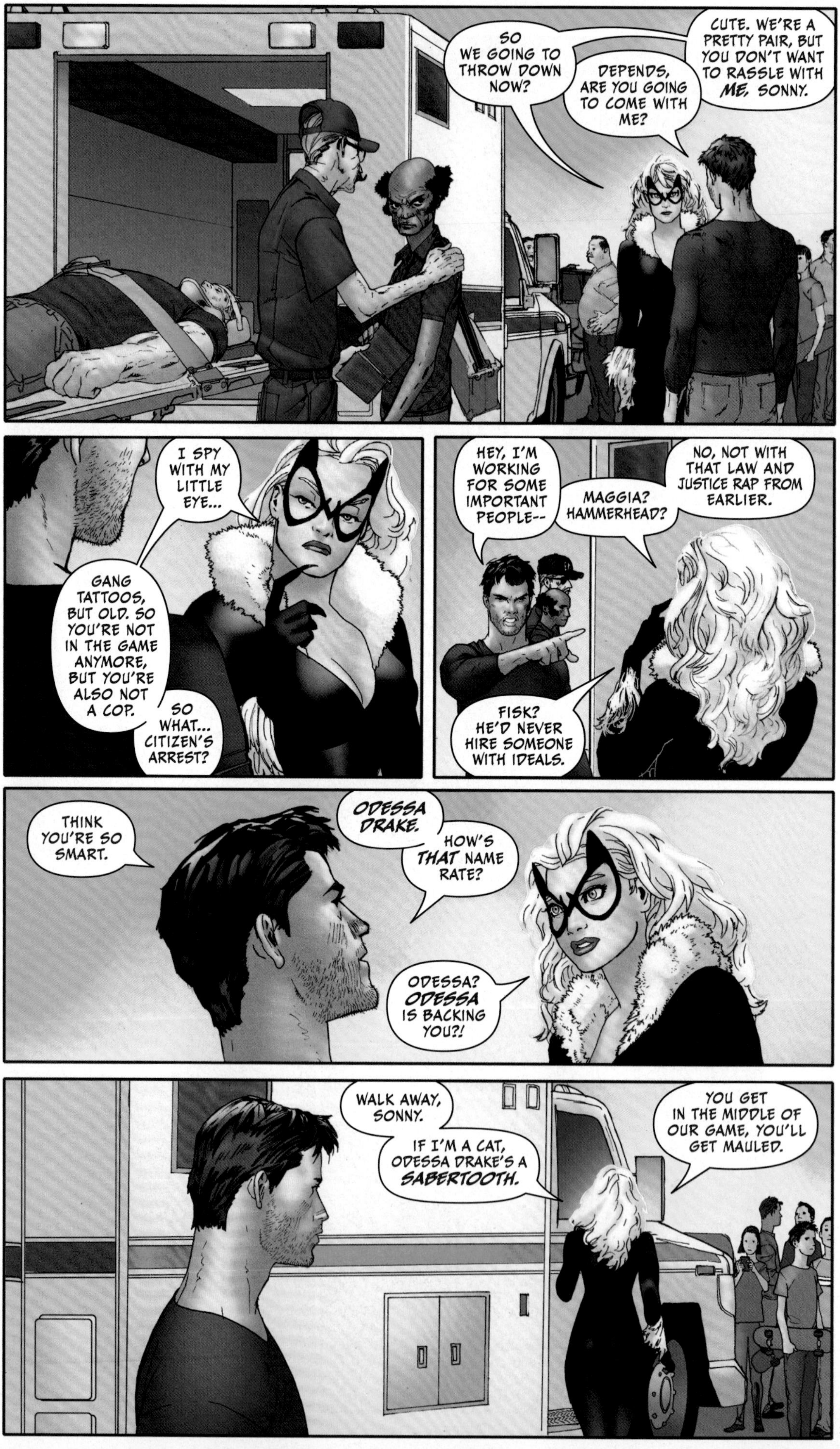
SO WE GOING TO THROW DOWN NOW?
DEPENDS, ARE YOU GOING TO COME WITH ME?
CUTE. WE'RE A PRETTY PAIR, BUT YOU DON'T WANT TO RASSLE WITH ME, SONNY.
I SPY WITH MY LITTLE EYE...
GANG TATTOOS, BUT OLD. SO YOU'RE NOT IN THE GAME ANYMORE, BUT YOU'RE ALSO NOT A COP.
SO WHAT... CITIZEN'S ARREST?
HEY, I'M WORKING FOR SOME IMPORTANT PEOPLE--
MAGGIA? HAMMERHEAD?
NO, NOT WITH THAT LAW AND JUSTICE RAP FROM EARLIER.
FISK? HE'D NEVER HIRE SOMEONE WITH IDEALS.
THINK YOU'RE SO SMART.
ODESSA DRAKE.
HOW'S THAT NAME RATE?
ODESSA? ODESSA IS BACKING YOU?!
WALK AWAY, SONNY.
IF I'M A CAT, ODESSA DRAKE'S A SABERTOOTH.
YOU GET IN THE MIDDLE OF OUR GAME, YOU'LL GET MAULED.

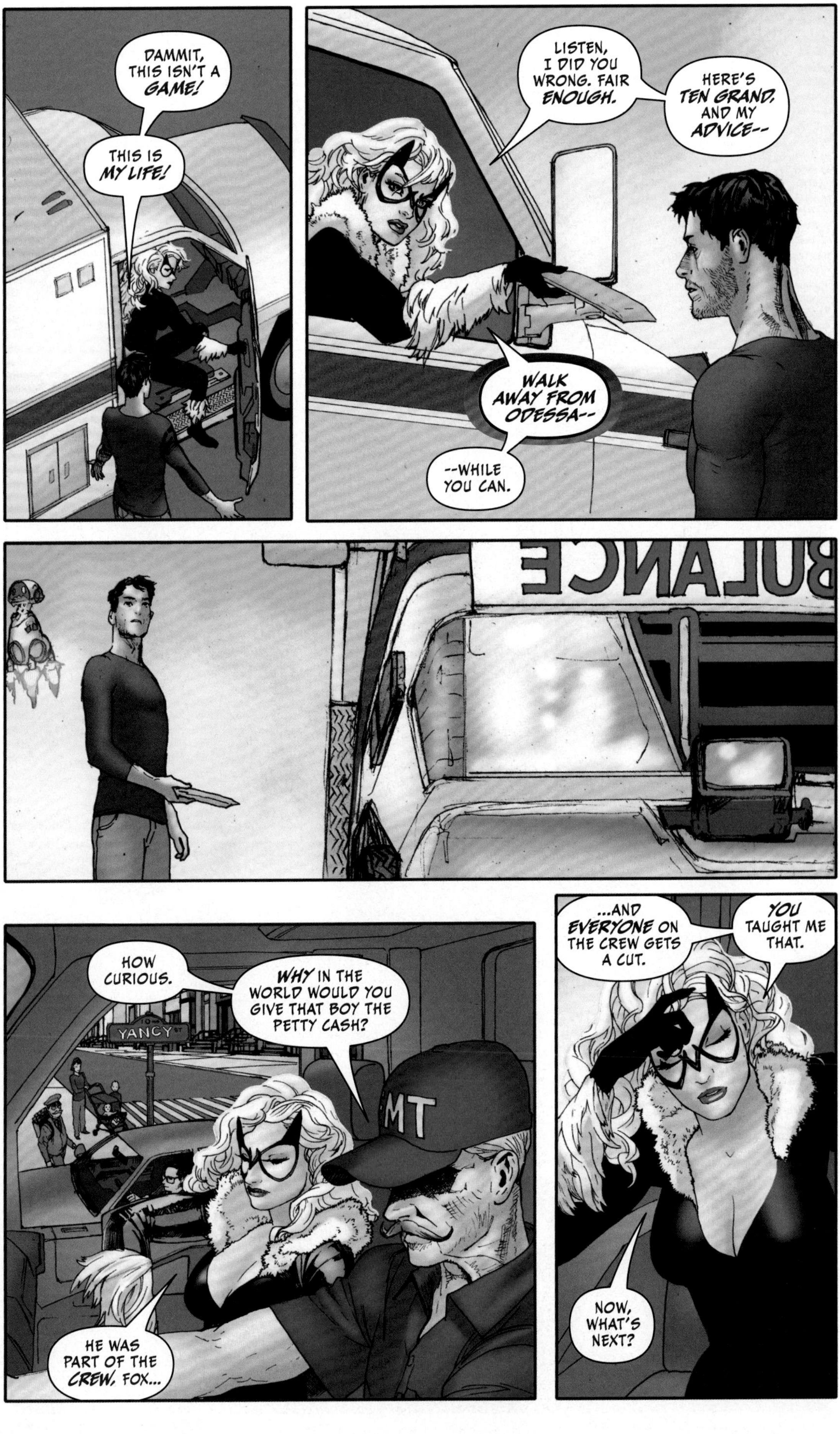
DAMMIT, THIS ISN'T A GAME!
THIS IS MY LIFE!
LISTEN, I DID YOU WRONG. FAIR ENOUGH.
HERE'S TEN GRAND, AND MY ADVICE--
WALK AWAY FROM ODESSA--
--WHILE YOU CAN.
BULANCE
YANCY ST
MT
HOW CURIOUS.
WHY IN THE WORLD WOULD YOU GIVE THAT BOY THE PETTY CASH?
HE WAS PART OF THE CREW, FOX...
...AND EVERYONE ON THE CREW GETS A CUT.
YOU TAUGHT ME THAT.
NOW, WHAT'S NEXT?

LATER.

...OCAMPO IS OFF THE BOARD, MS. DRAKE. HARDY GOT TO HIM.

DO YOU WISH HIM DEALT WITH?

NO. THE OCAMPO GAMBIT WAS MERELY HIGH SPIRITS, TURNING UP THE PRESSURE ON OUR WAYWARD KITTEN.

HE IS OF NO CONSEQUENCE.

WE HAVE OTHER NEWS, MS. DRAKE.

GOOD NEWS, I HOPE.

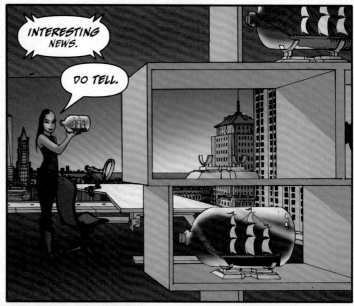

INTERESTING NEWS.

DO TELL.

IT'S ABOUT WHATEVER HARDY IS UP TO.

MS. DRAKE...

...SHE'S WORKING WITH THE BLACK FOX.

HE'S BACK.

KRASH!

MS. DRAKE...?

TAKE HIM. BRING HIM TO ME.

YOU BRING THAT COWARD TO ME!

TO BE CONTINUED.

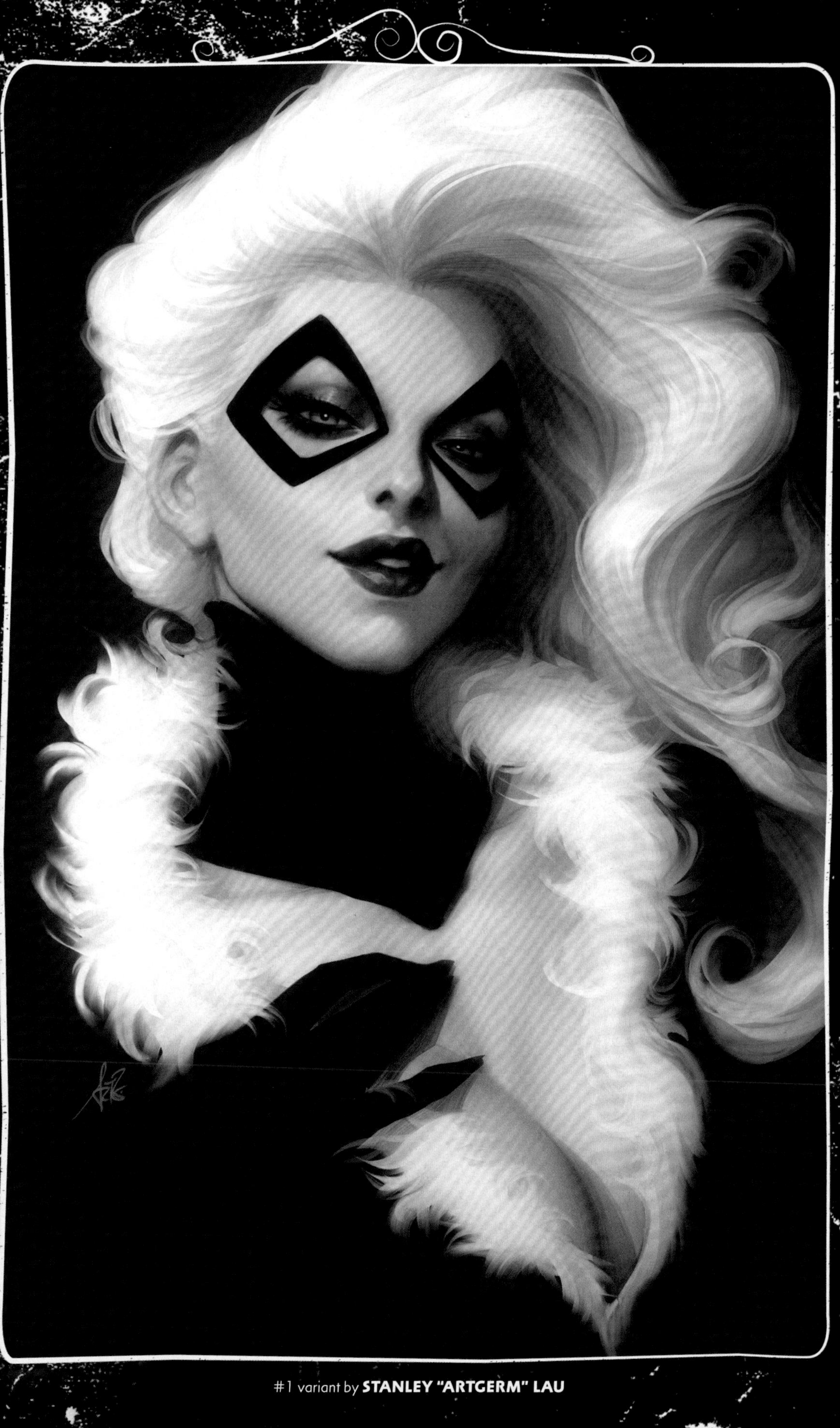

#1 variant by **STANLEY "ARTGERM" LAU**

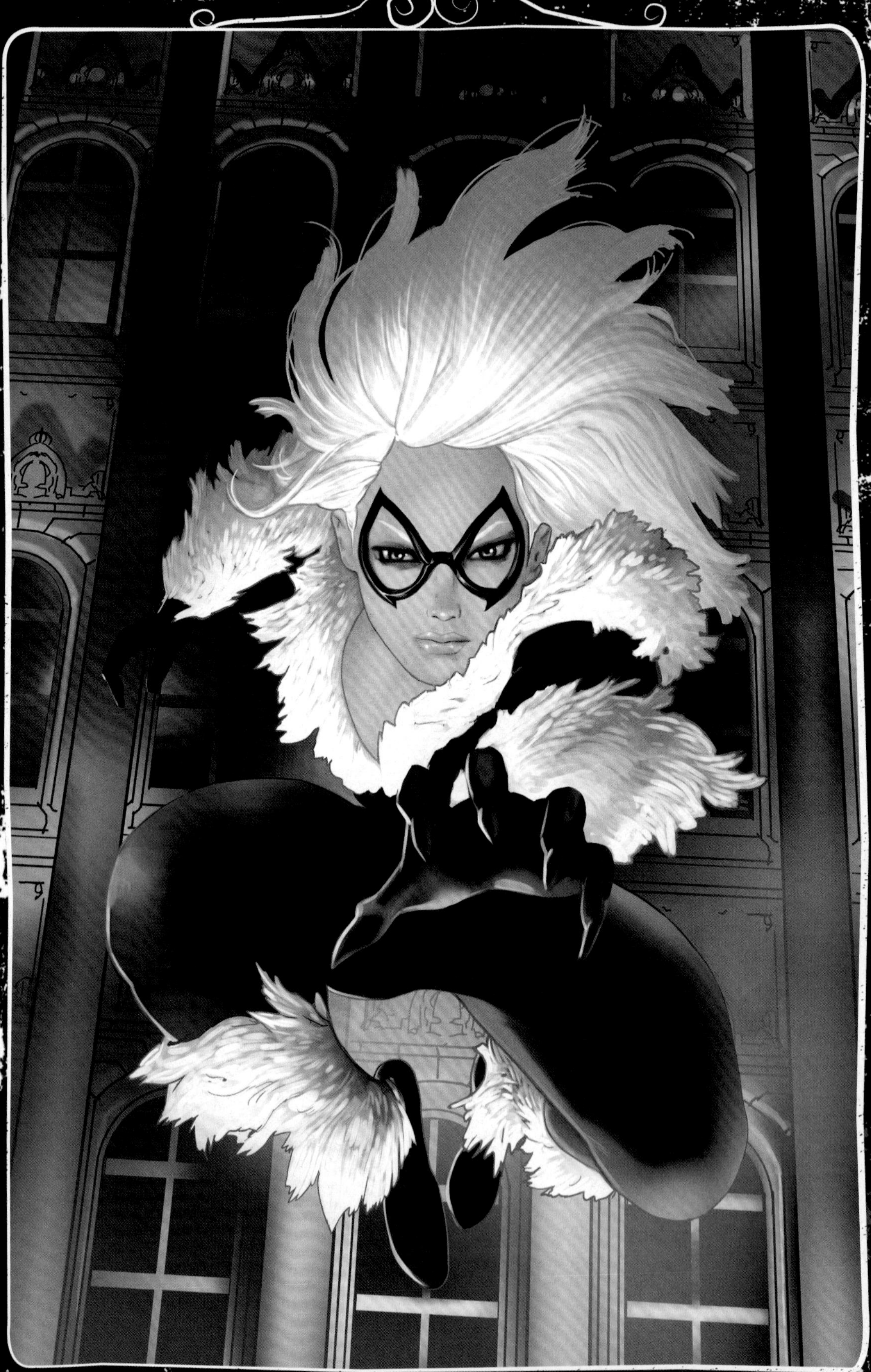

#1 variant by **TRAVEL FOREMAN** & **RICHARD ISANOVE**

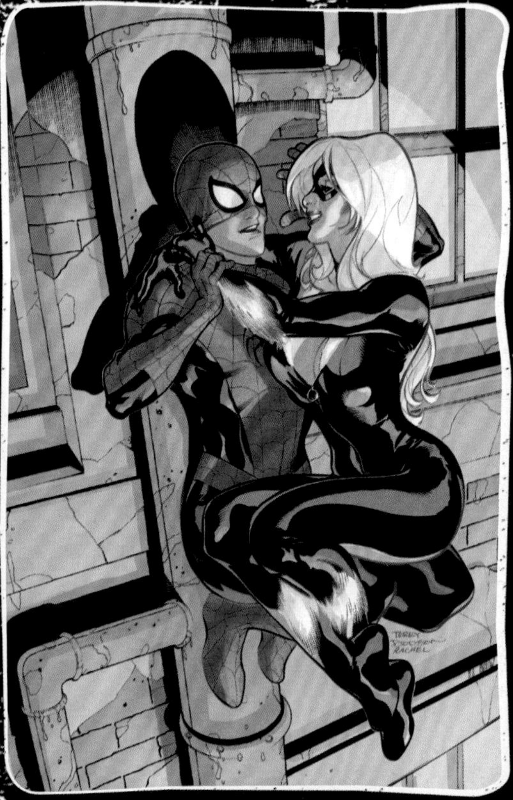

#1 Hidden Gem variant
by **TERRY DODSON** & **RACHEL DODSON**

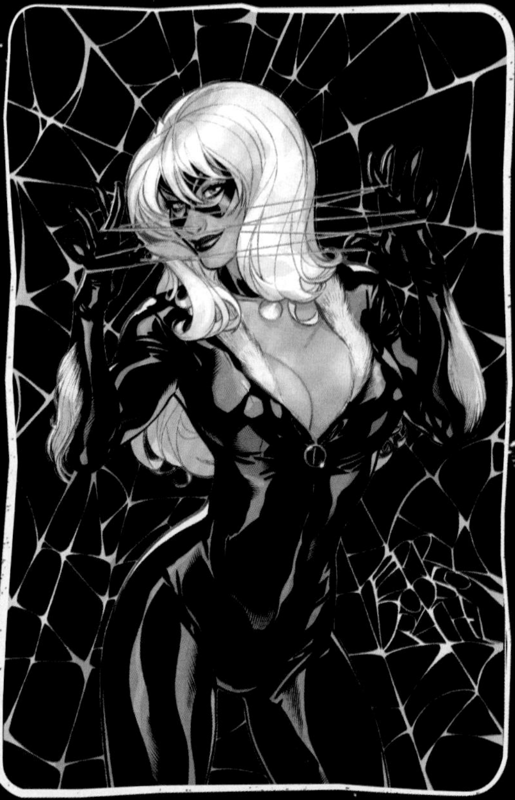

#2 Hidden Gem variant
by **TERRY DODSON** & **RACHEL DODSON**

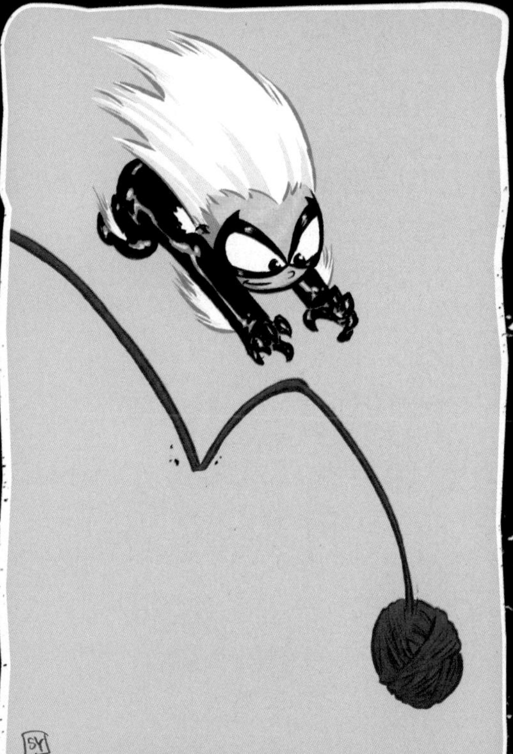

#1 variant by **SKOTTIE YOUNG**

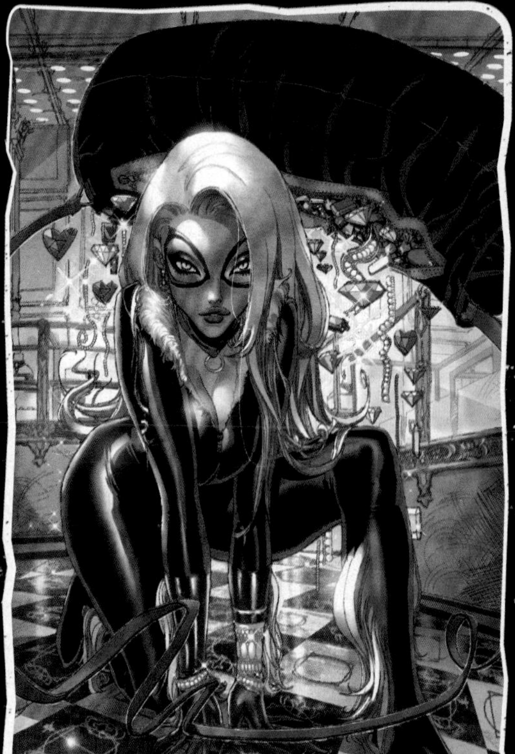

#2 variant by **ARIST DEYN**

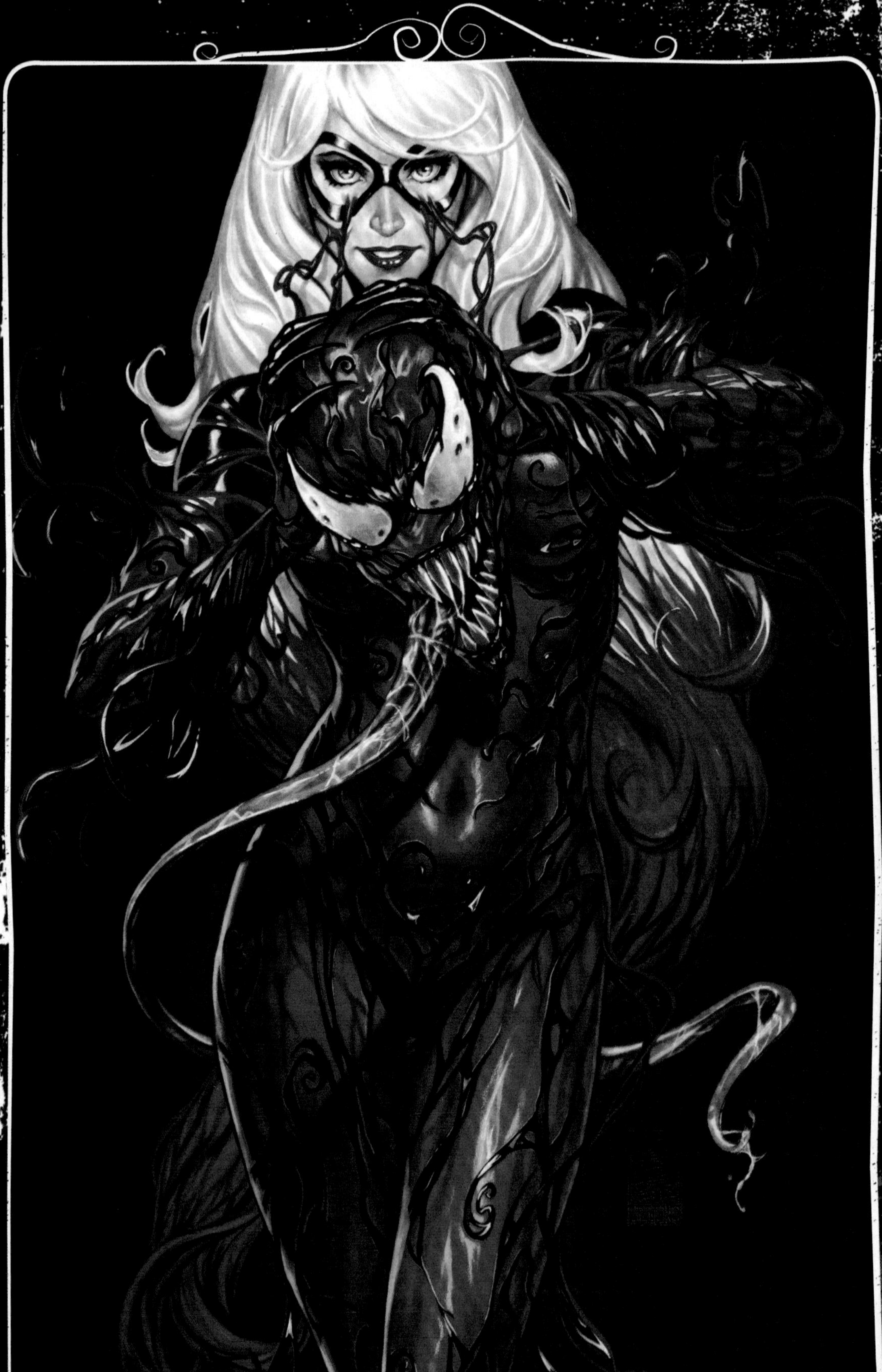

#2 Carnage-ized variant by **MARK BROOKS**

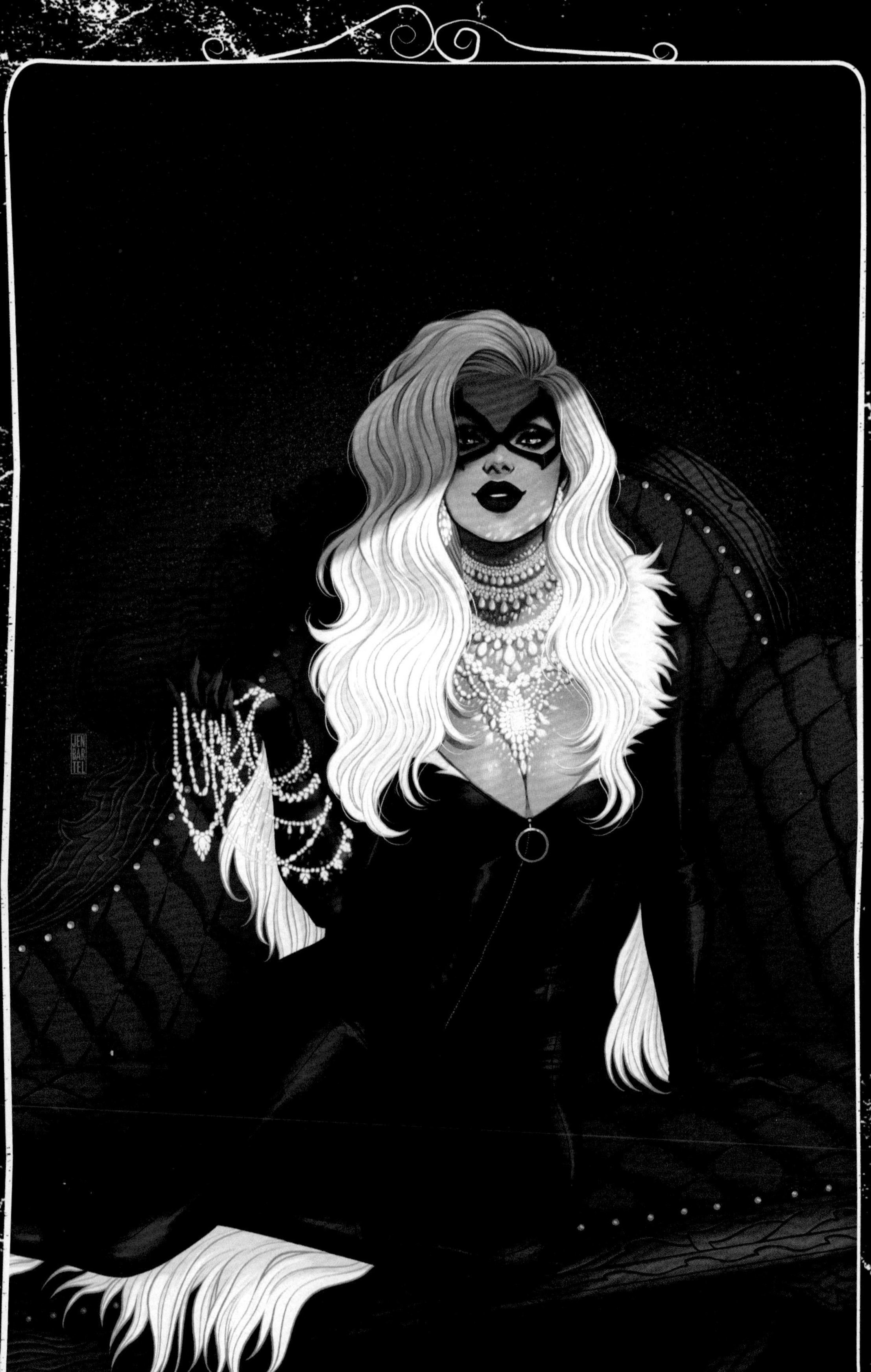
JEN
BAR
TEL

#3 variant by **JEN BARTEL**

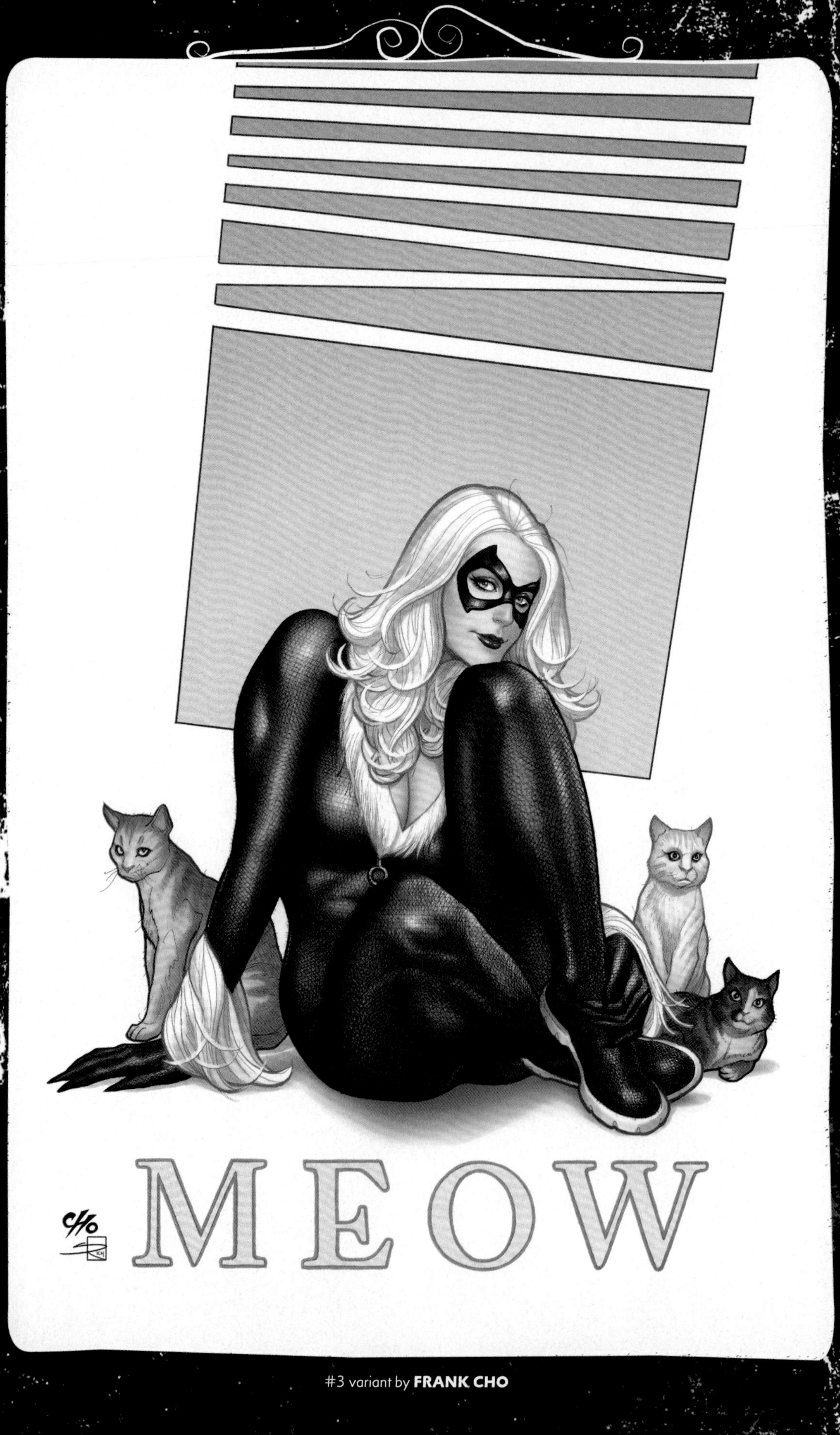
MEOW
CHO

#3 variant by **FRANK CHO**

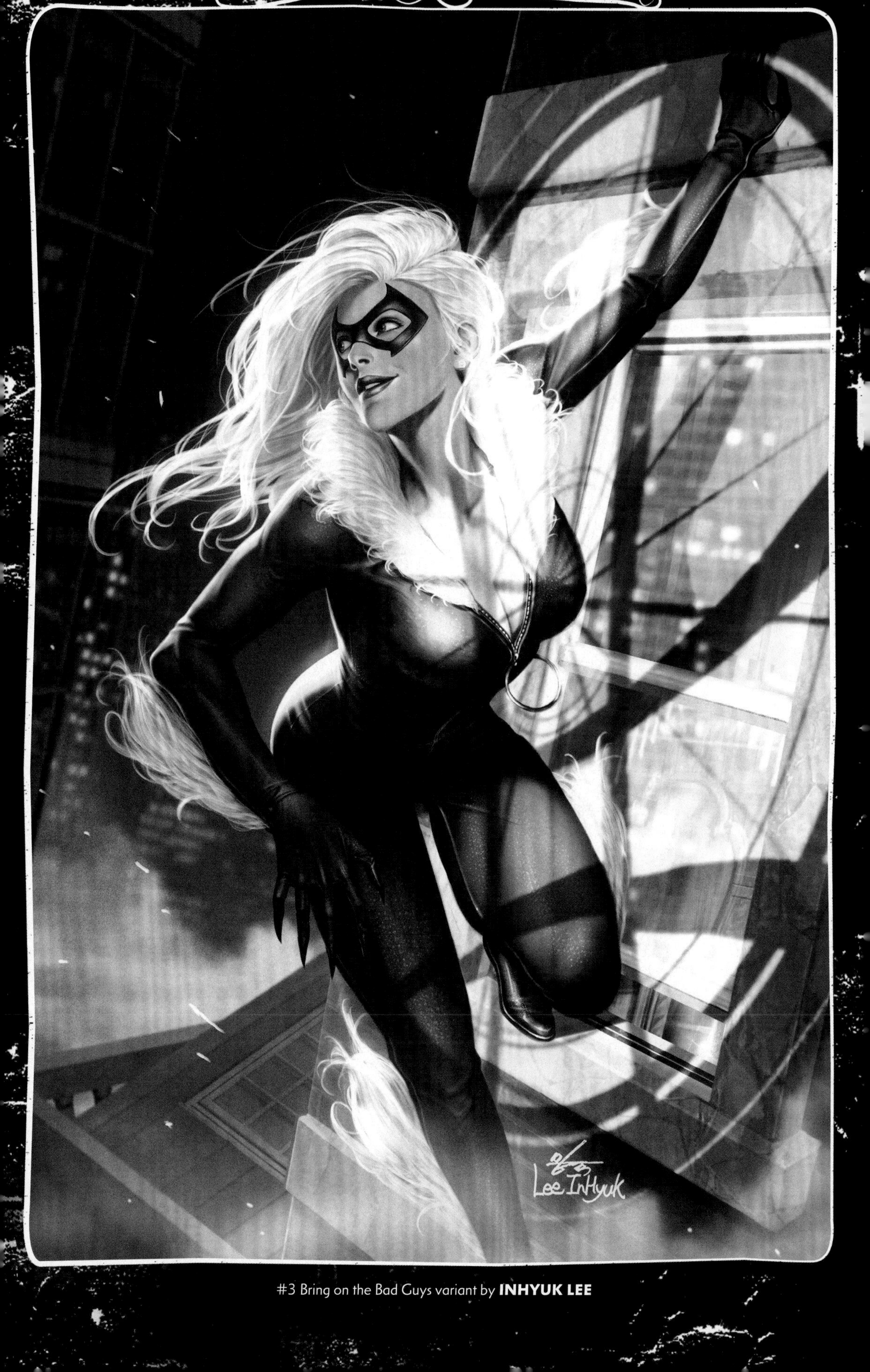
Lee InHyuk

#3 Bring on the Bad Guys variant by **INHYUK LEE**

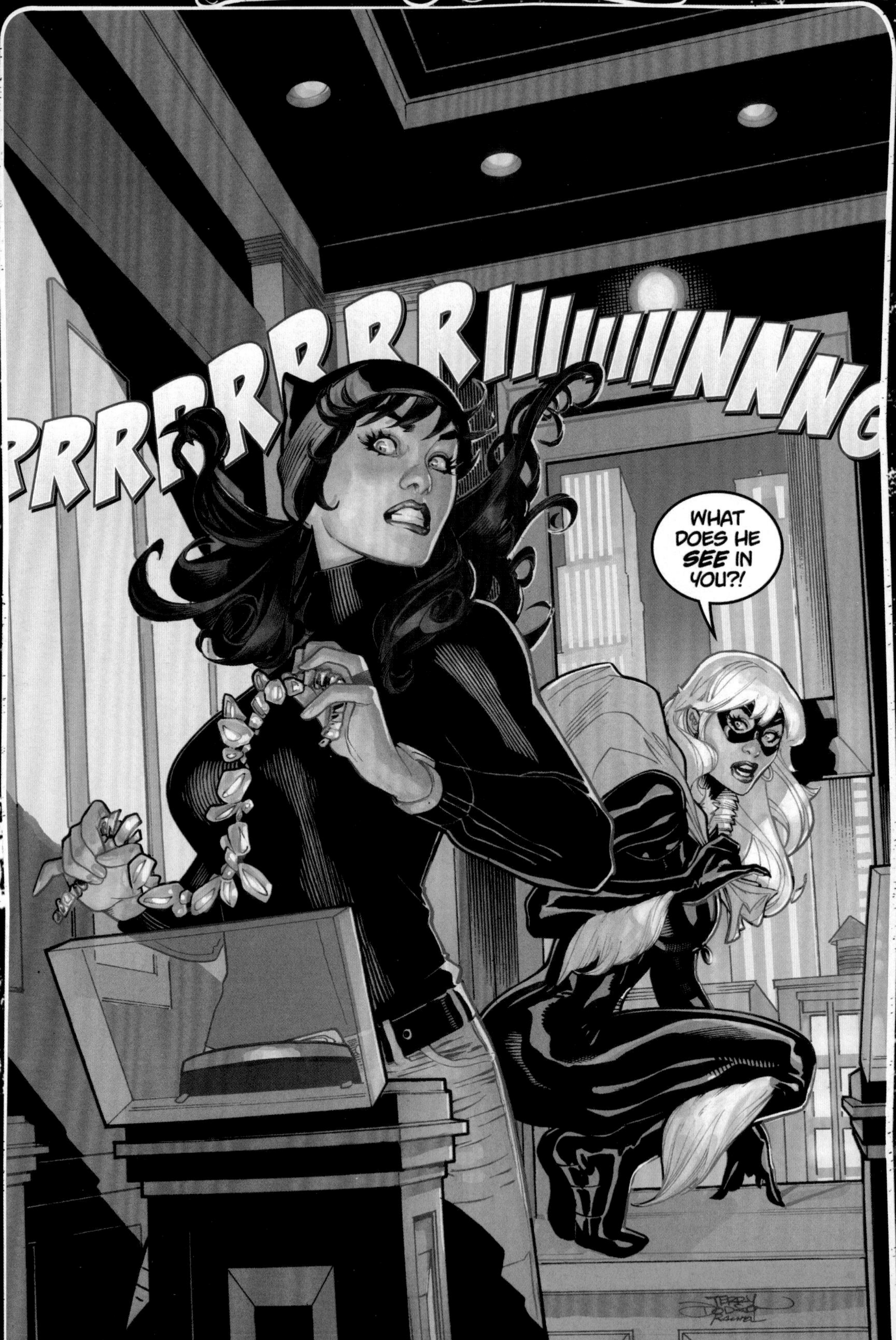
RRRRRRRRIIIIIIIINNNG
WHAT DOES HE SEE IN YOU?!

#3 Mary Jane variant by **TERRY DODSON** & **RACHEL DODSON**